Mother's Love from Beyond

A Healing Journey of Grief and Loss

Haneefa Mateen

Copyright © [2021] by [Haneefa Mateen]

All rights reserved.

No portion of this book may be reproduced in any form without written permission from the publisher or author, except as permitted by U.S. copyright law.

ISBN 9781737721918

Cover art: Haneefa Mateen

Disclaimer: the author of this book, *Mothers Love from Beyond*'s stories, experiences and opinions are from her perspective and are not intended as medical advice or the use of any techniques as a form of treatment for physical, medical, psychiatric, mental health problems either directly or indirectly. The intent of the author is only to share of her experiences in a general nature in her quest for emotional and spiritual wellbeing. In the event that you use any of the information in this book for yourself, which is your constitutional right, the author and publisher assumes no responsibility or liability whatsoever for readers or purchasers of this book.

Mothers Love from Beyond is a non-fiction story. Some names, locations, and other identifying information were changed to protect privacy of individuals.

Contents

Introduction	1
PART ONE:	3
Chapter 1: Childhood Fun	4
Chapter 2: Church of the Spirit	15
Chapter 3: Everything Changed	23
Chapter 4: Help Wanted	31
Chapter 5: No Baby Yet	41
Chapter 6: Aftereffects	50
Chapter 7: Second Marriage	56
PART TWO	64
Chapter 8: Counseling and Therapy	65
Chapter 9: Alternative Healing Therapies	71
Chapter 10: Momma Reappears	84
Chapter 11: Healing Assignments from Momma	96
Chapter 12: Spirit Messages from Other Relatives and Friends	107
Chapter 13: Apologies	133
Chapter 14: Forgiveness	144
PART THREE	152
Chapter 15: Unexpected Tasks	153

Chapter 16: Being Muslim	161
Chapter 17: Not Done Yet	170
Chapter 18: Ancestor Worship	179
Chapter 19: Medical Intuitive	191
Chapter 20: Mediumship Classes	201
Chapter 21: Spirit Helps Write This Book	213
PART FOUR	223
Chapter 22: Coping with the COVID-19 Pandemic	224
Chapter 23: The Healing Process	232
Chapter 24: Spiritual Growth	238
Chapter 25: Accepting the Green Cloth	246
Conclusion: Mission Accomplished	255
Epilogue	259
Acknowledgments	265
Books Mentioned in this Book	267
About the Author	270

Introduction

After my mother passed on and learned that she could communicate through a medium, she began guiding me from the Other Side and quickly made up for forty-three years of lost time. With her newfound ability to comfort, nurture, guide, and teach from the Other Side, she pulled in other helpers along the way. Accordingly, my life keeps changing dramatically as I'm healed at a quickened pace emotionally, physically, and spiritually from grief, domestic violence, racism, and other trauma. You will be taken along on my journey beginning from the perspective of a child, through gaining insight as an adult, to the later wisdom of an elder, all with the help of loved ones and guides from Heaven. This is a true story: my memoir of healing, forgiveness, renewed faith, and the awe of continued miracles.

During the COVID-19 pandemic and before, many people, or someone they knew suffered losses of family, friends, employment, health, perhaps homes, routine, sense of security, and their previous lifestyle. Perhaps you've also lost a sense of self and purpose for living along the way. Yet you also learned and gained new ways of coping and connection. How do you integrate these new experiences? How do you pick up and keep going in spite of losses and feeling overwhelmed? If you've had shifts in how you see the world, and the old ways of living no longer make sense, what do you do with the new you? Perhaps you had people dear to you that died, or almost died but were saved by doctors, or spontaneously woke up healed from a near-death experience? If that is you or someone you know, this book may help.

The story begins with a scene from a spirit circle I attended in 2014. What I was told by the mediums there started me on a renewed journey of healing from childhood memories. The memories are bittersweet. Be ready to breathe deeply, do some stretching, walk away, pray, and then come back to this book. Be forewarned that some of the middle chapters may be difficult to read and are marked by TRIGGER WARNING. However, this book is an honest acknowledgment that for many people, domestic violence and abuse are all too common and ignored. These are often unspoken topics, yet the voices of those who have lived through these experiences need to be heard. Domestic violence happens to mothers, sisters, nieces and granddaughters. Shhhhhhhh! It also happens, of course, to boys and men. The 'MeToo.' movement continues. I take the risk to keep the discussion open.

This book can provide relief from loneliness for many people who feel that they are the only ones. I've benefited from reading many other people's memoirs over the years, so now I'm sharing my story in appreciation and risking talking about culturally unspeakable topics that other people have not written much about yet: near-death experience and its aftereffects, different types of counseling, psychotherapy, healing, graduate school, Muslims, miracles, mediumship, everyday simple spirituality, and hope from a Black African American woman's perspective.

For curious readers and professionals, this book also provides understanding, inspiration, and hope for your own life as well as ways to assist other people. I have progressed from grief, despair, and just surviving while overcoming challenges to being a new person now, who is mostly peaceful and calm, knowing that love is ever present. Come along on my healing journey that is full of unexpected and pleasant surprises. Learn as I learn. Have patience—as my life story unfolds, many of your questions will be answered. Towards the end of the book, there will be many current controversial topics and concepts opened for discussion. Be prepared to debate and share.

PART ONE:

SPIRIT CIRCLE

Chapter 1: Childhood Fun

It was my third time participating in a spirit circle that summer. The evening's spirit messages came through much easier than in the previous two weeks. We were more relaxed after the facilitator explained more about what a spirit circle is. "In the old days, before television, radios, and smartphones, people used to socialize around the kitchen table. Women gathered together with their knitting and other crafts to have fun talking, sharing stories, and playing games. Occasionally, as spirit moved them, someone would spontaneously tell the group what messages they were being given for someone else in the room."

Haneefa, may I come to you?" The medium sitting across from me asked.

"Yes, you may."

"I'm seeing you sitting back, relaxing in the sun and enjoying it. I also see a beautiful, pastel-colored carousel. A mother or female relative is with you. Does that make sense to you?"

"Yes." As she was talking, I had the mental image of going slowly up and down on a pastel-rainbow-colored horse on a pole. "There used to be small street carnivals. But I was afraid of the roller coaster and the other rides. I only liked the carousel."

"But did you like it a lot? Because is your mother deceased?"

I nodded. "Yes."

"Well, she's showing me all these fun things she used to do with you."

Images came to my mind of going to the big holiday parades downtown. Giant, bigger-than-life people, animals, cartoon and Disney characters on large, rolling truck floats slowly passed by us. Children sat on the curb or stood with their family on the sidewalks with little fancy balloons on sticks and lots of treats to eat. I had forgotten this.

I did remember our old neighborhood in Philadelphia. During the fifties and sixties, there was a Ferris wheel and a carousel truck that came down our street during the spring and summer. No lie, the Ferris wheel would stop in front of our house. Momma would give us each ten cents. We gave it to the driver and then climbed three short steps to the inside and sat in the colorful seats. Another truck with amusement rides, had the Whip It. The Whip It is similar to a carousel except it went around in an oval and then gives a quick jerk as it turns the corner at the two narrow ends of the track. As children, we called the Whip It a merry-go-round too. However, while the Whip It had colorful seats, the carnival carousel had horses. Riding on the carousel put me in a magical space. Some horses were painted with different-colored designs alongside the natural brown, black, white, or pinto horses. The bright lights at the top and bottom of the carousel, along with the combination of the slow up-and-down motion of the horses on the pole while the carousel turned a bit faster, lulled me into a trance. I was always disappointed when the ride was over. My mother had to pull me crying from the horse.

There was also food on wheels such as the famous East Coast, mostly Philly, hot pretzel truck that came down our street. The pretzels were huge soft, yet chewy. The only time that I liked mustard was on hot pretzels. Then there were Mr. Softee ice cream trucks and Mr. Freeze. Of course, the milkman delivered milk in glass bottles that my grandmother saved and returned for more milk. Some neighbors got blocks of ice from the ice truck for their iceboxes because they didn't have refrigerators.

Most of the houses on the block on each side of the street are connected to each other. They called these rowhouses. We could hop or climb over most of the railings between porches all the way down the block if we chose to. Of course, there were neighbors who didn't like us doing this, but most would allow us. Although each home had a backyard, we mostly played on our own or friends' porches or on the sidewalks in front of our own stoops. There were block parties, where everyone played games together and competed for easy prizes. Of course there was food. I remember the small, individually wrapped blocks of frozen, evenly striped, pink, white, and brown ice cream that each child was given.

Two blocks down the street, on the way to the grade school, was a drugstore that sold penny candy, homemade fudge, and ice cream. The woman or man behind the counter would give us several pieces of candy in a tiny paper bag. Lollipops, black licorice, malt balls, Kool-Aid sticks, Squirrel nut chews, and fake cigarette candies to name a few. I never figured out how to make it work so that the candy would come out of the Pez dispenser one by one.

All the adults on our street were to be like our parents. So were the teachers and the adults at schools, churches, and mosques. They cared for us, guided, dressed, fed, and disciplined us. They kept a watchful eye on us to protect us as well as yelled at or smacked us if we did something wrong. News traveled fast, because by the time we arrived home to our mothers and fathers, we could receive another full yelling and spanking!

The neighborhood I am describing is my grandmother's—Momma's mother. Grandma's house had a living room, a dining room with a china cabinet and mantel, and a kitchen with a pantry downstairs. Upstairs was my grandmother's bedroom in front, then the room where Momma and we three children slept. My older sister, Kani, and I shared a bunk bed, with her on the top. I was such a rough sleeper that even with the wooden railing, I would fall out of the bed in my sleep, so I slept on the bottom bed. There was another bedroom for when my uncle came to visit.

Kani is one year older than I am. Some people asked if we were twins since Momma dressed us alike. She grew out of her shoes and clothes faster than I did. To me, she seemed much smarter than me in school as well as smarter and more coordinated in games. Kani won more games than I did. She also had more friends. I was shy and followed her around everywhere, copying most of the activities that she did. I was her shadow. With the usual sibling rivalry, Kani would snatch toys from me or hit me.

Momma didn't allow us to fight each other. She taught us that we were to care about each other. The only rule that came with a threat of a spanking—besides no lying and no stealing—was no hitting your sister or brother. Momma stomped her feet loudly as she walked when she was upset. We knew when she was coming and that we were in trouble.

CHAPTER 1: CHILDHOOD FUN

My brother Emin is three years younger than me. My first introduction to Emin was when he was in my mother's belly. Our grandmother and Momma had a black cat named Blackie. The cat would sit on top of Momma's big belly. I didn't like the cat because I was afraid of it. When Emin was old enough to crawl and toddle around the house, he could do anything to that cat, and the cat would just sit there. If I came anywhere near Blackie, he would hiss and strike out at me, often scratching me. Those scratches hurt, so I learned to keep my distance.

We also had godparents. One of our father's younger sisters was my godmother. I called her Aunt Deanie. Our godparents would bring us birthday and holiday gifts and take us out to the movies, trick-or-treating, and to haunted houses, small carnivals, and amusement parks. My many other aunts and uncles would also come along or took us each separately to events. Both of our grandmothers were very active in our lives.

Although Momma's favorite color was green, she dyed her clothes to match each year's fashion color. After bleaching out the previous year's color, she would use Rit dye to change a pretty blouse to pink, for example, or black. She wore jewelry—pearls, rhinestones, rings, bracelets, necklaces, clip-on earrings—and Avon perfume. She used to mix the perfumes. Momma wore poodle skirts and dresses with layers of crinolines underneath. Kani and I wore dresses with crinolines too for special events. Momma's favorite cigarette brands were Pall Mall, Winston, and L&M, which she smoked a lot. I disliked the smell of cigarette smoke on her breath and clothes, especially because the smoke, along with the strong perfume scents to cover it up, frequently also took my breath away.

She had three monkeys carved out of light green jade that were connected. One monkey had his hands over his eyes, the next monkey had his hands over his ears, and the other monkey had his hand over his mouth, representing see no evil, hear no evil, and speak no evil. She would tickle our little feet and our bellies, making us giggle and laugh.

***

Momma's Sayings

If we woke up in a bad mood crying, arguing, or with temper tantrums, Momma would say, "You woke up on the wrong side of the bed. Go back to bed and try again!" I would stand there wondering which side of the bed was the right side, especially since I slept in a bunk bed close up against the wall so I wouldn't fall out. There was only one side of the bed that I could get out of.

Since Momma didn't like fighting, she taught us, "Sticks and stones may break my bones, but words will never hurt me." To me, Momma would say, "You have an inferiority complex." At the age of six or seven, I didn't know what the word "inferiority" meant. Kani picked on me, calling me names. Sometimes she told me that I was black, ugly, and nappy-headed. She had a much lighter complexion than me, but her hair was just as tightly curled as mine. I don't remember Momma or any other relative calling me or anyone else black or nappy-headed. I thought I was actually black as a shoe. Thereafter, when I looked in the mirror, I saw my skin as black. So some words do hurt. We weren't allowed to fight over name calling.

Another of Momma's sayings was, "If they jump off of a cliff, would you do it too?" This I did eventually understand as if my friend did something wrong, would I follow them and do it too? But I didn't know what a cliff was. Sometimes Momma said "bridge" instead of "cliff."

Overhearing Grandma and Momma saying about our uncle, "He's always in a hole," made me scared. I imagined him being outside at night, cold and shivering in a hole in the ground. I wondered if that could happen to us too.

Momma sure could cook. She made homemade hamburger patties. I watched her put spices in the red ground beef, then chop onions and green peppers to mix in. She shaped handfuls of it into large balls and flattened them into perfect rounds. I used to wonder and fret over how the burgers got all lumpy and misshapen while sizzling in the hot, black, cast iron skillet. But they were delicious! Especially after Momma put the thick, juicy burgers between two slices of white bread. I can still smell the hamburgers as they cooked and feel the crunch of the crispy outside contrasted with the sweet, soft white bread. Ummmmmmmm! Momma also satisfied our sweet tooth and hers. She had candy cookbooks, but she also used recipes passed down to her. The cast iron skillet was used for making peanut brittle and plain brittle. When it cooled and hardened, she would carefully break it with a hammer covered in a cloth. Then she gave us each a piece. She used clear and dark Karo corn syrup to make taffy too. She made a wonderful, creamy chocolate fudge and rice pudding, bread pudding, and tapioca pudding from scratch. For school field trips, she would treat us to store-bought packages of Oreo cookies. As the television advertisement said, "Because a kid will eat the middle of an Oreo first and save the chocolate cookie outside for last!"

Momma was also an artist. She would do simple sketches for us—small, almost cartoon-like. I asked her to draw me a picture of a baby over and over and over again. Sitting next to me on the bed, she would grant my requests. Momma let us join her while she did paint-by-number oil paintings. She didn't seem to be concerned about us messing up her picture or getting oil paint on our clothes, or the furniture, or the walls, although oil paint leaves stains. She made sure we had crayons and modeling clay.

Left to our own creativity, we created masterpieces as we melted crayons all over the hot radiators by the windows. We shaped clay into people and animals and stuck them on the walls. I don't remember being spanked for this. Our holiday and birthday gifts were usually art supplies and books. I had dolls, but they were frustrating to me because when I combed my baby doll's and Barbie doll's hair, they quickly became bald. Barbie also became headless and armless! But I loved paper dolls. Sure, the dolls and the clothes could tear. Perhaps because I knew this, I was gentler with them. Momma also brought us paper dollhouse kits and helped us gently push out the furniture along the dotted lines for the living room and bedroom and kitchen appliances and the outside of the house. She would then help us fold and assemble them.

Momma would sit on the floor with us and play different games. She showed us how to play jacks. The game consisted of ten metal jacks that had six spikes and looked like pretty stars to me—until I stepped on one with my bare foot! They were either all plain silver or in pastel colors, and they came with a bright red-orange ball. To play, you shake the ten jacks in your closed hand and then let them fall on the floor in front of you. Then you throw the red ball up in the air close to you, then reach and grab one jack before the ball bounces one time as you catch the ball. You put the jack you grabbed behind you. You continue this way until you have picked up all the jacks one by one. Next, you do the same by grabbing the jacks two at a time, letting the ball only bounce once, until you pick up all the jacks. Then by threes, fours, fives, sixes, sevens, eights, nines, and last, you pick up all ten jacks at once. The rule though, is that you can't touch the other jacks while you're trying to pick up, for example, only three jacks at a time.

We sat, stood, or kneeled around jigsaw puzzles on the table or the floor. I liked the way the often, dull picture on the puzzle box became a large, brighter-colored picture after putting the puzzle together. Momma allowed us to help, although I remember accidentally bending or breaking the tips of the puzzle pieces by forcing them into places where they didn't fit or by playing with them. But by the age of seven, I was able to correctly put pieces into the puzzle. Erin was four years old at the time, and he helped too.

Another game was Chinese checkers. I mostly liked the bright colors of the triangles with holes in the round center of the playing board. The marbles that came with the game were solid colors. We also played regular checkers on a square board with alternating black and white squares. You get to jump over your opponent's checkers when you have a king. A king is two checkers together, one on top of the other. To me, Chinese checkers was more fun, although I didn't understand the strategies of either game!

We played some of these games with our friends. Outside, we also played marbles, Chinese jump rope, hopscotch, jump rope, double Dutch, and hula hoop. At six or seven years old, I was learning how to turn the two ropes evenly and high enough to go over the bigger girls' heads. Chinese jump rope was more complicated. We tied together rubber bands of assorted colors and sizes to make a long oval. The rubber band loop was placed around the ankles of two children standing on opposite sides. Then we took turns gently lifting one side of the rope with only the tip of one foot to put it over the other side. When we got fast enough, we looked—and felt—like we were dancing.

We did other activities, one that only the girls played. We would link our arms together and stomp our feet up the sidewalk, chanting:

We are rough.

We are tough.

We are the girls from Hobart Street.

So, take off your shoes, and smell your feet.

Pew We!

Because we are the girls from Hobart Street.

Hand games we usually played outside paired up facing each other, either sitting or standing, and clapping, high-fiving with both hands, crisscrossing, and other moves to the tune of songs like "Take Me Out to the Ball Game." We would also play outside in the rain wearing sunsuits or just our little panties, screaming and squealing but enjoying the rain as it cooled us on hot days.

Erin tried to play along. Momma and Grandma bought him a blue kiddie car that he pedaled up and down the sidewalks.

Bedtime Stories

What we also loved, probably the most, was Momma reading bedtime and anytime stories to us because she would act out the parts of the storybook characters. She would change her voice. My favorite stories were "The Elephant's Child," "Ali Baba and the Forty Thieves," and "Rikki-Tikki-Tavi." For "The Elephant's Child," Momma would pinch her nose shut while she said, "'Let go of me! You're hurting me. Let go! You are hurting be!' The Elephant's Child sat back on his little haunches and pulled, and pulled, and pulled, and his nose began to stretch." I could see his nose stretch and felt sorry for his sore nose.

When she read "Ali Baba and the Forty Thieves," I loved her saying "Open sesame!" I could see the huge stone door moving out of the way. It is a very, very long story. I would ask my mother to read it over and over again. She had a large, black, hard-cover book of *The Arabian Nights*. *Sinbad the Sailor* is another book with a very long story with four voyages. Each voyage is also a long story. But Momma would still read it.

Rikki-Tikki-Tavi is a mongoose that looks like a cat, but his head is weasel-like, with pink eyes. Momma would wiggle her nose and make the sound of Rikki-Tikki-Tavi. I loved the way she changed her voice to sound like a little boy, then the boy's mother, and then his father. The little mongoose is a boy too, so he also had a lot of curiosity, similar to the elephant's child. Rikki-Tikki-Tavi makes trouble by accidentally knocking things over, but he isn't punished.

Momma made the sounds of the other animals in the garden as they talk to each other. Of course, we couldn't wait to hear what was going to happen next. Would Naj, the big cobra, kill Rikki-Tikki-Tavi, or would he kill the snake? Scary, but we wanted to know. Not only at bedtime, Momma would read us stories anytime.

When there were thunderstorms, Momma and Grandma turned off all the lights and the television too. We sat together in the living room in the dark. I was afraid of the dark and even more terrified of the booming, shaking sounds of the thunder and the crackling snap of the lightning. I'd hide under the covers in my bed, except that I was too scared to be alone. It didn't help that Momma told us stories about people who were electrocuted by lightning, like the one about the woman whose hair stood permanently straight up on her head after she looked out an open window and got struck by lightning. Then there were bogeyman stories. The bogeyman was invisible and always creeping closer and closer. He could be found under the bed, in the dark closet, or in the basement.

The stories that I, unfortunately, believed the most were Momma's tall tales about spiders. As a result, for most of my life, I was afraid of spiders. The daddy longlegs that were as tall as the large metal washtubs that she took a bath in down on the farm. She heated the water in a large pot on the stove, and then poured the hot water into the washtub. She had to go back and forth and back and forth with pots of hot water until the washtub was half full. While she was sitting in the washtub, the daddy longlegs would come close to the washtub! Another farm story she told us was that one day, she was out in the garden standing by a fence. She was talking to someone and not really paying attention to what else was going on around her. When she did, she looked down and said, "Oh, what a beautiful green bracelet. Where did it come from?" She stood there admiring her new bracelet until it started moving. She jumped and screamed. It was a little green garter snake wrapped around her wrist! I don't know how I slept after any of these stories since I often had nightmares after watching scary movies and TV shows.

I was even afraid of Godzilla and King Kong! Of course, everyone was terrified and had nightmares after seeing Alfred Hitchcock's *The Birds*! Momma took us to the latest movies. The movie with the giant tarantula that was almost as tall as buildings certainly didn't help me with my fear of spiders—even tiny spiders or harmless, delicate daddy longlegs.

After the movie, she would take us to a restaurant, and we would sit and have a Philly hoagie, sub, or a Philly cheesesteak. Each of these sandwiches was served on a long "submarine" bun. Momma was proud that occasionally she could treat all four of us to a milkshake and hoagie for $1. Milkshakes back then were so thick with ice cream we could barely suck them through a straw. Sometimes she would get chop suey in little white boxes from a Chinese restaurant. We would carry the Chinese food home and eat it.

We rode buses and trolleys, but most of the time, we walked. It seemed like we walked everywhere. At the museum, I remember the mummy the most. The mummy was scary. He looked like a real man, but he had on raggedy, dirty clothes. His face was very dark, with small eyes.

Going to the park was my favorite activity. Fairmount Park is huge. There were also smaller neighborhood parks with monkey bars, swings, slides, and merry-go-rounds. I loved playing in the water. In the summertime, Momma let us play in the huge fountains. We splashed in the water at the bottom and enjoyed the gentle spray or forceful shower of the water that shot out of the holes in the sides of the fountain. Kani and I wore sunsuits on those days or took off our clothing, except our panties. The sun would dry us on the way home.

Momma told us to make a wish and gave us a penny to throw in the bottom of the fountains or other shallow pools. She would sing the popular song "Three Coins in the Fountain." Sometimes Momma would bring a blanket and a picnic basket. She would spread the blanket on the grass, and we would sit and eat sandwiches or fried chicken. In the fall, I loved the smell of the autumn leaves from the maple, oak, and chestnut trees unique to the East Coast—our little feet kicking up the dry leaves and feeling the crunch as we purposely stamped our sneakers on them, the leaves gliding over and around our ankles, and how it felt to lie on a pile of them.

The only parts of the parks that I didn't like were the playgrounds. I hated the merry-go-round because it made me dizzy and sick. I hated not having any control over when I could get off or how fast it was going. I would cry and beg to get off. I begged the boy that was running and pushing the merry-go-round faster and faster to stop. Often the child initially pushing the merry-go-round would get it going fast and then jump on and ride along with us. Then we were at the mercy of the merry-go-round, waiting for it to eventually slow down by itself. Sometimes a larger child would put their feet down and stop it. The swings also made me dizzy. My arms weren't strong enough for me to reach from monkey bar to monkey bar. I only liked the slides. Back then they were shiny metal that burned our little legs sometimes in the bright, hot sunshine.

It was warm enough in Philadelphia, since it's near the Atlantic Ocean, to have beautiful flowering trees and bushes. We would suck the tiny drop or two of honey out of the flowers of the many honeysuckle bushes along the sidewalks. In the summertime, we chased fireflies with their colorful blinking lights during the dark nights. We caught them in glass jars and then wondered why the fireflies stopped blinking! Yes, now I remember the fun we had with our mother, but somehow, I completely forgot about going to the big Thanksgiving and Christmas parades.

Chapter 2: Church of the Spirit

One Saturday, the facilitator Diane Willis of the Chicago IANDS announced that there was a church located on the Northside of Chicago that everyone should go to. She approached me later and excitedly explained that the Church of the Spirit was wheelchair accessible. Soon after, I went to the Sunday services. It is a small church in the middle of the block. So small, that although it has the usual stain-glass windows and the roof shaped like a church, you might pass by it thinking that it is house. I went inside and sat in the back. Since I arrived a half hour early, I was there for the 10:00 AM guided meditation. Gradually the pews began to fill with people casually wearing jeans, t-shirts, summer dresses or shorts. The service began at 10:30 with a brief opening prayer, recitation of the Spiritualist Principles, the Prayer for Spiritual Healing, another brief guided meditation by the assistant pastor. We were invited to do a few minutes of standing and hugging and greeting those near us. The organist, Joan, rang the chimes for us to return to our seat. She played a hymn and we sang along from little blue books. In the back of the sanctuary, two healers stood behind tall stools and provided energy healing as members took turns sitting on the stools.

Pastor Marrice gave the welcome and asked, "Anyone new to the church? Raise your hand. You don't have to stand or tell us your name or anything." Are there any announcements?"

Then she gave an inspirational sermon. Two people on both sides of the pews passed the collection plates. Everyone stood up for another louder invigorating hymn "Every Time I Feel the Spirit." This song signaled the message portion of the service. Then Pastor Marrice and the other mediums on the platform stage took turns giving spirit messages. A medium went to the podium, looked out into the congregation and chose someone.

"Mary. Mary may I come to you?"

Mary stood up in front of her seat and stayed standing during her message.

"Will you say your name aloud for me? The sound of your voice helps me to have a better connection."

"Mary."

"You're at a crossroads right now feeling like giving up. Just stand still for a bit and then keep going."

Then Mary sat down and another person was called.

"The person in the back with the dark blue shirt and glasses. May I come to you?"

And so on, until that medium got tired. Then another medium stepped up to the podium. Pastor Marrice went last. Occasionally she gave messages to people who already received one earlier.

"Anyone not get a reading yet?"

I sat still and they didn't raise my hand. I didn't understand what they were doing.

Each spirit message lasted from 2 to 5 minutes, sometimes 10 minutes. A brief "greeting" Pastor Marrice explained that if you want a longer reading you can make an appointment later for a private reading with a medium.

The service ended with a benediction prayer and the congregation singing, "Let There Be Peace on Earth." The lyrics are different from most other churches. As Joan continued playing the instrumental part of the song on the organ, we filed out of the sanctuary stopping near the doorway to hug the pastor and the assistant pastor. After the services, as people were starting to leave, a tall stocky man introduced himself as Assistant Pastor Rik and asked me to wait.

"May I give you a reading?"

"What's a reading?"

"A spirit message."

"Okay."

CHAPTER 2: CHURCH OF THE SPIRIT

"There is a spirit of an African-American woman here. She stands to your right. She's short, round, strong with strong-arms. She makes scarves, but she doesn't knit them. She sews them. She puts medicine in the scarves and put them around your neck. You're going to have to have patience. You're going to jump through some hoops. They're showing me a little black dog jumping through three hoops. This month June will be okay, but in July you will have to be patient and just do what you have to do. Be patient."

Afterwards, we gathered downstairs at the large tables to chat and enjoyed a home-cooked meal that was made from scratch and begun early in the morning in an old fashion kitchen. There is a huge black cast-iron stove with double ovens that are slow to warm up. The electric wiring is old too, so that the cooks have to be careful how many appliances are plugged in at one time. Otherwise all the lights would go out. As the service was ending, we smelled the brunch coffee, pancakes, quiche, or lunch tomato sauces, spices, soups, meats, cooked vegetables, salads, fruit, and fresh baked desserts. Past the kitchen, in the back hallway are two small beautifully decorated bathrooms that were initially labeled men's and women's. Later, the women's bathroom was enlarged to make it wheelchair accessible. All this was very different from any church I'd gone to previously.

Rik's message didn't make sense to me. After I arrived home, I called Mother Dear. She said, "I don't know any short, round woman. I'm the only one I know that sews in the family. Nurses taught me how to make the mustard plaster that I used to put on your chests as children. My mother (your great- grandmother) is the only one I know who was short and round, and she was talented in many areas so she might have sewed."

What did make sense to me later was the extra hoops I would have to jump through later that summer and fall as I prepared for resume and cover letter writing and hopefully interviews for practicum training. I was in my second year of a clinical psychology program at a university in downtown Chicago. Students are required to take summer classes. The first years of any doctoral program is grueling. It's difficult to know what each professor expects causing me anxiety. Overwhelmed with reading four textbooks and twenty assigned journal articles of twenty pages each throughout the semester for each course. Then that many more new textbooks and journal articles we had to find and read in order to write the research papers and case studies for midterm and final exams. I felt like I was married to my computer during my every waking hour. I often went to bed past midnight when my eyes would not stay open any longer, and then be up at 5:00 AM to type some more. I read on buses and trains. With seemingly endless deadlines, I worked on school assignments almost 24/7 even during my sleep I was typing, analyzing, and planning. Very frustrated as PowerPoint presentation slides zoomed in on key points again and again until I yelled out in my sleep, "I got it! I got it! I understand. Now leave me alone and let me sleep!"

Although I enjoyed the classroom discussions and role-plays, I felt lonely because the time spent doing school assignments didn't allow for socializing and relationships. Gradually I learned how to take time for fun activities and being around people going to the Church of the Spirit was a start. I was there most Sundays regardless of the weather as members of the even pushed my wheelchair through and across the snow.

What Is a Medium?

Over time I learned that a medium has the ability to bring messages from those who have passed over to people who are living on Earth. These spirit messages may be given to the medium as pictures, words, thoughts, feelings, or memories. Often they are given quickly, in a way that the mediums may not understand—but you do, because you knew the your relative or friend. Sometimes the message may not make sense to you at first. Usually later in the day or during the week, you'll understand as you remember or ask family questions about the item or person that was described to you. The medium may give you advice from your loved one or someone that you knew, after describing this person to you. They can tell you in what ways your loved one attempts to communicate with you when you are at home.

A psychic is different because the message mostly focuses on you. They will tell you how you've been feeling, what you have been doing recently, and what may happen to you in your future. A medium may also include some psychic messages, but a true medium's focus is on what your deceased loved one is doing and wants to communicate—not about you!

The mediums who initially gave me spirit messages were strangers. I've been very careful not to talk about my life with any of the mediums at the Church of the Spirit, so what they tell me they could not have known previously, and many events I'd forgotten. Therefore, no, the mediums could not have been reading my mind! I usually breathe deeply and try to keep my thoughts in the present moment while I'm with the medium. I also keep my facial expressions to a minimum.

First Messages from Momma

Most of the following short spirit messages were given during Sunday church services. The medium Cher gave me this message from my mother and Grandma:

"The energy around you feels good it's a healing energy. Not only for you but more for the people around you. Like your helper at home. As you heal yourself you heal them. I have your mother here on the left side smiling and a woman on your father's side perhaps an aunt. You've been hearing your mother's voice, haven't you? She's been singing." (From the medium Cher).

I know when Momma is around me when songs that she used to sing pop into my head. Reminds me of her love of music and, of course, her beautiful singing that she was famous for. Any family member who knew my mother mentioned her beautiful voice. Often to soothe us children, Momma sang "Summertime" from the opera *Porgy and Bess*. The words as I remember them are:

Summertime, and the living is easy.
Fish are jumping, and the cotton is high.
So, hush, little baby and don't you cry.
Your daddy's rich, and your mom's good looking.
So, hush, little baby and don't you cry.

That is all of the lyrics that I remember from childhood, but singing the song is still enough to calm me now. Momma sang Andy Williams songs such as "Moon River," Negro spirituals like "It's a Me My Lord Standing in the Need of Prayer," popular tunes from the fifties and sixties like Nat King Cole's "Unforgettable," The Platters' "Smoke Gets in Your Eyes," Brenda Lee's "Only You,"

Frank Sinatra's "Fly Me to the Moon," and many more. If I'm remembering correctly, Momma also played the piano and sang along.

When she sang "Itsy Bitsy Spider," she would climb her fingers one by one from our chest up to the top of our heads and then let them fall down with the rain. We would smile and giggle. She also, of course, sang, "Lullaby and Good Night" at bedtime. Another fun song was Harry Belafonte's "A Hole in the Bucket" because she changed her voice for the part of Liza and then the young man, Henry. A less happy song that Momma used to sing was "Sometimes I Feel Like a Motherless Child."

Other times, I knew when my mother's spirit was around because I would smell her perfume and even her cigarette smoke. I've always disliked the smell of cigarette smoke, and one day I asked her to please not share that with me, and she stopped. The mediums described to me the other ways my mother made her presence known.

"Your mother is here with an aunt. She's been around you, giving you support. Especially at night. You'll feel her around you at night putting her hand over your forehead, over your third eye. She says you've been overextending yourself. She's also showing me a little white kitten. You might not have had the kitten. But she's bringing the image of the kitten for comfort." (From the medium Cher).

No, I don't have a kitten, but I have felt comforted at night, as if I'm not alone in my bed, but not in the specific ways that the mediums mentioned. Momma's spirit warmed me in bed when it was freezing cold in my apartment. There was little or no heat in January and February, sometimes in April and October too, when the heat was lowered before the summer weather or not turned on soon enough when the weather was turning cold. I had four blankets and covers on my bed and wore a thermal top and pants under a thick jogging suit, and I still felt very cold. I prayed for relief and cried for comfort from my mother. To my amazement, I was soon very hot! Too hot. So hot that I threw the two top layers of covers off. I offered up a prayer of gratitude.

I had heard of yogis being able to warm themselves. I also heard about Native Americans and medicine people in Africa being able to pray for rain. I got the idea, years ago, to pray for sunshine and a dry journey when rain was forecast.

It worked! My journey would be dry all the way home, and as soon as I arrived safely in my apartment, it would start pouring rain!

Your mother is here with your mother's mother. She is showing me a desk that's messy. She says if you clean it up, then your work will be easier. Your father is here too, but at a distance. There are other loved ones here too. Your mother wants you to go to bed earlier. She wants you to take better care of yourself and shows me greens. Whatever that means. Perhaps you need to eat more greens. (From the medium Cher).

It was true—my desk at home was messy, with too many papers from school assignments and other important things to do. I did cook and eat a lot of collard, mustard, and turnip greens the previous week. My mother was letting me know that she was seeing and caring about what was happening in my life.

"How are you? Your mother is here, and she's the one asking. Asking you, how are you? She has glasses that she's pouring and mixing a concoction in. She said you haven't been feeling her around you the past two days. You need to listen more. She is showing me and having me feel arthritic fingers. Perhaps she had arthritis in her fingers, and perhaps it's been passed on to you. She's showing me she's helping with putting together a concoction. She's covering your ears. Like you're overstimulated. You don't have to listen to everything. Including something with your writing. Know that it is already done." (From the medium Cher).

My fingers hurt when they were cold, or a breeze from a fan was blowing over them, and from constantly typing. But I didn't know my mother had arthritis. Two rheumatologists who did x-rays and blood tests told me that I do not have arthritis. Later doctors diagnosed me with Raynaud's disease which is when fingertip capillaries are extremely sensitive to cold and painfully spasm and swell. Some people's fingers turn blue. Mine doesn't. Momma was showing me that she knows that my fingers cramped and hurt while typing on my laptop in the freezing cold classrooms at the university. I asked my doctors to write a letter to the teachers for ADA accommodations. Gratefully soon afterwards I discovered it was a lot easier typing on the smaller Apple keyboard and my hands felt much better.

"Your mother and father are standing behind you. Both say that they were too slow to respond to your needs when you were young. But your mother is with you now. She makes her presence known with household sounds in the evening and the sound of walking in flip-flops. She gets in the bed with you at night and lies next to you." (From the medium Rik).

"Your father is here too, but at a distance. He might have died when you were at a young age. Anyway, they're showing me him at a distance. There are other loved ones here too." (From the medium Cher).

My father is standing at a distance because he was not in my life during my childhood.

Chapter 3: Everything Changed

It was almost a year of attending Church of the Spirit before my mother brought through a full message for me. Seeing that I was no longer afraid of or skeptical of spirit presence and was comforted by her brief messages Momma decided that I may now be open to accepting her as part of my life after forty-three years without her. But first she had to ask me to accept her apologies.

The spirit circle medium facilitator Cher interrupted. "Yes, it *is* your mother. She is showing me a pretty green cloth she wrapped around her head. A silk, shiny, satiny cloth. She is saying, 'It was a big, huge mistake.'"

Tears came to my eyes, and all I could do was nod. Other memories came to my head too. Momma took us to several different mosques. I liked the one that had a blue swimming pool with a diving board across the street. I used to look out the window and watch people go up the ladder, walk across the long, white board, and with a bounce, do beautiful dives, usually headfirst into the water. Fascinated, I wondered how they did that and thought that I'd like to do it someday. I also liked the aroma and taste of the spicy chicken and rice that they served us. The colorful designs on the huge, beautiful, red prayer rug had me crawling and exploring the room.

Then she met a man at the mosque. He was a few years younger than her, tall, dark, and handsome. At my grandmother's house, both my grandmothers took Kani and me into the large kitchen pantry and told us not to let anyone touch us down there. To not let our new stepfather, do that. My grandmother placed her hand lightly there to show us where she meant.

They got married in the mosque. She was wearing a green sari made of a silk cloth long enough for her to wrap it into a one-piece dress. We watched as Momma smiled while she struggled to tuck it so that it stayed on. She was finally getting married. She was excited as any bride would be in a traditional white lace wedding gown.

Then we moved to an apartment above a storefront mosque. Kani and I had our usual bunk beds, and Emin slept in a bed in the same room. It was a large room with a beautiful, light-colored wood floor. We went to a new school nearby. I was in the second grade.

Arrival in the Midwest

We went to our stepfather's parents' home. We could barely eat. On the white wall in front of us, we kept seeing scenes of cows and the rows of corn fields on the farms from the windows of the Greyhound bus moving along the highway. It was like watching a movie. Our new grandmother-in-law cooked dinner. We were so tired that we began falling asleep at the table.

Our new home was a few streets from our new grandparents-in-law. It was a duplex, meaning that there was an apartment upstairs and we lived in a similar apartment downstairs. As you came in the front door, you would see the living room, walk through the dining room, then the bedroom, the hallway with the bathroom off to the right of the kitchen, and then the back porch. There was a factory yard with a high chain-link fence across the street. It was a quiet neighborhood. One day, there was an explosion at the factory. We heard the loud booms and the fire engines coming and coming and saw the orange-red flames going high up in the sky. We watched from our living room window. Our home was okay. Later the sonic booms of the new jets that went much faster than airplanes scared me too.

We were poor. Often there wasn't hot water. Stepfather cut one large bath towel into six pieces and gave each of us one piece for our face towel. We didn't have individual bath towels. Our face rag became what we washed our whole body with and then dried off with afterward. He bought our clothes from the five-and-ten-cent stores, otherwise known as Woolworth or Ben Franklin. I hated wearing the cheap panties—the elastic stretched out of shape, so they fell off of me and quickly had small—sometimes big—holes in them. I had to safety pin my panties to try to keep them up.

We didn't have a telephone. In emergencies Momma would have Kani or me run to our new grandmother's house to tell her what was wrong. She then called for help on her phone. One time, I saw sparks through the wood slats in the wall above the bathroom sink. I told Momma, and she told me to run and tell Grandmother. The firemen came and broke a big hole in the bathroom wall to put the fire out.

Roaches dropped off the ceiling onto the kitchen table while we were eating. The tops of black-eyed peas reminded me of the black tops on the roaches. I could hardly eat them. My stepfather would exterminate upstairs and downstairs. There was a strong smell of roach spray. But the roaches were horrible.

New Rules, New Religion

Our stepfather was a new convert to Islam. Momma was a Muslim too, but she did not try to force it on us young children. Kani was eight, I was seven, and Emin was four years old. In Philadelphia Momma read the Quran and the bible to us at night, the same way she read us storybooks. We watched her place her prayer rug or towel on the floor, then stand, kneel, and sit in the different prayer positions five times a day. We children observed and copied what Momma did. But she didn't make us make prayer. At night we would kneel by the side of Grandma's bed and pray with my grandmother before going to our own beds to sleep. I loved this time with Momma, Grandma, and God. It gave me a love for God.

In contrast, Stepfather made us get up at three thirty in the morning to make Fajar prayer and stay up late at night for Isha prayer. He yelled and punished us for falling asleep while sitting on the prayer rug for hours as he read chapters from the Quran, first in Arabic and then in English, during Ramadan. Both the languages were foreign to me because of the Quran translation is old English. One day he actually threw the Quran and hit me on the head with it because I kept falling asleep. It was preached how sacred the Quran was. The Quran was to be stored on a high shelf in the home, to be only touched with a clean right hand and to have a cover on it to protect it. Yet Stepfather threw the Quran, breaking the book's back. Even as a child, I saw the contradiction and hypocrisy of his actions. I began to not like Allah or being a Muslim.

Everything we used to do with my mother before she met him became a sin. We were forbidden to play children's card games like Concentration and Old Maid because playing cards was "gambling." He punished me for telling a woman at the mosque that that day was my birthday because Muslims don't celebrate birthdays. He told me I was too old to play with dolls. All I had was a monkey sock doll that I slept with. He tried to take that away. We were not allowed outside to play or to have neighborhood friends because they were not Muslims and he didn't want us to be influenced by them.

Kani and I had to start wearing pants under our dresses, although it was against the school rules for girls to wear pants. Stepfather told us at nine years old that our pullover sweaters were too tight. We also had to wear scarves, and Emin had to wear a small cap on his head. We were poor, so Kani and I wore the same green scarves day after day.

The neighborhood was probably safe—I wondered why he didn't let us go outside and play. Kani, Emin, and I played with each other inside the house. We made our own games and toys. For example, we made paper dolls and pop-up furniture out of notebook paper. We created cities on the bedroom floor using dried green pepper seeds to line the roads. Our imaginations grew. But Momma no longer played with us or read to us. She didn't take us anywhere alone anymore. No more long walks, or museums, or libraries, or playing freely in the park. Momma's marriage to my stepfather was a big, huge mistake. He was mean to her and her children.

Don't Hit

(TRIGGER WARNING for those who experienced past trauma this section has descriptions of abuse).

Momma was pregnant soon after we moved to the Midwest. She had morning sickness—if you could call it that, because she was throwing up all day and night. She licked salt and smoked cigarettes because she said it stopped her from having so much nausea. One day, she threw up on the prayer rug. My stepfather yelled at her as if it was the worst thing in the world she could have done. Another day, she fainted on the prayer rug. He yelled at her for that too! Momma had always been anemic. Stepfather criticized and yelled at Momma for almost everything all day. He called her stubborn, but Momma, after a while, didn't say anything. He would still hit her.

Stepfather also beat us. My mother rarely ever spanked us unless we did something very wrong, but he always seemed to find a reason to beat us. It seemed like he would beat me at least every other day, if not every day. He would come in the door asking my mother and then us what we did wrong that day. Kani would tell Stepfather that I was the one who did it. It was as if he would make up reasons to beat me. If I said, "I didn't do it," he wouldn't believe me, and if I lied and told him that I did do it, he still wouldn't believe me. He beat me anyway. So I vowed to myself to just stand there and take it. I refused to cry for something that I didn't do. He used an extension cord to beat us. We went to school and to the mosque with puffy welts on our arms and legs. That was the way that parents disciplined their children in the southern part of the Midwest. We had to say "yes, sir" or "yes, ma'am" to adults.

He made us stay seated at the kitchen table for hours until we finished our greens, turnips, beets, or whatever bitter vegetable. Sometimes I wondered, but didn't say to my mother, "Momma. Momma. Momma, don't you see me anymore? Momma, don't you believe me anymore? I'm still your little girl. I'm scared, Momma. Are you scared too? Tell him I didn't do it! Momma! You used to say that I did not know how to lie. Why does he keep saying that I'm lying? I can see that he's the one who's lying, Momma. Tell him to stop it, Momma. You told us not to fight, Momma. Why is he always hitting you, Momma? Why is he always hitting me? Make him stop, Momma! Make him stop! Do you hear me, Momma? Do you hear me?"

I wanted her to say, "I'm here, Haneefa. I am here. Momma sees you. Momma doesn't like fighting. Momma is going to take you away from here."

Even when he wasn't there, our mother no longer did activities with us. Sure, she cooked, cleaned, and fed us. Now pregnant, anemic, and constantly nauseated, at twenty-eight years old, her home responsibilities were no doubt a struggle. Almost everything that we used to do with our mother stopped. It was as if she ceased being our mother. As if we no longer had a mother, except in body. She cooked and cleaned, did laundry, and dressed us. She made sure we got off to school in the mornings on time. She still made the big, thick cornmeal pancakes that she called hoe cakes for breakfast. I would eat three hoe cakes, now with honey because Stepfather said, "The Prophet Muhammad ate honey." She also made cornmeal mush and other hot cereals such as oatmeal and occasionally Farina, Cream-of-Wheat, and Maypo for breakfast. Sometimes she mixed two or three hot cereals together to have enough to feed us. Breakfast was my favorite meal. She made wonderful oatmeal cookies. But she was no longer the mother we knew before.

More

Momma had a baby boy. Obadiah is nine years younger than me. She was even more busy as she boiled glass baby bottles and filled the cooled bottles with formula made from canned cow's milk. Powdered cereal was added to the bottles as the baby got older. Sometimes I helped wash dishes and the baby bottles. I liked swishing the bottle brush up and down, making lots of tiny white bubbles.

She washed baby clothes too. Momma had us help her wash clothes in the bathtub. She gave me the job of dunking the poop out of the baby's diapers in the toilet water and then putting them in the smelly diaper pail to soak. I hated washing white handkerchiefs in the bathtub because although initially the mucus would have dried hard and stiff on the handkerchiefs, in the water, it became endless slime that stuck to my fingers.

Out of the House

The only places that we went were to the Jumah services on Fridays and sometimes to a Muslim sister's home for lajna meetings for women. An elder woman taught Kani and me how to knit. We practiced knitting at home using pencils or chopsticks. The elder gave us a bag of leftover yarn that we patiently taught ourselves how to untangle and tie the loose ends together to make a useful ball of yarn. We kept knitting and knitting. Other times, Stepfather would take Emin with him and leave the rest of us at home.

Occasionally, on Sundays, we went on drives around the city, mostly ending up at the park. But it was very different. We often just played near the car, under our stepfather's watchful eye. Sometimes we would visit an older woman who lived in a wooded rural area in a suburb. Our family also went on long road trips to the Muslim convention. This was before expressways were built. We traveled on highways that mostly went through the main streets of cities and towns. There were only a few main highways with speed limits on long stretches of roads without stoplights. We saw lots of farms with red barns, cows, horses, and chickens, and rows of corn, wheat, vegetables, and fruit. Munched ate Momma's homemade oatmeal cookies along the way.

Then Momma was pregnant again. Stepfather got a new job. We got in a U-Haul truck and moved again, to another city. Two adults and four children in a tiny one-bedroom, single-story house. Momma had a baby girl and then a year later was pregnant again.

All Too Much

Then Stepfather came and took his children. Stepfather told us that he took the younger children away because Momma accidentally burned our new baby sister Marzia's leg while trying to bathe her in the small bathroom sink. The cold and hot faucets were separate. Plus, there were times when we didn't have hot water, only cold water. Stepfather said that he divorced Momma by declaring, "I divorce you" "I divorce you" "I divorce you" According to his understanding of Islam law all he had to do was to announce that he divorced her three times with us older children as witnesses.

Momma had a nervous breakdown. Being divorced, having her babies taken away, having to go on welfare, and the move to another strange city away from her family and hometown were all too much, not to mention how he constantly criticized her. Momma sat in the green chair in the corner of the living room and did not get up except to go to the bathroom. There she would repeatedly flush the toilet while cursing Allah aloud. In the living room chair, she talked aloud to herself too. It was as if she didn't know we were there.

There wasn't any food in the house except cold cereal. I fainted one day at school. The school nurse asked questions. Kani and I were asked to help provide information to put my mother in the hospital. I felt guilty for ever telling the nurse. We were sent to a private foster home. A Muslim family was kind enough to take all three of us in. Momma was eventually released from the psychiatric hospital, initially into a group home and then to her own apartment. She visited us at the foster family's home, but it was not the same. She bought us gifts. Momma was quiet, kind, and concerned, but they made the rules. She felt like a visitor, not my momma.

Momma used to sing "Sometimes I Feel Like a Motherless Child." At that time, I didn't know that my mother felt like a motherless child. She had a living mother, however it was an aunt, who we called Grandma that raised her. We didn't know that we would also feel like motherless children.

Everything in our lives changed after getting on that Greyhound bus. We went from the Northeast to the southern Midwest to my stepfather's hometown to the upper Midwest. Yet much more changed than our geographic location, and it changed forever.

Chapter 4: Help Wanted

Help wanted. Cook. No experience necessary. Will train.

I called the number in the newspaper ad and scheduled an interview. It was located on the far south side of the city, near the airport. I was surprised that the interviewer was wearing a military uniform and his name was Sergeant. He was young and cute, so I relaxed some as he explained that he was an Air Force recruiter. I didn't know what a recruiter was. I just wanted to be a cook.

Emin was in a high school program where he apprenticed as a carpenter at a private company affiliated with the community college in the morning and attended regular academic classes in the afternoon. Kani and I attended the same high school, but we were three years older than Emin. It may have been a new program. When I heard about it, I begged my foster parents and Momma to let me finish my senior year with the collaborative program through the local community college too. I saw there was a baker training program there. But my parents and high school counselors at the time didn't believe in women, especially Black women, going to college. Although I took some college-bound classes and received good grades, they told me that it would be a waste of time and money because women were just going to get pregnant, marry, and raise a family. Otherwise options for other women in the 1970s were teacher, nurse, or secretary.

I was a good baker as a teenager. My foster mother taught us how to bake. I enjoyed being in the kitchen with her. At first, I watched her as she baked, and then she let me help and later trusted me to bake alone. Kani made the best biscuits. She got up early on Sunday mornings and made three dozen biscuits, some thick, some thin and crispy, for everyone's personal taste, buttered and dipped in Mrs. Butterworth's or Alaga syrup. My specialties were cakes, yeast breads, and cookies. The cakes I beat by hand, two hundred strokes with a wooden spoon. We had an electric mixer, but the cake's texture was better when beat by hand. I used the electric mixer for making bread during the initial five minutes to beat together the flour, milk, eggs, yeast, salt, and sugar. For me, the best part was gradually adding more flour and kneading the dough by hand on the kitchen table. Often I made six loaves of bread at a time, enough for a family of eleven people plus company. We would eat some of the bread and freeze the rest or later. During the holidays, I sold my homemade cakes and cookies.

Anyway, I missed a lot of what the recruiter was trying to tell me as my mind was on one thing, becoming a cook. I missed understanding that this wasn't just any job in a kitchen. Not only was the training for the Air Force—it was a branch of the military. I sure wasn't thinking military. While I was enlisted in the Air National Guard, most likely I would be called to serve within the United States, but if there was a war, I could be sent away too! Seeing my shocked expression, the recruiter explained that I could enlist as a conscious objector, meaning that I personally did not agree with fighting and going to war.

Somehow I also missed him telling me, luckily he called me later on the phone, that in a month, I would be going away to boot camp for basic training in Texas for six weeks, and then I would go to tech school in Colorado for three months. I panicked and wanted to change my mind, but I had already signed the enlistment papers. I was very scared as the time neared because I'd never gone away from home before! I'd also never been on an airplane before. The Air Force would make the travel arrangements and pay for the plane tickets. It was a half-hour ride on the airplane before going to a bigger airport to get on a jet. A passenger sitting next to me chatted to keep me calm as I felt sick and my ears popped when the airplane went up and came down and taxied on the runway. To my amazement and relief, the jet was a much smoother ride.

Basic Training

We arrived at midnight, from many different U.S. cities, at the Lackland Air Force Base Basic Training Reception Center near San Antonio, Texas. Men were sent to one side and the women to the other side. The men had their hair cut, then shaved off with huge clippers. Women's hair was not to touch their collars and was tucked up under baseball-style caps. My hair was thick, so it barely fit. We received multiple immunizations in both our arms. They took urine samples, which I later learned was for drug tests. It was a very long night as we stood waiting in long lines while they issued us metal dog tags with our name and serial number on them, uniforms of green fatigues, dark blue work trousers, jacket, coat, sweater, T-shirt and shorts, canteen, belts, two pairs of black work shoes, and combat boots for everyone. Then we were measured and fitted for dress suits of light blue shirts or blouses, royal-blue pencil skirts or trousers, and dress shoes or pumps. Each of us received a huge green duffel bag to put all of these in plus a small briefcase for other items like flashlights. Exhausted, we boarded a bus to the women's open-bay barracks—white buildings with thirty beds along two walls of one long room divided by a center aisle. We were called by our last names and assigned to a bed and a locker. Grateful, we were finally allowed to sleep.

The next day, we were awakened before sunrise by the sound of a bugle playing Reveille and the woman training instructor (TI) yelling for us to hurry and get up and take our communal showers and to remember to holler "Flush!" before we flushed the toilet so that whoever was in the shower didn't get scalded. Our personal areas had to be neat and clean, with all our belongings either in our small locker with a small drawer or our duffel bag. Everything had to be folded exactly to six inches, the length of a dollar bill, to fit in the drawer. On the bed, the dark green wool blanket and white sheets had to be tight enough so that a quarter could bounce off them. Thankfully, my foster mother had taught us how to fold hospital corners at the ends of the bed at home, so I did less trembling with that task. One of the other women showed us how to lie on the floor on our backs under the bed to pull the blanket and sheet as tight as possible through the metal bedsprings. I learned to carefully wiggle in and out of my bed at night so as to not have to take too much time in the morning. Someone else showed us a trick of leaving our underwear and bras tightly folded in our drawers and putting the underwear and clothes that we were going to wear the next morning on the top of our laundry bags. All of this had to be done before we left for breakfast at the chow hall (dining hall/cafeteria) at seven. The TI was always yelling at us to hurry. We only had ten minutes to get ready.

We learned to say, "Yes, ma'am or sir," and "No, ma'am or sir" and how to salute all the "brass," the officers. In the beginning, not being able to see the tiny brass wings attached above the officers' chest pockets, we saluted everyone.

When we started marching. I seemed to have two left feet. After a while, they assigned me a personal drill instructor (DI) to practice "Right face, left face, about face. Hut two three four. Hut two three four," plus sing a chant. Part of the problem was with the drill sergeants' Texas accent, the word "face" sounded like "hace." It was like a foreign language to me. Yes, me, a Black African American, had to be pulled aside to learn how to march. I was only one of a few in the sea of white faces. My personal DI was of Mexican descent, Sgt. Garcia. He was patient. Eventually, when I got it, I got it! I loved the sound of boots hitting the ground in a unified rhythm, a dancing drumbeat to my ears. Soon the drill sergeants were yelling at me, "Mateen! Stop bouncing!"

Sixty women marching in unison, arranged by height with the shortest in front and the tallest in the back. We often passed groups of sixty men doing the same thing. Sometimes men and women marched together in one group, and it was awkward trying to get us sized correctly. Often we were off cadence until we were near our destination. It probably wasn't that I naturally had two left feet and couldn't learn but mostly that I was shy, and being yelled at by the TI triggered memories of being yelled at at home, which made me more self-conscious.

I never got punished in basic training, but I witnessed others being humiliated or sent home. We nervously stood stiff, straight, and still at attention while the TI went down the center aisle checking that every hair was in place, our uniforms clean and pressed, and our shoes properly shined. We spit-shined our shoes every night. The woman TI was harsh but gentler than the male TIs for the men. Oddly, the Mexican drill sergeant assigned to teach me marching was kinder than our dorm leader, Sgt. Tywkwinski, when he occasionally did dorm inspections. She was tall. He was short. Sometimes she would fail me for dorm inspection. He would pass me. I am very organized and neat, almost a perfectionist, so I didn't do anything less since I didn't know who would do the inspections or when.

The dining halls were located on the first floor of thousand-bed dormitories. It was all-you-can-eat. I could go for seconds and thirds or more on several choices of meat, chicken, fish, spaghetti, lasagna, bread, and desserts of cakes, pies, cookies, and soft-serve ice cream. The breakfast French toast on thick-sliced Texas bread I found irresistible. And so were the occasionally available pecan pie slices! This amount of food was a huge difference from the food divided equally between nine children when I was in the foster home. A long loaf of Butternut bread had fourteen slices, which meant each child could have exactly one and a half peanut butter sandwiches, with an end piece left over.

I went into basic training at one hundred pounds and came out at one thirty! It was solid muscle weight, I'm sure, because we marched or walked almost everywhere. We ran regularly and had to be able to run around the whole track four times to equal one mile by the end of the six weeks of basic training, plus there was the obstacle course. We walked to the firing ranges to learn how to shoot the M-16 rifles that felt bigger and heavier than me. The kickback was so strong I had bruises on my left shoulder. Women who were going to be stationed overseas after basic training had to hit the bull's-eye at least eight out of ten times. Since I was in the Air National Guard, my score wasn't crucial. This was good because I wasn't a good shot.

I got homesick after the shock of the new, fast-paced routine wore off. It was a couple of weeks before we were allowed to make phone calls and write letters home. I cried in my bed at night while trying to quiet my sniffles. Occasionally the tears came during the day. Everything around me and what I usually did were now completely different. The TIs and DIs yelling and screaming at us, pressuring us to hurry up and to do it right, didn't bother me as much as it did my dorm mates because I was used to years of being yelled at by my stepfather and foster father at home. However, I really longed for my sisters and brother.

Toward the end of basic training, we were allowed to travel around the base and into town alone on the weekends. Air Force bases are like small towns. I loved the small-community feeling. The BX was similar to present-day Super Walmart or Target stores. The prices were discounted with a military ID, so most of our biweekly earnings stayed in our pockets because we didn't have to pay for rent, food, or transportation. I sent money and gifts home to my family. Friends accompanied me to the theater, bowling alley, and other activities on the Air Force base.

Technical Training School

I flew in another Southwest Airlines jet to Lowry Air Force Base, United States Air Technical Training Command Center, near Denver, Colorado. Here, we lived in modern, high-rise dorms. Life here was very different from basic training. We didn't have roommates. We had private rooms. Yes, there were still rules. This was emphasized when we were startled awake as the military police (MPs) brought dogs through our dorm rooms in the middle of the night to sniff for drugs. Did I say private room? They still did weekly and random inspections for cleanliness.

We got up early and went to the technical college to learn to be chefs or for other on-the-job training (OJT). The evenings and weekends were ours to do what we wanted. It was a stepping-stone to a normal civilian life with a nine-to-five job, self-discipline, and eventually my own apartment and budget. This was newfound freedom for me in comparison to the isolating, punishing, tight restrictions of my family, even basic training had been better than home.

This was an exciting, fun time for me. I loved learning and discovering that I was indeed smart, dependable, respected, and competent. Not dumb and stupid like my family frequently told me. At the technical college, I received high grades on quizzes and exams as well as performance—in a kitchen with huge grills, mixers, and pots and pans almost as tall as I was! We wore white uniforms and aprons with mandatory hairnets.

"Order up!"

"Next?"

"Pancakes."

"French toast."

"Two eggs over easy."

"Fried hard."

"Scrambled."

"Order up!"

"Omelet."

"Just give it to me two in a glass."

"Huh? What do you mean?"

CHAPTER 4: HELP WANTED

"The eggs, just pour them in this glass." The customer smiled as he put a clear drinking glass near my face. I slid the raw eggs into the glass. "Thank you, ma'am."

"Next?"

I was thrilled that I could keep up with the fast pace. I stayed five orders ahead so that by the time the person arrived in front of me, their plate was ready. It gave me an adrenaline rush of satisfaction.

The meal that I loved preparing the most was breakfast, although we had to report to work at three in the morning to make food for over a thousand hungry people. This meant opening crates full of dozens of eggs, cracking them five to a small glass bowl so if an eggshell or rotten egg fell in, we didn't waste as many. The glass bowl also made it easier to slide two eggs at once out on the grill. Browning the potatoes that we'd peeled and cooked the night before for American fries or hash browns. Seasoning the ground beef and combining it with gravy to go over toast for SOS (I won't tell you what SOS stands for; hint—it's not a cry for help). Long strips of bacon amazingly crisped on sheet pans in the ovens.

We made lunch and dinner too. Every day, lots of spuds (instant mashed potatoes) that we drizzled more butter on before putting the pan on the steam table. Occasionally rice and the other foods served in Texas and standard at most Air Force bases: a variety of meats, chicken, fish, vegetables, potatoes, pastas, breads, and desserts of cakes, pies, cookies, and soft-serve ice cream. They still served the occasional pecan pie slices, which I eagerly looked forward to.

I had made new friends among my classmates and the other trainees on base now that I had opportunities to socialize. I was, however, "a square."

Robert, the only other Black person besides me in the class of ten students said it one day. "You're a square."

"What's a square?"

"You don't go anywhere or do anything except work. You're boring. You don't smoke. You don't go out with us."

Robert and the other classmates introduced me to tequila sunrises and strawberry daiquiris at the Airmen's Club. I took a few sips and spit them out. I exclaimed, "Why would anyone drink this stuff? It tastes and smells awful!"

Especially beer! It was the same the one time I tried marijuana—that only gave me a headache. My classmates threw a twenty-first birthday party for me at a private home. They passed around joints and drinks. I declined. Soon everyone else but me was sitting on the couch or a chair with their eyes closed, stoned. Eventually I got tired of being bored and lonely. At least at children's parties, people played musical chairs or pin the tail on the donkey! I grabbed my coat and I left. A little later, behind me, I heard one of the men call out to me and offer to walk me to my dorm building. It was dark and late at night, so I agreed. He was quite a gentleman. I arrived home safely.

I stayed a square. They invited me to discos with a large, flashing, colorful ball hanging from the ceiling. Again, I was bored. It was a different style of music than the R&B that I was accustomed to, and after my friends had a few drinks in them, they no longer talked or danced, no matter what the music was. Boring. How could this be partying? Instead, I enjoyed hiking and long drives with friends through the Colorado mountains, having intimate discussions along the way or just sitting silently, listening to the sounds of birds and allowing ourselves to be startled by huge or tiny creatures. I loved the smell of the pine trees.

All too soon, I returned to an Air National Guard base in my home state, and the rest of my airmen classmates went off to active duty in different parts of the world. They were upset and disappointed that they were not assigned to any of the Air Force bases in the United States or overseas that they had chosen before basic training. Recruiters are required to get us into the military, not necessarily tell us the truth. Most of my classmates really didn't even want to be trained as cooks. They explained to me that they were assigned to the kitchen based on their scores on the Armed Forces Vocational Aptitude Battery test (AFVAB). After signing on the dotted line, we were owned by the United States government and could be sent anywhere.

Apparently, I received a high enough score on the AFVAB that the officers at my local Air National Guard base tried to talk me into becoming an administrative assistant. They introduced me to a tall, beautiful, young Black woman who also tried to persuade me. But my heart was set on becoming a cook, and I insisted. In high school, I took a typing class; however, I wasn't interested in becoming a secretary. My older sister took typing, shorthand, and key punch classes. I only copied off of her in typing. At the time, being a secretary seemed lonely based on TV stereotypes from Mary Tyler Moore and I Love Lucy shows. Although I tended to be quiet, I knew I was really more of a people person and didn't want to be shuffling papers.

Weekend Warrior

The National Guard or Reserves members are called "weekend warriors" because one weekend out of the month, members report for duty. Once a year, they go away to other military bases in the United States for two weeks of training. During the rest of the year, they work at regular civilian jobs unless called out for active duty during state or national emergencies or wars.

I returned to my hometown and the nearest state Air National Guard base. Probably because the pots and pans are tall and heavy, requiring a man's strength to lift them, I was the first female cook in the Air National Guard kitchen. However, I was able to lift the smaller pans with ease and slide heavier pots onto carts to transport them across the kitchen. Twenty-five pushups and sit-ups a day in boot camp prepared me well! There were two young Black American men. I vaguely remember being introduced to them before I was sent off to basic training. I also was the first to go to technical college—the men were trained in the kitchen at another local Air Force base.

The first Saturday, I reported at 0700 to the staff sergeant in the kitchen to be assigned my tasks for the day. They had an interesting hierarchy, different from the kitchen at the Air Force base in Colorado. First, you make fresh salads, then you graduate to starches and cooked vegetables, and then the higher-ranked staff cook the meat. So I started out making salads. It took two people four hours to fill up a huge, stainless steel salad bowl that was almost chest high on the tabletop and three feet across. Most of the time, the other person was one of the young Black men. We talked as we washed and cut up crate after crate of lettuce, tomatoes, cucumbers, radishes, green peppers, and onions. I got to know Roy the most as we laughed and enjoyed each other's company. He often spoke up and protected me from the other men and unreasonable assignments I would have unknowingly agreed to do with my eagerness to achieve and be accepted. Otherwise, Roy was quiet and shy with me.

After months of making salads, I graduated to making other parts of the lunch meal when the staff sergeants understood that I had already been trained at a beginning chef's level to prepare almost anything on the menu. The Air Force granted my wish to become a baker by enrolling me in a correspondence course for baking. I learned, mostly from baking manuals mailed to my home, how to use the kitchen equipment and calculate appropriate recipe measurements. The staff sergeants allowed me to choose what to bake. People gave me plenty of compliments for the desserts I made. But to me, the huge batches didn't ever taste the same or as good as homemade.

In emergencies we had to be ready at a moment's notice but couldn't tell anyone, not even our families, when or where we were going. When the state employees went on strike, the national guard was called out to take their place. We cooked for one of the large state institutions for people with physical and intellectual disabilities. After we finished our shift for the day, we had free time. Back then, there was a lot of prejudice, especially in rural communities, so Roy and I stayed on the institution grounds and got to know each other even more. No hanky-panky, though. It's been said that the way to a man's heart is through his stomach. Well, Roy fell in love with me after I made a couple of loaves of bread from scratch.

"I didn't like you when I first met you six months ago," he told me.

"Why?"

"You were so skinny. And shy."

"Oh." I nervously giggled with relief, although I felt he was holding back from telling me his other reasons.

Roy was so shy himself that I was the one who proposed to him on the telephone. We married a year later and completed our six years of enlistment in the Air National Guard together. Emin, Kani, and I all married within a year or two of each other. Our mother went home to our family in Philadelphia for Thanksgiving and disappeared. Family there looked for her, even contacted the police. No one heard from her after that.

Chapter 5: No Baby Yet

In the earlier years, there was love, caring, and affection in Roy's and my marriage. We enjoyed doing activities together. Roy liked cooking on the grill outdoors in the parks. He would put small, dry branches that we found on the ground on the fire to get a delicious, natural wood flavor. Went hiking in state parks and even tried camping. We worked and traveled together in the Air National Guard. We went to family events and reunions together.

Sex was caring. However as my father-in-law warned, his penis was way too big although Roy was on the shorter side of average height. Extended, it often hit the back of my pelvic bone in my back, the pain taking my breath away in the wrong way.

Roy and I had been married for four years, and I hadn't become pregnant yet. We weren't using contraceptives or taking precautions. I came from a large family, and my sisters and friends were having children. At twenty-five years old, I very much wanted to have my own baby. Each summer was really sad for me as I watched other women with their big bellies.

While I was working at a hospital, I decided to go to an obstetrician-gynecologist who was a fertility specialist. This doctor initially told me that my husband had to come to the appointment with me and have medical testing too. But Roy refused. After I begged and persuaded, the doctor agreed to treat me alone. He gave me a little box and instructions. "This is a special basal thermometer. As soon as you wake up in the morning, take your temperature—before you move around in bed and before you get up—record your body temperature each day on the charts in the little booklet inside the box." He further explained, "This temperature chart, along with observing your vaginal mucous secretions, will let you know when you are ovulating. During ovulation is the best time for you to have sexual intercourse, since, hopefully, your eggs will be ready and waiting for your husband's sperm."

Month after month, we tried. I started hating to see the usual monthly period. I was almost ready to quit trying. Then the doctor suggested two procedures that he could do to help. "Both procedures could increase your chances of getting pregnant. The first one is in the radiology department and involves the doctor there inserting a colored dye that will go up through your uterus and out through your fallopian tubes. The X-rays will show if they are open or not. The fallopian tubes are very tiny, so the force of the dye could open them up wider."

This test showed that my fallopian tubes were partially blocked. The doctor explained his second option—a laparoscopy. "I will make a half-inch incision a little below your navel. Then I will insert a long tube with a light so that I can see your fallopian tubes and do corrective surgery as needed." It took several hours for me to wake up from the laparoscopy procedure, so I didn't get the results until a follow-up appointment the next week.

"Mrs. Mateen, the ends of most women's fallopian tubes usually have little, tiny, fingerlike flower petals that reach out and grab the eggs released from your ovaries. But instead, I'm sorry to tell you, your fallopian tubes are scarred and look like baseball bats. I did cut away some of the adhesions and scar tissue. I also put more dye through during the laparoscopy. Hopefully, along with the dye that was put into your fallopian tubes a week ago, this may open them up enough. Some women have become pregnant. Go home and try." He ended the visit with, "Make an appointment to come back in six months." The sad expression on his face showed that he really didn't expect me to conceive. As the meaning of "come back in six months" sank in, I was sad too as I realized he probably meant for a gynecology follow-up appointment, not an obstetric one!

Well, my next period was five days late and scanty. Usually my menstrual cycles were regular, which is pretty exasperating when one is trying to get pregnant. The doctor didn't believe me, so he made us wait another month. Hooray! No period. The doctor finally ordered a pregnancy test. The test result was positive. The following Sunday, I woke up with a sharp pain in my left side. I called the doctor, who told me to make an appointment so that he could examine me to see if the pregnancy was in the right place.

In his office, he explained, "Your pelvic bones are large enough and positioned correctly to carry and birth the baby. Also, your womb has grown to a three-month size. Therefore, your pregnancy is progressing normally." I left his office happy.

A couple of days later, there was a little dark red blood in my panties. The doctor put me on bed rest. I worked in an emergency room department as a nurse's aide at the time, which required a lot of walking, running, and pushing wheelchairs and gurneys, along with lifting patients. My mother-in-law told me to come stay with her since Roy was working. She was a retired licensed practical nurse.

The following Sunday, I woke up during the night with painful cramping in the front of my lower belly. I called the doctor, who told me, "If the pain doesn't go away by eight o'clock in the morning, go to the outpatient department. I will meet you there." Well, the pain increased to almost unbearable. Looking down at my belly, I noticed that with each cramping, it looked like there was a hard ball the size of a grapefruit under my skin that appeared and then went away, then reappeared. My mother-in-law comforted me, but she looked very worried. After a while, she offered me to give me an enema. Shortly after the enema, I had a bowel movement in the toilet. To my surprise, the pain went away. Naturally, I did not bother to go to the outpatient department in the morning.

Two weeks from the day of the obstetrician's appointment, when he told me everything was okay, I woke up with bright red bleeding from my vagina. He told me to go to the emergency room. They admitted me to the hospital and ordered an ultrasound. Shortly after I returned from the ultrasound department, two young medical interns came in. One of them told me, in a very matter-of-fact way, "The fetus was not in the embryonic sac. You had a miscarriage."

I began crying. The other intern then said, "Don't cry. You will be able to have another baby."

I silently sobbed harder. It felt like that was the cruelest thing anybody could tell me. Hadn't he read my medical chart? Didn't he know how long my husband and I had been trying to have a baby? The humiliation and unbearable suspense of infertility workups? The doctor not expecting me to have gotten pregnant this time? I didn't tell the intern any of this. I just continued to cry. He walked out of the room with the other intern.

Beside me, on the nightstand, was a small booklet that my mother-in-law had given me with an inspirational story and short prayers. In the back of the booklet were some names my husband and I had thought of for the baby. Clutching it, I cried even more.

Routine Procedure

A nurse came in with several consent forms to sign and an explanation. "A D&C procedure is usually done after a miscarriage. We will take you to the operating room early tomorrow morning. During a dilation and curettage (D &C), the cervix is opened to allow entrance to the inside of the womb in order to scrape out any fetal tissue still left in the womb. This helps prevent infection and continued bleeding."

I told the nurse I wanted to see the baby, no matter how tiny it was. My husband and mother-in-law called to ask how I was feeling and what I wanted to eat. We agreed on Mo's fried chicken. Roy brought it to me. It was delicious. As we ate, we talked and joked some about the chicken. Then he went home. Later that evening, I started to get really horrible gas pains in my belly that went up into my chest and shoulders. I felt embarrassed as I vomited up the chicken and coleslaw. Although I put on the call light several times, no one answered. With an urgent feeling to move my bowels, excruciating pain caused me to walk doubled over to and from the bathroom. I guess my roommate couldn't stand to watch me struggling, so she also called the nurse. I began to bleed heavily again.

The doctors decided to give me Pitocin to slow down the bleeding. This meant keeping my uterus contracting throughout the night. The hard, round shape in my lower belly now stayed rather than disappearing. What initially was painless bleeding, became constant cramping. The nurse finally came in and explained that I was having contractions. A middle-aged nurse's aide stayed with me, counting the contractions as the pain worsened and occurred more frequently. She rubbed my back. The more she rubbed, the more I felt like I was going to lose control and start screaming. I didn't tell her my fear. I just asked her to please not rub my back.

She offered to hold my hand and comfort me. "No, thank you," I told her. She asked me if I was sure. "I'm sure." She left the room. In my head, I was thinking if she held my hand, I would be screaming, and screaming, and screaming. The pain kept increasing. I didn't want to lose control, especially since I had a roommate.

I don't know how the idea came to me to pick up the newspaper by my bedside and, throughout the night, find and circle all the As with a pen. Then all the Bs, then Cs, Ds, et cetera, in order. Then I started over again with the As. I don't know if I made it all the way through the alphabet again before falling asleep. The nurse came in often to check my IV, blood pressure and pulse, the frequency of my contractions, and my sanitary pads for the amount of bleeding. Sometime during the night, the pain and the bleeding gradually subsided.

After the D&C, I woke up in the hospital room with a throbbing headache and was very, very tired. I lay in bed most of the day. During the afternoon, a nurse came into the room to wake me. "Most women go home within a couple of hours after a D&C. You need to get up and walk around." I told her I had a bad headache. She left and returned with another nurse. Together, with one nurse on either side of me, they sat me up a while on the side of the bed and then stood me up. They walked me slowly toward the hallway. We only got as far as the doorway to the hospital room before I fainted. They helped me up into a wheelchair, then put me back in the bed with the side rails up.

That evening, a doctor came in. "Your blood count is very low. You need a blood transfusion. We don't know why, because you didn't lose that much blood during the D&C procedure." The nurse started an IV with a bigger needle and tubing. She hung a small bag of blood. The blood going into my arm was cold, making my already chilled, anemic body colder. My head throbbed with each heartbeat. The nurse checked on me regularly, and by the end of the night, the bag of blood was completely infused into my body. Thankfully, the headache and chills were also gone. But I still felt very weak.

The next day, they gave me another unit of blood. I still didn't move from the bed, and I don't remember eating. I dozed in and out of consciousness. The headache, heart palpitations, and chills returned, along with cold sweats that night. The belly pain returned the day after that, except that by now, my whole abdomen was swollen and hurt too much for me to move myself even a little bit in the bed.

Since it was during the Christmas holiday, my doctor's partner came to examine me. He asked me to rate my pain on a scale of one to ten, with ten being the worst. "A ten," I told him.

"Is this the worst pain you've ever had?" he asked.

"No, it is not as bad as the pain I had with the contractions on the first night that I was in the hospital."

I guess he didn't believe me since I didn't scream and jump up to the ceiling when he pressed on my belly because I lay there another night without receiving any other treatment.

Emergency Surgery

I lay in that hospital bed for four days. On January 4, 1982, my obstetrician, who had been out of town on vacation, came to exam me. Roy was sitting in a chair beside me. The doctor explained to him, "Your wife is in serious condition. She needs emergency surgery. We need you to sign the consent form for her to have the surgery."

All this time, I had been alone at the hospital. That weekend, Roy had been out of town attending a cousin's wedding, plus he didn't like hospitals or seeing sick people.

The doctor pressed on my belly. Next thing I knew, I was floating on the ceiling and looking down at my body in the hospital room. The severe belly pain and headache were gone. An overwhelming feeling of incredible love and peace and total acceptance filled me up.

I looked down to see and hear the doctor yelling my name. "Haneefa! Haneefa!" He was shaking me hard. "Haneefa!"

Confused as to why he would be yelling at me, I softly and weakly answered, "Yes?"

I was going in and out of consciousness and what seemed like dreams, except that it felt like I was really living in the dreams. Some scenes were of endless fields of bright red, glowing flowers that filled me with peace as I looked at them. A few other scenes were frightening arguments and being chased. Later I woke up with the question "What have I been doing with my life??" repeating again and again in my head.

When I was conscious enough, my obstetrician told me, "You had an ectopic pregnancy. Your baby was outside your uterus. Instead, it was growing inside your left fallopian tube and ovary. These ruptured after being stretched to a size large enough to surround a three-month-old fetus and placenta. That's why you were bleeding internally. We gave you two more pints of blood during the surgery. I'm sorry, I had to remove your left fallopian tube and ovary." The next day, they gave me another pint of blood.

Complications

While in the hospital for an additional week, other complications threatened to take my life. A night shift nurse sat me on the side of the bed, listened to my chest with her stethoscope, and then had me breathe deeply and cough. Deep breathing and coughing, of course, hurt my lower belly and my chest.

She said, "You have pneumonia. You can't just lie here in bed. You have to get up and walk." She walked me to the bathroom, where we discovered that my urine was bloody. Lab test results showed that besides an infection, there were sickle cells in my urine. Each night, until I was strong enough to walk alone, this nurse got me up walking. She emphasized again and again how important it was for me to get up and walk every day.

So I did. I walked up and down the hospital hallways. One night, I even visited the staff in the emergency room where I worked. It was located on the other side of the hospital, so that was a long-distance walk. But a couple of days later, there were sharp pains in my incision that felt as if someone had stuck two pitchforks in my lower belly and were pulling them in opposite directions. One pitchfork pulled upward, the other downward. I could barely walk across the hospital room. Certainly I could not walk in the hallways, where the day shift nurses were used to me smiling and greeting them. Unfortunately, when I complained of the pain, they didn't take me seriously. One nurse noted that my temperature was up and said, "The flu is going around. You might have a touch of the flu."

My mother-in-law called every day to check on me. I told her about my new pains and what the nurse said. Eventually, she got angry. "I'm calling the hospital administrator."

Later that day, my obstetrician came and examined my belly. By then the incision was red, hot to the touch, and had several white pimples with pus on it. I also had a high fever. Roy arrived for yet another emergency as the doctor told us, "We will have to cut Haneefa's belly open again. Because she has an infection in the wound, we cannot take her to the operating room to do it. The wound will have to be left open so it can heal from the inside out."

He cut me open in my hospital bed without anesthesia! He did stick a needle in the incision and inject it with epinephrine, the usual local anesthetic given for minor skin injuries. But I was awake and felt the pain as he used a small scalpel to slash me three times across the incision. Even though he didn't like seeing people sick or in pain, Roy somehow held my hand. He yelled at the nurse's aide when she brought my dinner tray in while the doctor was cutting me! He stayed with me through it all.

When my obstetrician-gynecologist came in after the ectopic pregnancy emergency surgery, he proudly told me, "I gave you a 'bikini cut' across your lower belly instead of a vertical cut. This means that the scar won't show because it will be under your underwear or bikini. We also used staples—that's a new procedure—to close your incision. The staples also leave less scarring than regular suture stitches." Perhaps experimenting with staples on me was not a good idea after all!

The doctors put me on IV antibiotics, and I stayed almost three weeks in the hospital. They discharged me to my mother-in-law's home with the wound still open. They wanted it to close naturally from the inside out. It was a very deep wound, approximately two inches. Initially it had a grayish discharge, which the doctor said was a normal reaction to the silver nitrate that I was supposed to apply three times a day. However, I couldn't bear to look at it for even a second. Roy, of course, was too sensitive and empathetic, so he didn't even try. So, my mother-in-law did the treatments after the visiting nurses told us that it would be too expensive for them to keep coming. I was off work for three months before the wound closed all the way.

CHAPTER 5: NO BABY YET

I didn't know that I had died. Dying didn't hurt—it felt as if I had simply faded away. I was grateful to be alive and knew that I could have died if I hadn't gone to the hospital. I could have died anytime during those initial four days in the hospital, when it was short-staffed between Christmas and New Year's Day and my obstetrician was on vacation. Other opportunities for dying occurred after the emergency surgery. Yet I didn't know the significance of almost dying—or how my life would change.

Chapter 6: Aftereffects

Immediately after the emergency surgery, and for the following year, I grieved for my baby. I cried every night for three months and then less frequently. I also had memories of the trauma from the events leading up to hospitalization and the hospital experience itself, including the surgeries. I didn't talk with my husband about what had happened because he couldn't stand to see people suffering. Also, I hid my tears from my mother-in-law since she didn't talk about her own feelings, tending to instead express anger and blame. Keeping it all inside, I didn't talk to other family or friends either about my grief.

Yet I also felt almost blissful. Perhaps I brought back some of the peace I had experienced on the other side. I became more outgoing and less shy. The question "What have I been doing with my life?" remained in my head. I began changing my life accordingly.

I decided to enroll in the community college, Registered Nursing Program. It required a lot of reading and writing assignments web clinical practice however I discovered after awhile that I really didn't need to study because I was falling asleep whenever I opened a textbook. Yet I still excelled on tests. It was like I inhaled the lectures, although they included subjects with a lot of details such as pharmacology, applied algebra, microbiology, anatomy, and physiology and, of course, nursing as it related to each disease from infancy to old age. And with a new social life as students studied together in each other's homes.

Roy couldn't deal with the changes in my life or my blossoming personality, probably because he was no longer the center of my attention now that I had new interests. I still cared for Roy and our home, but I now had a life too. Basically, he was wasting his life out in the streets at night, not home much anyway. I chose not to enable him anymore. For example, I used to make sure he was awake to go to work after he had been out all night. We had three alarm clocks in the bedroom, each clock set at a different time, and he still wouldn't get up unless I poked and yelled at him. My nursing clinical training rotations were on different shifts the next semester, so I often left early in the morning. I stopped covering up for him, and things went from bad to worse. We divorced soon after I graduated.

There were two other reasons why we divorced. One is that Roy really didn't want me to get a college degree. Since he only had a GED, he was afraid that I would make more money than he did, although I told him that I wanted to adopt a child and only work part-time. We made an appointment to start the adoption process. But a few months later, Roy admitted that he really didn't want to adopt a baby. He didn't want children at all. At the beginning of our marriage, he had said that. Now, eight years later, he was the one who suggested adoption or having a woman friend have his baby. Then changed his mind again.

Living with Roy would frequently feel like I was living alone and talking to a blank wall. He was emotionally absent and later became physically absent by staying away for nights and days on end. Roy had reason to be depressed. His father allegedly killed his mother when he was four years old, lying next to her in bed. When he was a teenager, his father got out of prison and took custody of him and his two sisters. Then his father committed suicide by sitting in the car with the garage door closed. I did not know what depression was at that time. Roy would stay in bed sleeping for days. After a while, I learned to pick an argument with him by the fourth day in order to get him out of bed. Roy lost a lot of jobs. The longest he kept a job during our marriage was a year and a half.

Looking back, I realized Roy probably felt that I was the one nagging or verbally abusing him. I probably was because I did criticize him a lot and bossed him. While I complained about him being irresponsible, and at times not caring because he would forget my birthday, I never really gave Roy the opportunity to do much, even when I asked him to do tasks, because I was always doing everything. Being the responsible one, I managed the home, paid the bills, bought furniture, and sewed our clothes and household items like curtains and pillows. I was unaware that his foster mother did the same because her husband didn't have much education and was considered intellectually slow. My father-in-law worked hard at a factory and brought the money home to her. We were both in our twenties and were just copying what we saw our parents do.

Neither Roy nor I even knew how to be a family. My sister and brother and I sure didn't know how to even be siblings after my mother married my stepfather. Previously we did before, while we were surrounded by a loving, attentive extended family of grandparents, aunts, uncles, and cousins and our community in Philadelphia. Later we felt incredible loneliness as our stepfather took up all our mother's time with his criticism, arguments, beatings, and bossing her around and keeping her pregnant and busy with babies. We older children were on our own, often having to sit very still in silence at a distance from each other. We played together when Stepfather wasn't there and while my mother was busy, but our play was limited because we were always afraid that we would be stopped or later told that we were doing something wrong and get punished.

During my marriage to Roy, money also started to go missing from my bank account. One day I went to the bank to withdraw cash, and the teller said there was only $11 remaining in my account. This did not make sense to me. My paycheck was direct deposited the day before! I always saved a third of each check, so there should have been much more money in my bank account. Later I realized that Roy must have taken my ATM card at night while I was sleeping or busy in another room during the day, withdrawn money from my account, and then put my ATM card back in my purse or pocket.

At that time, I knew very little about the behavior of drug addicts. I thought there was another woman in the picture. And there was! I discovered her when I returned to our house to get my belongings a week after Roy roughed me up a little and I fled in fear. This was the first time he had ever abused me. In only a week's time, he had moved a woman and her little children into the house that I had furnished and paid rent for! Then Roy had the nerve to try to sue me during the divorce for spousal support after he was the one who kept losing jobs! Although our marriage was not physically or verbally abusive, it was abusive in that, for all nine years, I was often the main provider and decision maker.

Other Changes

When I returned to work in the ER department, I found that I had even less to say during break times and downtime when the staff would chat. I lost interest when everyone at the lunch table was talking excitedly about what they had recently bought, or the color of the bridesmaid's gowns for an upcoming wedding, or, of course, what their children were doing or what they'd bought for them. It was already difficult being the only Black person sitting at the table. It was already difficult for me to relate to their conversations and different lifestyles, especially their jokes using stereotypes and myths about their patients of other complexions and cultures. They would tell these jokes as if I weren't sitting there at the table. I'd end up laughing at them for being so ridiculous but thinking, *You are not talking about anybody I know!*

My personal values had changed. I also didn't want to hear my family and friends bragging about what they'd just bought, nor was I interested in what I could buy. I wanted to talk about my new spiritual experiences, which were all I really thought about. Becoming increasingly more psychic and intuitive—knowing about events before they happened—began to bother me the most.

Near-Death Experience?

Eight years later, in 1991, I went to a New Age store that I frequented for handmade jewelry, semiprecious stones, crystals, and Native American items. It had some books, but until I wandered to the back of the store and into a separate room, I wasn't aware that it had a used book section. I went directly to a bookshelf and pulled out the book, <u>Heading toward Omega: In Search of the Meaning of the Near-Death Experience</u>. This is the first time that I learned of the concept of a near-death experience. Sure, I had nearly died. But this author told stories of people who died, went to heaven, and came back to tell about it.

Most important, he explained what happened to their lives afterward. I believe God gave me this book that day because I had been praying and praying to God in the past few years to please help me understand what was happening to me. My whole life had changed. My values, religion, friends, interests, my career as a nurse all felt different, and other events were happening after my near death experience that no one could explain to me. I cried aloud with joy as I read, for the first time, other people's similar stories. I no longer felt alone, or weird about fitting in or questioning my sanity.

The Soul's Journey, based on the Islamic scholar Ibn Al-Qayyim's *Kitab al-Ruh,* also gives a description that is often recounted by near-death experiencers. The Angel of Death comes to the dying person to take their soul. Both the dying person and the Angel of Death communicate with each other, but not by physically seeing, hearing, or speaking. Souls of deceased relatives that are in the Garden of the Next World come to meet the new soul that recently died. The angel takes the soul from one heaven to the next to be with Allah. The angels there are as bright as the sun and gather around the new soul.

A typical description of a near-death experience is floating above one's body, or flying while seeing one's body below and what other people are doing, and traveling from place to place. Going through a dark tunnel toward a bright light. Being greeted by deceased relatives and other loving spiritual beings. More is described in the book, Image Heaven, which includes references from the bible.

Being shown a review of your life is commonly referred to as Judgment Day in the bible and Quran. The Quran also explains that you judge yourself. Those who returned to tell us about it describe how you will be made to see and feel all that you did and said that affected other people, the good and the bad, therefore being able to see and truly understand other people's perspectives and life situations. The life review determines your need to return to Earth life based on your deeds and what you've learned. After the freedom of not being restricted by time or space, plus experiencing the beauty, love, and peace of the heavenly paradise garden, most people are reluctant to come back to Earth life.

Most near-death experiencers may have only some of this ideal scenario. Each may be very different. Some may briefly go to what they consider a hellish place, or just a darkness or void. Others may go to other places they consider wonderful or intriguing.

Please note that what happens during a near death experience depends on individual beliefs and cultural influences from the country that you live in. African American stories for example are different. Considering that African Americans may have a higher proportion of near death experiences due to increased health disparities with life-threatening illnesses from increased racial stress, and lack of access to adequate healthcare along with exposure to systemic violence. This may be why there aren't many African Americans coming forward publicly telling their stories. There is only one book that I know of, *Good Clean Dark: African-American NEAR DEATH Experiences*. Stories may be different for other minority groups within the United States or other countries, or where there are ongoing wars, or in contrast with peaceful socialized or remote indigenous cultures.

But the aftereffects and changes upon return to Earth are similar for everyone. In, *Beyond the Light*, P. M. H. Atwater describes these possibilities and she also explains the physical, mental, spiritual, personality, and relationship changes people commonly have afterward. Although I didn't have an exciting story to tell about relatives that came to greet me, or the classic bright light and dark tunnel, my aftereffects were the same as those Atwater described. She explained that men, more than women, tend to have the more elaborate heavenly or hellish stories to tell because men are usually skeptics and have to be shocked to be convinced.

Physically, those who have had near-death experiences frequently have low blood pressure and digestive problems and experience new food sensitivities, such as I did, to wheat, meat, and other allergens. It seemed like I became allergic to almost everything—cats, dogs, rabbits, mold, dust, medications, none of which bothered me previously. Bright flashing lights, most music, and violent movies or television shows made my body hurt, as if my nervous system couldn't tolerate the vibrational shocks. Energy surges from my body and aura blew out my wristwatch batteries and screwed up computers. After a while, I gave up and stopped buying wristwatches. We had DOS computers back then, so if you made one little mistake, you had to start all over again, setting up your spreadsheet on a plain black or blue background. I stayed away from computers too for a while. Now using a PC spreadsheet is easy and forgiving of mistakes. You simply click Undo. Modern computers are not as sensitive to power surges. Still, I buy expensive power backups for my desktop computer for added protection.

Chapter 7: Second Marriage

(TRIGGER WARNING for those who experienced past trauma this chapter has descriptions of abuse).

My second marriage was a rebound marriage, meaning I married again six months after my divorce. It was a living nightmare and an instant replay of the constant verbal and emotional abuse of being told how stupid and ugly I was by my stepfather and foster father. My second husband, Sameen, talked nonstop, not letting me even open my mouth as he belittled me. To him, I was timid and quiet—after all, he was six foot three!

There weren't the almost-daily beatings that I and my mother received from my stepfather when I was a child. But having sex forced on me by my husband reminded me of the beatings. It also reminded me of the sex I was exposed to and forced to perform on my foster father as an adolescent. When I went downstairs to use the sinks in the laundry room to wash my period panties, my foster father would call me to a dark corner in the back of the basement, expose himself to me, and make me perform oral sex on him. Occasionally he would take me in his room, close the door, and commence to yell and scream and slap me around for some made-up misbehavior and then have intercourse with me. Very confusing and shameful for me as an adolescent, it was the only personal attention that I received from him. So, ten years later, it was equally confusing for me when Sameen would say he loved me, yet never give me any say, ignore my needs, and force sex on me without kind words, affection, or foreplay.

CHAPTER 7: SECOND MARRIAGE

Sameen also isolated me in the house, gradually preventing me from leaving to go to work, the mosque, grocery shopping, to visit friends or family, or even talk on the phone alone, just as my stepfather had done. When Sameen was not home, his two children stood watch to keep me from using the telephone. This was an instant replay of how my foster parents initially were nice to us, let us eat all we wanted, let us play with their own children, but later made Kani, Emin, and me stay in one room of the house. We could not come out of that room except to go to the bathroom and clean the house for them while their children got to play and go outside. They brought us their leftovers to eat inside the room. Can you imagine cold, lumpy oatmeal for supper?

Luckily, I only lived with Sameen for two months. Two months of hell. He cut my clothes, threw things, and called me bad names. He constantly lectured me on what a good Muslim wife and mother was supposed to do. And after all, I was a nurse, so I should understand his and his children's behaviors. He asked me why I didn't do my hair, although he'd previously praised me for leaving my hair natural—not to mention the fact that being afraid of what he was going to do or say next took up all my time and energy! Sameen wouldn't let me sleep or eat. I was stuck in paralyzing memories of similar abuse from my stepfather and foster father and in fear for my life.

Eventually, I asked him, "Why didn't you just marry an intellectually disabled woman (although no one should ever be abused) if I am so stupid that you have to tell me everything to do? I'm going to get you a sex toy doll with a vagina." I didn't even know if such a thing existed.

Sameen took his children and went down south after my cupboards and bank accounts were bare and he'd run up my long-distance phone bill. But the terrorizing reign had only begun. He called my home phone almost nonstop. I couldn't even use my own phone. I couldn't stand to hear Sameen's voice. He would call and say he loved me and ask if I loved him. Because I was his wife, I was supposed to come down south with him.

I called the telephone company and told them I was being harassed. He was also using my calling card, making very expensive calls on my home phone bill. Customer service told me to get an answering machine so that I could record and screen his calls. But then I still had to listen to his voice. Then he started calling Kani and my Muslim best friend Kameela, harassing them. Finally, Kameela and her husband convinced me to go see him down south. Kani also pressured me by telling me that Sameen was my husband, and therefore, I should go to him.

I Return to Him

Sameen met me at the Greyhound bus terminal and took me from there to a motel. From the motel, he took me to different places in the southern city, including to see his children. The children had been bounced from home to home, always a kindhearted woman or family. The woman at the home where I saw the children hardly said a word. She looked like she had also been abused. The children begged me to take them with me. But I really wanted no part of him. I like children, and I felt sorry for them, but I knew I could not do anything for them. He had taken them away from their own mother.

Back at the hotel, the horror intensified as Sameen raped me all night. As the sunlight woke me, I struggled to get off the bed. I felt like I was gonna lose my mind if I stayed with him another moment. I went to the window and broke it with my hand. Numb, I didn't feel the pain or care about the blood.

Two police officers came shortly and asked, "Is this a domestic dispute?"

My torturer replied, "Yes." The police turned, opened the door, got in their cars, and drove away. I did not know what a domestic dispute meant or why they had left.

Somehow, I managed to grab my hand luggage and run out the door. Fortunately, I'd kept my money stashed in the long knee socks that I slept in. After walking down the main road a ways, I hailed a taxi and told the driver to take me to the train station. Little did I know that the train and bus station were in the same building!

Sameen caught up with me there, grabbing my still-bleeding wrist and pushing the small pieces of glass deeper. I had to pull us over toward the train tracks and threaten to go under the train before anyone would come help. The police came later and asked if we were married. I told them no, which wasn't a lie because we were married at a wedding ceremony but never legally married by a judge or a notarized official. Even though he was insisting that we were married, thankfully, the police took him away. I was able to get on the Amtrak train and go home, twenty-four hours away.

When I returned home, I was confused, in shock, and my life still felt like a nightmare. I went straight to the hospital emergency room to have the glass removed from my hand and wrist. These services were financially covered by a program for rape survivors. There wasn't much else they could do since it happened in another state and it was over twenty-four hours after the rape. Two weeks later, when I had an appointment with a female doctor, she told me that my vagina was still healing from the many internal tears and cuts from the rape. It took years for my hips to feel like they had begun to return to their natural positions.

Fatherly Advice!

"You should have come to me for advice. I would've told you not to marry any of your husbands. You don't marry people just to righteously have sex! If you're going to have sex, just have sex. Your mother was very gentle and kind. She would not have even hurt a fly."

I stared at my father while I listened to him in disbelief. I didn't say, but should have yelled at him, "Well, if my mother was so beautiful and gentle and kind, why didn't you marry her? And stay with her?"

It was as if I met my birth father for the first time at twenty-five years old when I was with my first husband. He didn't advise me then. Where was he all those years? Kani told us stories about how she used to ride on his bike with him when she was five. I was jealous of her because I didn't remember him at all. Now, he was giving me advice about my life? If you had been my real father, my daddy, and stayed around and raised me, then I wouldn't have had a cruel stepfather and foster father!

While Sameen was far away down south or wherever, I read the book, *Men Who Hate Women and the Women Who Love Them*. The author explained how children in abusive households grow up and repeat the abuse in their adult relationships. The boys become men who abuse their girlfriends or wives. The girls become women who choose men who will abuse them! So when my father told me that I should have come to him for advice, I was so angry that I stopped speaking to him and refused to see him for a year. My family and friends couldn't understand what I was going through, and I lost my friend Kameela of six years because she was angry with me for not calling her and doing activities with her during my brief second marriage. Kani advised me not to get therapy because they will just drug me up and I would end up like Momma.

The Only Difference

My second marriage was a repeat of how my stepfather criticized and abused my mother, except that Sameen didn't hit me. I began to understand what my mother had experienced and why it was difficult for her to leave her husband, even if she wanted to. How he must have shocked and drained her energy. I'm sure she was shocked that anyone could be so cruel yet tell her that he loved her, and she must have been confused with how rapidly it happened. The day after my wedding, Sameen went from talking about how wonderful and beautiful I was to how ugly and dumb I was. He also criticized me out in public—the few times that we did go out together. Sameen too stayed away for days, sometimes weeks. Similar to going to the foster home as a teenager, my attempts at another marriage were like jumping from a hot pot to the frying pan and into the fire—while hoping and looking for something better!

The difference between my mother's marriage and mine was that I was employable and made a substantial income. I didn't have children. In addition, my sisters, brothers, and friends lived in the same city. So eventually, when I got past my embarrassment and shame, I asked for help. Although Sameen dwindled away my money, I was able to return to work and later get help through therapy.

Like Momma, I too lost my faith in Allah. I was very angry at Allah. I still did a silent prayer before going to bed, but I no longer read the Quran every day, or did my five daily prayers, or went to the mosque. All my piety for nothing! I prayed and asked Allah for a good husband. So when a Muslim couple introduced me to Sameen, I thought Allah had sent him to me! However, like my mother, my faithfulness and piety were used to abuse me. Previously, I'd enjoyed reading the Quran, especially since in the Quran, the Prophet Muhammad (peace and blessings be upon him) received revelations that gave rights to women, not take them away! What I'd understood of the commentary of the Yusuf Ali translation.

My grandmother taught me from when I was a little girl to not say "I hate you" to anyone. Even then, I understood her to mean that we should not hate, and I thought I never would. I was a good girl and a believer. However, Sameen was the only person that brought hate into my heart. I knew that if he ever returned, he was not waking up in the morning. When I heard that a hurricane was near where he was down south and that hurricanes can spawn tornadoes, I prayed to God, asking for a tornado to strike him.

After a while, I would automatically cringe and have terrible memories from being abused by a Muslim stepfather, then a Muslim foster father, and later a Muslim husband anytime I saw an oriental rug or any man with a beard or a kufi or Kenya cap on his head, or a Quran or any Arabic writing. The idea of strict prayers and religious routine brought automatic inner conflict. I needed help.

Battered Women?

The emergency room worker referred me to a free community counseling service. It was located in the basement of what looked like an old school. The counselor listened but didn't say much. It was as if she didn't understand what I was telling her. Perhaps she was a student. Somehow, I also found out about the Battered Women's Task Force support group. I had never heard the term "battered woman" before. There, the teacher educated us about how to see the warning signs of abuse during courtship or dating.

The warning signs were there. How he made me walk home with him out in the rain late at night, ignoring my suggestions to take the bus or to go inside somewhere until the rain slowed or stopped. He put pressure on me to have sex, even though we were Muslims. I wanted to be righteous and not have sex without being married. We got married only two months after we met. Some friends who knew him introduced us. So, not knowing about men and without guidance—which is the American way of hooking up—I trusted them and him, similar to how my mother married my stepfather. We were married in a mosque, but it wasn't my regular mosque—it was a small mosque on the other side of the city with mostly South Asian and Arab men in attendance. Kani and her young children came to my wedding. I trusted his character.

A few weeks after our wedding, he started telling me stories about his life. He bragged about coming from Chicago, where he had been in gangs and a lot of fights, and how he broke wine bottles on other men's heads. I listened. I saw how he smiled and enjoyed being able to win those fights. Love is blind because I had not noticed the many scars on his face, although I'd been sleeping next to him all that time. Even in the sunlight, during the courtship, I didn't see his scars or his flaws. The constant shock of his criticism and pushiness with his often, expressionless face, except when he was angry, blinded me to the truth.

The battered women's support group teacher told us that forced, unwanted sex during marriage is abuse. He could keep a hard-on for a long time. He, like my foster father, expected oral and anal sex, and both were disgusting and painful for me. How nasty-tasting and gagging it was to have semen and a huge penis in my mouth and to not be able to breathe! I certainly didn't want to swallow it! I thought that sex was the wife's duty and what was expected in marriage. I remembered hearing my mother giggling and laughing in bed in the other room, in the dark with my stepfather. She rarely laughed during the day when he was around or even when he wasn't home. Were they having sex? I never enjoyed sex. It always hurt! Later I read that a possible side effect of cocaine use is an erection that can last for hours. Priapism is the medical word for it. It can be dangerous. A man can die from priapism. At that time, I wished he would.

Not Just Muslims

One woman in the battered women's support group said her husband was a respected leader at a Catholic church. He said he never hit her. People believed him instead of her. However, her many emergency room visits' X-rays showed proof of her multiple broken bones. In another support group for men and women, another woman said that she couldn't call God the "Father" because of what her own father did to her. He used bible scriptures to say that sexually and physically abusing her was okay. I could relate—I still can't think of God without seeing him as an awful man.

Addictive Relationships

Later a coworker told me about a twelve-week addictive relationship course. She was in the process of divorcing her alcoholic husband. Since I had been recently married and divorced twice, I decided to attend the course with her. The course met as a group. I also went to weekly individual therapy sessions with the facilitator. The therapist warned us that some of us would be tempted to go back to addictive behaviors such as drinking, gambling, or sex because therapy would bring up feelings and memories! I didn't drink or do drugs. I didn't run out and get a boyfriend. She advised us not to get into a relationship for three years. After hours of being raped, I was not interested in sex anyway. I did discover that not eating or only eating very little helped to numb my feelings. This became my addiction and resulted in me losing a lot of weight over the course of healing. Unhealed past memories are intensely painful. The way I had to survive all those years was to become numb. I could smile and say everything was fine and truly believe it. I did not like to allow myself to be sad for more than one day; after that, I was up and about as if nothing had happened. When I was an adolescent, I would accidentally walk into doors, or trip, or bump my knee and not feel pain. That is how numb I had become! In order to survive the abuse from my stepfather and foster father, I was like a zombie.

PART TWO
ON THE ROAD TO RECOVERY

Chapter 8: Counseling and Therapy

Going to a good counselor or therapist can help because having someone to listen to and understand your troubles calms you. You may feel this calming even at the first appointment. Knowing that help is available and learning that you are not going crazy, although you may feel that way sometimes, you learn that you are mostly overwhelmed by life's stressors. The stressors may be worries about not having enough money or concerns about employment or your boss. You could be concerned about your parents or other family members, illness or death, abuse—someone hurting you or criticizing or bullying you—or you may be worried about housing or safety. These are things happening to or around you, yet you may blame yourself by thinking that you're not good enough.

The counselor will help you by understanding the situation and showing you ways to cope, relax, and solve problems to help make the situation better. You may also experience healing of past hurts and traumas. Learning to connect to what you really feel and identifying your sadness, frustration, anger, grief, guilt, happiness, and joy help you get unstuck and feel alive again. By saying your thoughts and experiences aloud, you begin to understand yourself and become compassionate toward yourself and others. You will be able to make better decisions. The therapist can also help you begin to trust again and learn how to have healthy relationships.

There are many different types of counselors and therapists. Some mostly listen. Some give you exercises and homework to do so you can see what it's like to feel better and live life differently. The following are examples of some of the counseling or therapy and common emotional struggles that I experienced.

Individual Therapy

In the beginning, talk therapy was okay. I could just tell the therapist, little by little, what happened to me. But the more questions the therapist asked me, the more memories came up. The problem was most memories did not come up while I was in the therapist's office until the end of the session. That meant leaving the office and having to cope with intense feelings by myself as I was traveling home. The worst memories mostly came when I was home alone at night.

Initially I only remembered the good about my mother—the fun activities we did together, the places we went. Although I wondered why my mother didn't leave our stepfather and go back home to our family, I wasn't upset with her because I understood at a young age that she was being abused, and I protected her by trying to be as good as possible. I rarely asked her for anything so as not to add to her troubles.

Guilt and Shame

There was also the guilt and shame of the sexual abuse and allowing my foster father to continue to abuse me instead of running away from the foster home. It was several years before I told therapists about the sexual abuse, and some events I never mentioned. I believed it was my fault all those years even though therapists explained that children believe even a divorce is their fault. But abuse is wrong and never should be done to anyone. It is the abuser's or the rapist's fault. My foster father was eventually was lightly punished with several months of jail time during which he was allowed to go to work during the day and be in jail at night under the Huber Law. But I still believed it was my fault. As children, we were in a worse abuse situation with the foster family than being on our own living with my mother. Plus, my foster father always threatened that he would send me away if I didn't obey, which would separate me from my sister and brother. Of course we were each told this individually, so we were very good children, even as teenagers!

No feelings were allowed around my stepfather or in the foster home—except for the men's anger. As children, to even slightly lift an eyebrow or start to frown or lift a corner of our mouths to smile meant being hit upside our heads or finding ourselves up against the opposite wall without really knowing how we got there. Therefore, I didn't know what emotions were.

Memories and Nightmares

Along with the conscious memories brought up from the therapy sessions came brief intense rapid images one image after another of the trauma. Body memories of the sexual abuse were the worst. Feeling someone inappropriately touching, raping or beating you all over again. Although now in reality the abuser is no where near you. When these memories occurred in the therapist's office, I didn't know what was happening to me. I was so caught up in what I was feeling that I couldn't tell her. When I did try to tell her, she didn't know what I was talking about and yelled at me, "Haneefa! Pull yourself together!" I started to dread the weekly sessions, but I went anyway because I really wanted help. All I knew was that I dreaded going to talk to her in her office, where, somehow, I would maintain my composure, only to suffer during the rest of the week alone. But I looked forward to going to therapy because I honestly believed she could help me. I did the homework assignments that she recommended, believing that the more effort I put into them, the sooner I would get better.

Endurance

My foster parents didn't give us pain medication. No allergy medication, either. I remember working summers at the public library when I was fifteen and sixteen years old. The first week I was at the library, I came home with puffy and itchy eyes, probably from all the dust. But my foster parents refused to take me to the doctor or give me any allergy medication. Their reasoning was that taking over-the-counter drugs would lead to us using illegal drugs, so I had to go to work with puffy eyes. Eventually the swelling went down by itself.

Perhaps being beaten almost every day by my stepfather taught me to endure pain. I was determined not to let him see me cry or see my fear. This, of course, made him angrier, but inside me, I had my dignity. I knew I hadn't done anything wrong. So I stood my ground and took the extra whippings with the extension cord. As an adult, I didn't even think to take medicine and prided myself on my good health. None of the jobs that I had were sit-down jobs. All of my employment required heavy lifting. As a cook in the Air Force, I lifted large pots, pans, and bowls that were half my height and full of food. Later I lifted two-hundred-pound people by myself at a nursing home when I was a nurse's aide. Because we were often short-staffed, we were assigned twenty-four patients on a whole wing or side of the building to do alone. Running to the other side of the building to get another person to help with lifting would have taken too much time. But thanks to our class on body mechanics, I managed to not injure myself or a patient while lifting. I only weighed 125 pounds at five foot four inches tall then.

Both these jobs required a lot of standing and constant walking. I didn't ever have a car, so I walked long distances to the bus stop to and from work and carried my own groceries home. I endured the frigid cold while waiting for buses. I was unconscious of the toll on my body due to understaffing, not taking morning or afternoon breaks, or lunch breaks to eat, or even to go to the bathroom. I prided myself on doing my best in everything I did, especially when caring for people who were at the mercy of others. Eventually my body did break down after I became a vegan along with working two jobs. The gradual increase of back pain that I had from adolescence didn't allow me to sit for long. My lower back began to hurt when it rained. My knowledge of body mechanics saved my back but put extra strain on my knees. At thirty years old exactly, my knees began to hurt. Working and keeping busy was my way of coping with both physical and emotional pain.

The emotional strain is another story. The abuse in my second marriage broke me, along with two divorces and the strain of often being the only Black professional person in a department—or the whole building. It was easier to cope with the physical pain than the emotional pain and trauma. It appeared to me and others that I was successful since I was educated, working as a registered nurse, and making decent money. But working a job as a Black person meant literally being worked to death while being disrespected, with more and more demanded of you, no matter how dedicated and good you were. I suppose my ability to endure pain with a smile indicated to others that it was all easy for me.

I couldn't even get help from psychotherapists or counselors, especially white therapists—there weren't many Black therapists in the late 1980s and early 1990s. I didn't appear depressed enough. I got up and went to work every day. My hair was combed, and my fashionable clothes ironed, even when I felt suicidal because I couldn't endure any more emotional pain from the constant memories surfacing of the bodily memories of sexual and physical abuse. Exhausted from daily nightmares keeping me awake, I didn't know what to do.

A nurse coworker took me back to the ER and talked privately to the doctor. They agreed to admit me to the psych ward. In my records was the previous ER visit where the doctors treated the cuts on my hand that still had pieces of glass in them and the pelvic exam that showed that my vagina still had big tears in it from the rape. Using anorexia as a way of numbing the pain, I was very underweight.

On the psych ward, treatment was mostly eating meals together in the cafeteria and going to groups all day—groups that never talked about any of my problems. There were mostly white men and a few women patients. The counselors talked to the men about how they were going to cope when they returned to work. I had a white male counselor. Eventually I told him how hard it was being the only Black nurse on the job and in educational workshops. He assigned me a young Black female nurse.

But still the traumatic memories and nightmares weren't mentioned by the treatment team, although this was the main reason I was there on the psych floor. One day, they allowed me to go out on a pass. While traveling, I saw my foster father from a distance across the street at a gas station. He didn't see me. I hurried away. But this triggered body memories during the night. In the dark, it felt like I was being raped again, alone in my private room. I got up and found the nurse at the nurses' station. I told her how scared I was of the memories. She told me to return to bed. Later she came and gave me a pill, which put me to sleep.

At the end of the week, my psychiatrist came and said he was discharging all his patients. He told us it was because we weren't going to get any rest with all the noise of drilling and hammering from the construction in the department next to the psychiatric ward. He was concerned about the usefulness of my treatment since my body couldn't tolerate the medicine I was faithfully taking. My blood pressure dropped too low, and my heart rate was too fast. I was having dizzy spells and chest pains even with low doses of Haldol prescribed for the trauma memories, and Elavil, for the depression. A friend who came to visit me told me later that I talked and walked like a zombie. I probably did, just trying to stay upright!

Sent home with a prescription for both Haldol and Elavil, I was on my own. Home alone at night. The psych meds didn't stop the nightmares or the memories, so I gradually weaned myself off them in approximately a month. On my own, I had to find a way to cope with the memories. I prayed and prayed, and God showed me what to do.

It is often written that abuse survivors block out their memories. I don't personally think that is true. I remember back to when I was three years old. Unfortunately, I did and do remember most of the abuse. Patients are usually overwhelmed with the many memories all coming up at the same time. What therapists don't realize is that it's easier for us to say "I don't remember" than "I really don't feel that you're ready to hear what I'm saying. You keep changing the topic and interrupting me. You're looking elsewhere instead of at me. You seem to know before I even open up my mouth that I was about to tell you a secret. Yet I never told you anything before, so why are you afraid?"

From childhood we've become sensitive to other people's feelings and thoughts to know when to get out of the way of the abusive parent. The automatic terror surfaces now—that we could not fully feel as a child—when we were threatened with what they would do to us if we ever told. The other reason we don't tell is we are used to protecting our parents from our hurts, and therefore, if we care about the therapist, we don't want her to hurt as much as we hurt.

Chapter 9: Alternative Healing Therapies

As you can see—and may have experienced yourself—talk therapy, even with psychiatric medications, is often not enough for treating abuse and trauma. Memories get stuck in the body, along with intense emotions that are very painful. Other nontraditional, alternative therapies may be an option. Regular talk therapy alone only made me feel crazy. But having alternative therapies, in combination or alone, over the years helped me heal faster. Psychotherapists told me that many of their clients who experienced the amount of physical, sexual—including rapes—and emotional abuse that I endured either went insane or were strung out on drugs and attempted or committed suicide. They wondered why I didn't.

Sexual Abuse Therapy Group

A friend introduced me to a sexual abuse therapy group near my home. This new therapist used a much gentler approach. There were no desks or chairs in the therapy room. There were only pillows and stuffed animals on the floor. Her approach was to use visualization to heal by teaching us how to replace traumatic memories with positive images. This was, as she explained, an eastern technique used to treat Holocaust and Vietnam War survivors. She explained about post-traumatic stress disorder and what flashbacks were. And how women's flashbacks were different from those of war veterans. Finally! Flashbacks are intense images and body memories that temporarily make you feel like the trauma, disaster, or abuse is happening in the present moment. Other therapist didn't seem to know about flashbacks. It was comforting to have a therapist who understood and to be in a nurturing environment among other sexual abuse survivors. She kept us informed about workshops around the city. The sexual abuse therapy group also discussed women's issues. (TRIGGER WARNING)

Healing Flashbacks

After a while, I began to notice a pattern with the flashbacks. First, I would get a feeling of overwhelming anxiety, fear, and dread. Then, a few days later, I would feel the pain in my body of being beaten almost every day with an extension cord by my stepfather, or a hand in my panties, or gagging on the hard penis and semen in my mouth, or the rapes. Then, by the end of the week, I would see the abuse just like I was watching a movie, but thankfully, the pain and fear lifted. I would have relief from the memories. Therefore, I taught myself how to sit with the anxiety instead of trying to avoid the awful, painful body tightness and tension plus the fear of the emotions. I knew that I would get relief soon, a natural relief, without drugs.

The main point is that memories come up as feelings first, sometimes with a lot of anxiety, where you can hardly sit still. As you breathe deeply and relax, the memory comes up. But the memory itself won't hurt. You'll simply get an image of the memory. Relieved, you'll say, "Oh, that!" Then the hurt and the pain and the strong feelings just simply disappear and don't bug you anymore. Maybe a couple weeks or a month later, more strong feelings will come up as another memory surfaces, and you will breathe through it and know that you're not gonna die or go crazy from these intense feelings. It gets easier and easier each time. Then you'll have your peace and your joy inside for longer and longer times.

Holotropic Breathwork

A participant in the sexual therapy group told me about a practitioner who used a combination of Reiki, massage, and rebirthing breathwork. I started with rebirthing breathwork, during which I reexperienced the difficulties of my premature birth, the feelings of not being wanted, and the feeling of abandonment from spending time in incubators and repeated hospitalizations for pneumonia. However, these rebirthing sessions were not traumatic but nurturing and healing, because the memories are mostly like watching a movie of yourself. Events that come up are then remembered, healed, and released. After each session, I would feel as if a great load had been lifted. I would be almost blissful for the next two weeks, until it was time to heal another layer of abuse that had surfaced and was causing anxiety. This was the first time since my mother married my stepfather when I was seven years old that I could experience naturally what it was like not to have emotional or physical pain. Gradually, there would be longer and longer periods during which I felt well.

The rebirthing technique was developed by Leonard Orr. We often tend to automatically hold our breath when we are afraid and stressed, and we then forget how to breathe naturally and properly. Rebirthing breathwork helps us connect to a gentle, natural pattern of breathing. A rebirther is a person that sits next to you while you lie on a bed or floor and helps guide your breath rate. She is there to support you during your experience, which lasts approximately two hours. You are basically rebirthing yourself as you get into a flow with your breathing. There are different ways of rebirthing, but most occur in a one-on-one session with a trained rebirther sitter. I only did the rebirthing that used the breathwork technique.

Memories and feelings come up to be healed and integrated. Intense feelings go away with the breathing and are replaced by peace, calmness, and a sense of well-being and profound healing. Negative and limited thinking also gradually decrease. One theory about the benefits of rebirthing breathwork is that it heals birth trauma from when chilly labor-and-delivery rooms had huge, bright lights; babies were spanked to get them to breathe; the cord was cut too soon, depriving the newborn baby of oxygen; and mothers were routinely anesthetized, requiring force or the use of forceps to pull the baby out. Momma told me while I was a young child the story of my birth. She said that she was gassed and "knocked out" with "twilight sleep" during labor. Twilight sleep, I now know was an injection of morphine for pain and scopolamine so that there was no memory of the labor and childbirth experience. Women were often woken up and given their newborn babies while they were still sedated and sleepy, which meant they had difficulty bonding to them.

Since I was premature, I had to stay in an incubator at the hospital until I weighed five pounds. Momma was a cigarette smoker before it was discovered that smoking during pregnancy caused low birth weight and secondhand smoke caused asthma and pneumonia in children. She said, "You were red and so little that when I did get to take you home, I had to carry you on a pillow." According to the birth script theory, people born prematurely spend most of their life feeling as if they need to catch up with their peers. This has been true into my adult life, but I now realize that a lot of this feeling is also because of the social isolation that comes along with domestic violence and racism. Actually, I did well academically and in my careers, even surpassing some of my peers. But for the longest time, I didn't know that I was successful. I just kept working harder and harder, thinking I was dumber and had fewer advantages than other people.

A year after the rebirthing breathwork, I was introduced to holotropic breathwork, which is similar except that it is a rapid breathing technique often done in groups. It also induces memories of birth, but more often past-life memories. Past-life memory scenes are often distinguished by unfamiliar clothing, buildings, and vehicles from a different time period. For example during separate sessions, I saw 1930s cars, brownstone houses in the city, and myself as a little girl who died young, as a Native American woman during a ceremony, and as a woman hidden away in a monastery and then in caves. I've experienced myself as a white man many times. The last holotropic breathwork session that I had was different. I was in a red car speeding down the highway, in vivid color, going so fast that it was a blur.

Homeopathic Medicine

Homeopathy was introduced to me through an African spirituality church class that taught meditation, breathing exercises, yoga, health, and nutrition, including Chinese and Ayurvedic medicine. Good health not only improves how we feel physically but helps us to have clearer thinking, happier moods, better behavioral choices, and better relationships with other people. During my first appointment, of almost two hours with a homeopathic doctor, he asked me a lot of questions about my aches and pains, on what side of my body, food cravings and dislikes, hobbies, work, my childhood, and life experiences. Then he gave me a dose of a homeopathic remedy under my tongue. An hour later, I had an intense urge to cry. Not usually a person that will let other people see me cry, I went to another room to sob. Later I learned that the homeopathic remedy he gave to me was Ignatia. Ignatia is usually for grieving soon after a loved one dies. My grieving had been delayed twenty-five years—multiple losses beginning with my mother at age seven, leaving extended family and neighborhood friends behind in Philadelphia, the miscarriages of two babies, and two divorces.

Sweat Lodge

Every day on the way to work, I had to cross a bridge over a river. I had a strong urge to throw myself over the railing and into the river. It would have been easy since the railing was only waist high. Married for almost ten years, recently divorced, then divorced again after a rebound marriage of less than six months, I was, of course, sad and depressed. But I wouldn't rationally attempt suicide because I didn't want to end up worse off than just having emotional pain. I knew of young people who had been crippled by risky diving or car accidents, and I didn't want a similar fate. Plus I was afraid of any body of water bigger than a swimming pool. Yet I still had the strong urge to jump off the bridge.

One morning, as I was halfway across the bridge, something hit me on the left side of my head. This shocked me out of my thoughts. I looked up to see a blackbird chirping loudly and circling close above my head. Stunned, I was afraid to move. Would the bird attack me, like in the Alfred Hitchcock movie "The Birds?" The bird stopped circling and flew a short distance in front of me. Then he perched on the top of a tall streetlight and stayed there while I slowly, cautiously walked the rest of the way across the bridge. Thereafter, that blackbird with a red-and-yellow stripe on his wing flew alongside me every morning as I went across the bridge to work and escorted me back every evening. In the spring, when the weather was warmer, he introduced me to his mate. She was tan and stayed in a small vacant lot full of grass and bushes next to the river. On the way home, I would stop at the lot and sit and watch both of the birds.

In the fall, the red-winged blackbird no longer escorted me across the bridge, and he and his mate left the lot. Not knowing about their migratory patterns, I was sad, of course, but grateful for the comfort they had brought me. The miracle of this was enough to sustain me. Then, instead of one red-winged blackbird, three of them would appear anywhere at the same time! They didn't come every day, but seeing three birds together became a common occurrence, and not only when I was alone. When my birth father came to visit with my younger sisters and brothers from his other relationships, while we were in the zoo parking lot eating our lunch, three birds landed on the ground in front of us. Oddly, the red-winged blackbirds were the only birds that would not accept the birdseed or peanuts in the shell that I usually carried with me instead of tobacco to give thanks. They did not accept my family's food scraps, either.

Camping?

All of a sudden one morning, I got the urge to go camping, but I didn't know why. Roy and I had vowed to never go camping again after sleeping outside in just a sleeping bag in a state park. Our individual sleeping bags were too short, so the mosquitoes bit our scalps, faces, ears, necks, and hands as we tried to pull the tops of our sleeping bags up over our heads. In addition, since we were sleeping on the ground, we woke up feeling wet and cold because the morning dew wet the bottoms of the sleeping bags. Obviously, we didn't know what camping was.

I called a friend to ask her if our mutual friend Karen was going camping. This was odd because I had not previously gone camping with her. She said, "I'll call Karen and ask."

In the meantime, I went to a sporting goods store and asked the salesman for the longest sleeping bag available. He gave me a seven-foot sleeping bag with an attached head section. I also told him I wanted a sturdy tent to protect me from rainy and chilly nights. I bought what he recommended, and then I went home and waited.

Waited and waited until Karen called, close to nine at night. "Yes, I am going camping. I am heading to the grocery store now because we have to have enough

CHAPTER 9: ALTERNATIVE HEALING THERAPIES   77

food for three days. Do you want to come along? If so, you better hurry. The stores will be closing soon, and I will be leaving at three in the morning."

Because I had such a strong urge to go camping and had done everything else, including buying the sleeping bag and tent, and Karen did happen to be going, of course I said, "Yes!" I didn't even know where we were going, yet I trusted the inner signals and feelings given to me.

While we shopped at the health food store, Karen told me where she was planning to go. "It's a conference that's mostly for mental health professionals. You and I are registered nurses, so it should be okay. It's on an Indian reservation located far up north. You'll need a tent because we'll be sleeping outside. They'll give us one meal a day. It only costs $75 for the week."

"Seventy-five dollars!? I've paid over $100 for each day of a weekend conference! Without the cost of the hotel room!"

For the most part, the activities were similar to any conference with lecture sessions. However, the purpose of the conference was to help professionals as well as patients understand Indigenous culture and spirituality. This effort would, hopefully, decrease substance abuse on the reservation. We were introduced to the sacred pipe, talking circle, sweat lodge, and powwows. In the talking circles, we all sat in chairs in a large circle and took turns speaking, giving respect and attention to the person holding the eagle feather, who was the only one allowed to talk.

My most memorable lecture at the conference was about the sacredness of androgynous people. The presenter was androgynous, and I really couldn't identify them as either female or male. It was as if they switched back and forth between genders in speech, voice, and mannerisms. Yet even these stereotypical gender roles were subtle. The presenter explained that in Native American culture, everyone's goal in life is to have a personality that is balanced between feminine and masculine. Therefore, those who were born androgynous were often spiritual leaders and teachers in the community. People who were psychic, intuitive, and connected to the spiritual world were also valued members of the community, unlike societal beliefs in the rest of the United States that such people were considered odd or mentally ill and rejected.

We gathered for the one meal of the day, lunch, at wooden tables outside. The menu included Three Sisters Salad—made of wild corn, green beans, squash, and lettuce—hot squash-and-wild-rice soup, corn soup, fry bread, and fresh fish from the nearby lakes. The food was comforting, delicious, and satisfying—and enjoyed while surrounded by wonderful people.

The sweat lodge was inside a dome-shaped wigwam. We watched as the men moved huge stones off the fire into a small pit in the center of the wigwam. The doorway was then covered with heavy cloth. Small amounts of water were carefully poured on the hot rocks to fill the inside of the dark wigwam with hot steam. In the sweat lodge, an elder led perhaps six of us in prayers and songs. He explained the purpose of doing the sweat and how it aids in healing purification of body and mind. I had an incredible urge to throw myself on the large, glowing, red-hot stone in the middle. This, of course, was very distressing and frightening for me. I also had a strong, sad longing for my mother, yet I sat still and quiet. When we went outside the wigwam for a cool, refreshing break, I listened to other people's conversations about their experiences. I was too embarrassed to tell anyone what I was experiencing. After the second break, I stayed outside and waited. I was disappointed to learn that this was the last round. I could have endured one more round in the sweat lodge. When the elder asked why I did not return, I told him the truth.

He advised me to tell my story to a middle-aged medicine woman. She listened to me first, then gave me two tiny red cloth bags with tobacco in them, explaining that a pinch of tobacco is offered to give thanks and respect for anything that you have received from nature or a gift of wisdom from elders or a medicine woman or man. Tobacco is also offered to the Creator when making a prayer request. She sent me to a young medicine man. We walked along a wooded path as he talked to me in a spiritual way that only a part of me understood, with my soul understanding most of his teachings. Yet I felt that he understood me, and I was comforted. I asked him about the red-winged blackbirds. He explained that red-winged blackbirds can talk and the bird was my protector, probably sent by my mother. He asked if I had been to a powwow before, since there was one happening the next day.

I smiled. "Yes, and I like the drums and the dancing."

He nodded. "It is very similar to African culture. You may want to explore your own African culture."

He also suggested that I spend the rest of the afternoon in solitude out in nature, walking to allow more of the feelings and understanding that had started from my experience in the sweat lodge to come to me. These experiences at the health professionals conference on a Native American reservation helped me resolve and heal some of my feelings about the disappearance of my mother.

Karen drove very fast leaving the reservation on Sunday because she needed to get to work on time, and we had many miles to go. Her car was red. It was then that I realized that not only did holotropic breathwork allow us to see our past lives, it helped us to see our future too! At the end of my last group holotropic breathwork session weeks ago, I had seen in vivid color myself in a red car speeding down the highway.

When I returned home from the Indian reservation, people told me that I had changed. They said that my face glowed and I appeared taller. Soon after, a medical exam showed that I had indeed gained an inch! All my shoes felt too tight for my toes.

African Spirituality and Healing Rituals

It was the deep breathing that I learned in the Black women's group meditations that helped me lessen the intensity of my feelings and the flashbacks. I had been sitting and enduring the anxiety of the flashbacks because I didn't know about deep breathing. Somehow the deep breathing and meditation together gave me a sense of stability in the rest of my life.

Auset, the mother within and the Great Mother, healing meditations of the Ausar Auset Society Church use deep breathing, music with mantras, and guided visualization. Receiving the nurturing and caring devotion of a mother as you see yourself breastfeed. Quietly saying an intention to remember your childhood or your past to help heal the conditioned habits from your parents and the effects of trauma. The memories that come up are gentle, similar to watching a movie with you in it. There was an Auset meditation in which I saw and felt myself in the hold of a large ship with other African people dying on the floor around me. Surrounded by vomit, feces, urine. Dying of diseases, malnutrition, exhaustion, despair, and grief. Others had jumped overboard or fought to be killed. But I couldn't die. I felt so lonely and resentfully angry that I was among the few who stayed alive. Why was my will so strong? Why did I have to survive? At what cost? I seemed to be on automatic pilot, without thinking about the consequences of being alive. This past-life memory connected with and explained the deep sense of loneliness and perhaps survivor guilt. I had survived childhood and marital abuse and societal discrimination. There seemed to be no relief or end to the struggle, in spite of pushing and pushing toward my goals. This left me feeling even more lonely. Many people around me seemed to have given up or had enough sense to only do the minimum of what was necessary at the time.

In another Auset meditation that resulted in a past-life memory, I saw scenes of a large crowd of African people leaving a village. They were moving on. As the chief of the village, I decided it was my duty and responsibility to stay behind and preserve the traditional culture. There were feelings of great sadness, loss, and again loneliness as I watched my people leave. These healing meditations helped me to see repeated patterns in my life. The healing results were a great relief, very comforting and freeing. Other types of meditations and rituals, such as for HeruKhuti (Ogun), completely removed the obsessive negative thoughts of depression in my head.

Psychic Awakening

Well, after these different forms of therapy healed most of the pain of my past traumas, my psychic connection began to open more than after my near death experience. While the flashbacks had deceased, my new struggle was with knowing things before they happened. I knew what other people were thinking, which got to be really difficult when they were my friends because I really didn't want to know when they weren't telling the truth, that what they were saying and what they were thinking were very different. I prayed daily for this sensitivity to stop, and after two weeks, it did decrease to a manageable level. My access to people's thoughts ceased.

Being in crowds was uncomfortable because I could feel people's pain, both emotional and physical. I'd find myself in a distant chair in the room, trying to protect myself from the bombardment of other people's feelings. This happened even in a small group of only seven people. When I learned to meditate regularly my sensitivity became less painful. A balanced empathy, however, was useful while I worked with patients as a nurse because I knew before they asked what they needed and how to reposition them in bed or in their wheelchair so that they were comfortable and relieved of their pain. For profoundly disabled patients, I was able to communicate telepathically. Sometimes they would physically speak to me, but other people didn't believe me because these patients didn't usually speak to the other staff.

I knew about the Gulf War before it was announced to the public. Usually I didn't watch TV or listen to the radio because I didn't have time while studying in nursing school, and I preferred creative, artistic activities for relaxation. The other main reason I didn't watch TV or listen to the radio was because, like other near-death experiencers, the high-frequency waves and sounds physically made my body hurt. But one day, I got up and turned on the TV just in time for the news report that U.S. troops were being sent to Iraq. For months previously, I hadn't been able to sleep at night because I saw and felt the heat from bright, orange-red fireballs, the pain and screams of people—mostly women and children—running down the streets of Iraq. The United States only showed Star Wars–type technology scenes on TV, while insisting that they only bombed enemy installations with exact precision. I was shocked that I knew better. Four months after the war was over, the United States admitted to accidentally bombing civilians! I also psychically knew about the Oklahoma City bombing before anyone told me because I had a feeling of dread and anxiety that intensified around three that afternoon. Later I heard the details of what happened.

I began having dreams at night where I actually felt awake, but not fully awake. It was if someone were giving me step-by-step instructions in my dreams. But most of the information was way too complicated, like equations and chemistry formulas. However, upon awakening, I wouldn't remember any of it in my conscious mind, even though I would wake up responding aloud as if I understood. In my everyday life, I haven't been good at math. For sewing and art projects, to keep my basic arithmetic skills fresh, I frequently add, subtract, multiply, and divide using a pencil before checking the answer with a calculator. My answer is often correct, but then I don't know what to do with the answer afterward. The projects, for the most part, turned out beautiful, although I ended up figuring out the measurements by eye.

What helped me a lot with my heightened sensitivity was Bernie Siegel's book, *Love, Medicine and Miracles*. It was almost in front of my face—in my way on a display in the middle of the floor of a university bookstore where I had gone to get art supplies. Although I didn't have cancer or know anyone who did then, I found the book comforting as I read about synchronicity, spiritual flat tires, being awakened in the middle of the night by loved ones who died and were on their way to heaven—long before receiving the phone call—and birds communicating with people. Red-winged blackbirds were frequent visitors during this time. *Love, Medicine and Miracles* also gave me the courage to begin living my own truth and dreams. I learned to listen to, follow, and change directions instead of being a perfectionist workaholic who had to have everything planned just so, becoming frantic when things didn't go as planned. There is a right timing, in spite of what seemed to be delays and obstacles.

Miracles Begin to Happen in My Life

I was at work one day when a young man walked up to me and gave me a small item. Puzzled, I politely told him, "Thank you," of course. But I didn't know him. It was at a large neighborhood elementary school built to accommodate children with disabilities, and so it had a lot of staff. Perhaps he worked on the other side of the building. But what puzzled me even more was that he gave me an item that I had thought of as I was waking up that morning. By now I don't remember what it was. It was something that I desired, or maybe needed, but I didn't have to have. I had the money at that time to buy anything I wanted. I could've gone to the store and bought it myself or saved up the money.

This happened at a time in my life that was very emotionally painful. Yet these small miracles made me smile and increased my faith. Miracles began to happen more frequently, seeing the red-winged blackbirds, the red fox mother with her baby that I saw in the city park, and being guided to different ways of healing.

My creativity was also high. I would wake in the middle of the night from dreams that showed me ideas for beautiful dresses. Then I would get up at five, go to my sewing room, select the appropriate pattern pieces, and cut out the fabric. I sat and sewed until the dress I saw in my dream was manifested in my hands. The same thing happened with ideas for full-length, long-sleeved knitted sweaters, which appeared in my hands in about a week's time! So many ideas were coming to me in my dreams that I couldn't draw, sew, or knit fast enough! One night, I saw a computer screen that could be used to draw my designs and do calculations for different sizes for me faster. Back then, in 1990, the computer screens were black or dark blue with only the white characters that you typed showing on the screen. Now in 2020, there are easy software programs for clothing design that could help me quickly change colors and styles. I was also following the guidance from my dreams in the rest of my life. Whenever spirit gave me a strong urge to go somewhere, I followed it. The money and the way to get there simply appeared. That's how I ended up on the Indian reservation.

Chapter 10: Momma Reappears

One night, I heard my brother-in-law loudly abusing Kani, who lived in the duplex apartment downstairs. She invited me to move there after she told me she had put him out. It was a couple of years after my second divorce. Frightened I lay in bed trying to plan how I could get my two young nieces out of the house safely in the event that something happened to Kani. Not able to sleep, I got up and sat on the living room couch. It had quieted downstairs. I felt a presence sitting in the other chair in the living room. It spoke to me telepathically—to my mind, not by a voice. It felt like my mother. She had gone home to Philadelphia for Thanksgiving dinner and no one in our family saw or heard from her after that. We didn't know if she was dead or alive. I was terrified. The next day, I went to the house of a friend I had recently met for a previously scheduled hair appointment. While she was braiding my hair I told her what happened the night before. She shared with me that she often had premonition dreams of deaths of people she knew. I asked her if I could spend the night at her house. She told me, "No. Go home. You have a job to do."

I went home, and for three consecutive nights, my mother visited me. I never saw her. I just felt her presence, and I could feel the edge of my bed go down as she sat. Momma communicated with me telepathically. On the third night, I could feel her hand on my back, rocking me, the way you gently rock an infant. I relaxed and slept well. The next day, while I was washing dishes, I felt the same feeling of a hand gently rubbing my back. As I acknowledged that the presence of my mother was real, I began to cry.

CHAPTER 10: MOMMA REAPPEARS

That evening, when Kani came home from work, I went downstairs to her apartment. Her eyes were wild, as if she were about to have a nervous breakdown. I told her that Momma came to visit last night.

"Why didn't you tell me and Emin?" Kani yelled. "We would have wanted to see her too!"

I didn't know how to explain it to her. I told her that Momma gave me a message for her. "She loves you, and everything is going to be all right." Kani's face visibly relaxed, the wildness gone from her eyes.

The following day, Kani left a message on my answering machine, "You need to go and see a psychiatrist. You know how much I hate answering machines, but I have to tell you this."

Later my brother called, saying he had spoken with our grandmother. She called me and said, "I heard of such things happening." I was glad that my brother and grandmother believed me and gave me support.

Two days later, there was another message from Kani on my answering machine. "I'm going to go and get help and join a support group for families that have someone with a diagnosis of paranoid schizophrenia like my husband." Kani put her husband out of her house shortly after that. To this day, I don't remember what our mother's full message to Kani was. All we know is that the message was important, healing, and needed at that time. The bigger question was whether my mother was dead. We assumed that she was dead. How else could her spirit visit us?

Later when I relocated, Momma's spirit tried to visit me at night at my new apartment. I felt her presence. In the dark, I was scared. Like a little child, I pulled the covers over my head. Eventually I told her to go away—and she did. From Mary Summer Rain's book, *Phoenix Rising*, I later learned that mothers' spirits often unconsciously go out of their body at night to check on their children. It is possible that Momma's spirit came back to check on her oldest daughter through me. And twenty years later she found another way to make her presence known and to communicate with me in a more acceptable way. Chicago IANDS led the way

***

Chicago IANDS

Several years after my near-death experience I found the book, <u>Spiritual Emergency</u>, in a university bookstore, therein I read of the International Association of Near-Death Studies (IANDS). However, it was a couple of more years before I saw a magazine announcement for the Chicago chapter meetings. A friend, Calvin, who also had a near-death experience and I would take a bus, a train, another bus and then walk a couple of blocks to get there.

When I first attended Chicago IANDS, the meetings were located in the basement of a Unity church in Evanston, Illinois. It began as a support group for people who had near-death experiences and now includes discussions of other spiritual experiences such as out of body travels. On the second Saturday of every month from 2:00 p.m. to 5:00 p.m. Diane Willis the founder and facilitator started the meeting by playing her Native American flute as we meditated for a few minutes. We sat in chairs in a large circle back then. Diane asked us each to introduce ourself and answer the question, "Why are you here?" Those who had a near death experience were encouraged to tell what happened to them.

Trying to walk up and down the stairs became too difficult for me. I was glad when Chicago IANDS moved eastward on Central Avenue to Evanston Hospital which of course has ramps and elevators. It is wonderful that participation increased to fill the hospital's Frank Auditorium with over 200 people. often with standing room only especially when there were famous guest speakers. However there was no room for a cozy large circle. Nor enough time for sharing longer personal near-death experience stories when passing the mike across each row to give everyone the opportunity to answer the question, "Why are you here?"

A long wide hallway and foyer in front of the auditorium provided space for registration tables, refreshments and tables stacked high with recent and older books about near-death experiences, the afterlife, past lives, and spirit communication plus DVD's of past Chicago IANDS speaker presentations. Each month I couldn't resist buying one or more books during the refreshment and social breaktime. Diane would flicker the lights and ring a little bell to signal it was time for us to returned to our seats. At 3:00 p.m. a guest speaker would tell the story of what happened during their experience. These were often stories of going through a dark tunnel and seeing a huge, bright light, meeting with God, seeing the beauty of heaven and sometimes the terror of hell, and meeting deceased family relatives and pets. Curious people who had not had a near-death experience also came, such as doctors, nurses, counselors, professors, students and scientists hoping to learn about what people experience as they are dying, while they are dead, and if they return to life.

What was most interesting to me were how people's lives changed after a near-death experience. Many returned to Earthly life with new abilities and talents—musical, artistic, healing, intellectual genius and psychic. Mine were enhanced perhaps as not new abilities but enough initially to have me feeling overwhelmed. Being around people at Chicago IANDS and the Church of the Spirit who had similar experiences and therefore understood calmed me a lot.

Other people came to the Chicago IANDS meetings because they were grieving the loss of loved ones, even their children—some who died from suicide. They came to get answers. Why did they die? What is the Other Side like? Did they suffer? Are they okay now? What did I do wrong?

These questions could better be answered at a Spiritualist church and by mediums and that is probably why the facilitator Diane Willis recommended the Church of the Spirit is where everyone should go. It is the oldest Spiritualist church in Chicago. Founded in 1897, in the current building since 1914 located at 2651 N. Central Park Avenue. All this was very different from any church I had gone to. The Church of the Spirit practices a religion called Spiritualism. Similar to a Unity church, its members and visitors come from many different faiths—Christian, Jewish, Muslim, Buddhist, Hindu, and more.

Back then, I rarely went to church or any place of worship. If someone invited me, I went only because I believe prayers are stronger when many people are gathered together. So why was I going to church now? For weeks, I asked myself that question. Perhaps it is because inside the Church of the Spirit, you can feel the loving, peaceful energy surrounding you as soon as you step into the sanctuary with the pews on either side of a long, red carpet going down the center aisle. You feel this loving peace even when the church is nearly empty, before everyone arrives. It was this peaceful feeling that kept me returning to the Church of the Spirit, although I didn't understand its purpose for about a month. It is the only Spiritualist church where everyone in attendance gets a personal spirit message from the mediums on the platform stage. Other traditional Spiritualist mediums choose only three to five people during the service. However, they give longer messages with a lot of accurate evidence about the loved one who passed over. The whole congregation tends to benefit from listening.

At the time, I didn't consider myself grieving. I had been to therapy off and on for years. Therefore, I thought I healed most of my losses. Momma thought otherwise. During the spirit circle, besides reminding me there was no more fun after she married our stepfather, she was showing me that the fun stopped not only during my childhood but for most of my life. She used to take us to many to museums, big-top circuses, parades, and more. My favorite place was the park. Romping through the grass, crunching on the leaves, and playing in the water fountains. My mother could have shown me a park scene, but she chose to show me the street carnival at night, which I'd forgotten. But my mother also chose to show me the carnival to acknowledge my spiritual growth and healing. She brought up feelings of my fears of the roller coasters and the other rides. She also gave me the image and memories of the live pony that I was afraid to ride. After much encouragement from my aunt and my mother, I eventually got up on the pony and rode. This was my mother's way of telling me that when I finally got up on the horse, I discovered that it was okay. Not as bad and frightening as I thought it would be. It was the same now, I could get past my fears. The fears that were interfering with my graduate school studies.

Coping with Losses

With the spirit message from my mother encouraging me to do something about my fears, I'm reminded of an earlier therapy session. It was during a stressful time in my life with several major changes. I'd been feeling well for a while and was surprised by the sudden intensity of my feelings, an unwelcomed yet familiar anxiety.

I thought I was healed until 2005, when I had this awful emptiness. I told the therapist about it, that I didn't enjoy anything I used to do—not even my art. I had my own apartment. I should've been happy after five years of first being homeless, then living in transitional housing, my aunt's house, and then three months at an assisted living facility because there were no wheelchair accessible apartments immediately available. I should've been happy to finally have my own apartment. But I wasn't enjoying anything. Then I became very anxious. It was the type of anxiety where I was not able to sit still, so I made myself busy and dreaded going to bed. I had tension so tight my body hurt all over, making me feel like jumping out of my skin. Then I remembered what I learned over the years was that being anxious meant that a memory was coming up. Although this high anxiety is uncomfortable, I know relief is coming soon after I breathe deeply and allow the old memories and feelings to surface.

To my surprise, the memory that came up was about how I lived with my brothers, sisters, mother, and stepfather, but we rarely did activities together as a family. My stepfather's agenda and moods took precedence. This led to an awful feeling of loneliness in a crowd and now an overwhelming sense of aloneness as an adult, all connected to the invisible position we children had in our stepfather's home. Thankfully, the horrible emptiness and loneliness went away immediately after I recognized the memory.

"Why were you feeling so empty and lonely?"

"I don't know. That's what I've been trying to figure out myself." I wanted to say "Why do you keep asking me that question?" But she was gentle and nurturing.

"Perhaps this is due to losses."

She'd said that before. I'm impatient, worried, but I calmly continue. "It could be. The memory that came up related to my birthday is that before we moved to the Midwest, we had everything, but then everything was taken away from us. A major move. When I recently moved from the suburb back to the city, I again moved away from family in a neighborhood similar to where I lived as a child with fond memories. That suburb had become home to me. Now I had to move again."

"At the other apartments, you had a community. You were worried about losing friends there too. But you still have them. As a child, everything went away. As an adult, you can still stay in contact with people. These days, there's technology like email."

"Yes," I said, "but socializing is so hard. So tiring."

"Why is this so tiring?" she asked. "Is there fear there?" I turned away, thinking about it. "Is there fear there?"

I said, "Probably."

"Fear of losing them?"

"Yes," I said, "Well, you helped me to see that there are other people in my life," I said. She nodded. I continued. "I think what unpeeling the layers to heal the past did was make me grieve what I had not grieved from childhood. The emptiness feeling may have been a big flashback to the huge loneliness I must have felt as a child. But I don't remember feeling lonely when I was little."

"Feelings get suppressed as a defense mechanism," she said. "When you feel safe, like now, as an adult the feelings will surface."

"Thank you for sticking by me. I've really felt lost for the past six months."

She only nodded. "You're not ready. You seem to go back and forth on doing this. But that's okay. Next time, we will talk about school. You seem to have some issues about school from childhood. I can hear it in your voice."

"I didn't feel oppressed as a child when I was in school. I liked school. It was an escape from the chaos at home."

"You got more attention from the teachers."

"No, not really," I said. "I didn't get encouragement from school or home. Some of the white teachers did hug me. I was quiet and cooperative in school. I guess I'm still afraid that if I release any more of what was the old me during healing or therapy sessions, I won't be anything. Last fall, I got a few glimpses of feeling like a child who is free, vulnerable, and innocent. That's something to be excited about achieving as part of fully healing. But I didn't feel safe. I felt scared and anxious. So I pushed these feelings away."

That June, I'd been coming to psychotherapy sessions with her for two years. It required a lot of trust to allow myself to remember and feel. I had a tendency to tell her my story without feeling it. For some reason I did better expressing my feelings when we went outside, although sometimes people walked by or even sat on nearby benches. Perhaps it was because I was constantly reminded that I didn't feel safe inside her small office behind closed doors. Every time we talked about my childhood, the room seemed to get smaller and darker, even if the sun was shining through the large window.

CHAPTER 10: MOMMA REAPPEARS

Monica commented, "I have clients who say they can't come in because they are depressed. Well, isn't that the reason why they should come in?" She was probably asking me because I came regularly to therapy appointments with her. I always went to appointments with other therapists too, even when I paid out of pocket.

"Yes, but therapy can make people feel more depressed. It's a lot of work."

"Didn't it help you feel better?"

I hesitated. "Yes, it helped me feel lighter and less anxious. But when I was depressed, it was hard to see even a few peeks of sunshine through the pain."

"Were there times when you felt worse after therapy with me?"

"Most of the time no, except when you helped me release a big chunk when we were processing issues concerning my stepfather. The void feelings afterwards were awful. I don't feel that now. I just feel like I've lost a lot of what used to be me, or what I thought was me."

"The feelings of loneliness and emptiness for months in the fall—is that why you've been reluctant to do more deep work?" she asked.

"Yes. Michael J. Fox, the actor, said he lost a lot to Parkinson's disease, but good things filled the gap, even better than before. I'm hoping that happens for me too."

"Yes, and that is why we try to shore you up, to help fill the gaps."

When I got home, I left Monica a voice mail message explaining the reason why I often avoid her questions or bring up emotional topics near the end of the session. "I have trusted you from when I first came to your office, although I did say in session today it took a year. It took a year for me to let my guard down and let you help me. Although you often gently confront me, I always look forward to coming on Thursdays, except for last month, when we had too many—three short sessions in a row. Then I actually dreaded coming. The problem with short sessions is issues aren't worked through during the session, and then there is no closure. The client goes home wide open with memories, flashbacks, and feelings coming up all during the rest of the week, especially at night, without any support or guidance on how to deal with the overwhelming intensity. That's what I refer to as the snowball effect. It starts as a snowball in the therapist's office, but by midweek, it has already avalanched the client. That's why I will clam up or change the topic if you ask me a loaded question so close to the end of the session. You have helped me, and I've grown a lot. To answer your question, I do feel better most of the time after sessions with you. The quality of my life has improved tremendously."

I called Mother Dear that night, and we talked. It was easier to do after the day's therapy session unlike other days when I was so afraid to call and be told by a relative that she was very ill or had passed away. Anticipatory grieving of yet another loss I didn't know if my heart could bear. I do have friends and family that I talk to. I can talk about most things with them now. I've just been afraid to cherish them or be vulnerable with them.

I'm also recently reminded of when I told a friend that I was going to therapy, she told me that there was no need to go to therapy because God was all that she needed, and it really struck a raw nerve for me. After being invited to attend church one Sunday, I thought about churches' exploitation of people's misery without helping them improve their lives. I was reminded subconsciously about how religion was used to abuse me. If I had answered the therapist's questions about school, I probably would have talked about how my stepfather made us outcasts at school with the religious fanaticism that he imposed on us. How he didn't allow my mother to support us at school functions or encourage our education like she used to. Memories of when prior to the stepfather, Momma and my grandmother used to buy us new school clothes each year and funded school activities.

In my thirties, I did get kind of fanatical myself with meditating for thirty minutes once or twice a day and having a strict vegan diet. The food was healthy, but so coarse it was probably more suitable for farm animals. It also left me feeling very lonely. No one else was that strict with their life, although we belonged to the same religious group and heard the same rules. A loneliness I never knew before my stepfather came into my life.

Anniversaries

For years I would get depressed in the fall, starting in October, because I had too many losses or reminders of losses in that season. The divorce from my first husband was in October. Momma disappeared in November, soon after Thanksgiving. I had miscarried my baby in the month of December. The

CHAPTER 10: MOMMA REAPPEARS

following stories are other ways that Momma has helped in my everyday life, without a medium.

On Momma's birthday, which is April 22, I would feel especially confused and moody and have difficulty concentrating. It was only at the end of the day, usually at bedtime, that I remembered, "Oh! It's my mother's birthday!" It's not like I ever forget the date of my mother's birth. I just had a tendency as I got older to remember everyone's birthdays a few days before, but not on the day. However, it is only my mother's birthday that gives me such a strong reaction. I'd simply remember other people's birthdays in the next day or so and then call and wish them a happy belated birthday. My mother, however, wouldn't let me forget hers.

My cousin, who is an Uber driver, took us through our old neighborhood. Amazingly, the houses had not changed on the outside. That is the charm of Philadelphia. Later in the week, my uncle took us to Reading Terminal, one of the largest and oldest public markets. It was built in 1893. The first store we went in near the entrance was Sweet As Fudge, a shop that sells old-fashioned candy. Homemade fudge, peanut brittle, French burnt peanuts, coconut, malt balls, and licorice sticks. Of course, there were the popular "penny" candies such as Mary Janes, Squirrel nut chews, Tootsie Rolls, Bit-o-Honey, Chick-O-Sticks, Dad's Root Beer Barrels, Goldenberg's Peanut Chews, lollipops, gum balls, Lemonheads and assorted Brach's candies. There were fresh nuts, including Mother Dear's—and thus our family's—favorite, pistachios. My brother got tired of us *ooh*ing and *ahh*ing and saying, "Oh, look at this!" and "Do you remember this?" He moved on.

We found him later at the Bassetts Ice Cream counter ordering a butter pecan cone. I asked for the same with tears in my eyes, because butter pecan was Momma's favorite ice cream. My brother did not know this. He was too young when we first left Philadelphia. They served us three large scoops each. While the ice cream was incredibly delicious, it was too much for us to finish. I was lactose intolerant and allergic to milk, and my brother had diabetes. To my astonishment, I did not get sick!

We explored the rest of Reading Terminal. There were lots of meat and seafood shops and a large produce area with abundant fresh fruits and vegetables. I vaguely remembered coming here when I was little. Momma told us stories about being able to buy chocolate-covered grasshoppers and ants and fried frog legs there. I don't know if she was pulling our legs when she was telling us this, nor do I know if she actually ate these delicacies herself. I'm also reminded of her stories about an uncle who caught and cooked snapping turtle, raccoon, and fried frog legs, which tasted like chicken. Momma might have eaten these because she brought rabbit, pheasant, and oyster to us when we were living in the foster home. There are a lot of ethnic shops in Reading Terminal, but I didn't see any strange food there, and I wasn't going to ask. (Okay, I am now shocked after googling "chocolate-covered grasshoppers" just for the heck of it. You can actually buy them now, along with ants and other edible insects, in snack bags similar to potato chips or nuts from Amazon! Extra source of protein, I guess).

Our younger sister, Margie, put together a family reunion of my father's adult children and grandchildren. We went to Golden Corral, a buffet restaurant, on a Sunday. We arrived just as the restaurant was getting crowded with people coming from church. Our family is very large. It was good to have such a wide variety of food choices. After I finished eating, I looked down and was surprised to see a big blue cotton candy in front of me on the table! Margie had put it there. Tears came to my eyes as I remembered it was our mother's birthday. It was her gift to me on her birthday.

I was reminded of when I was five years old and wanted cotton candy from the vendor's cart at parades or in the neighborhood. It looked so pretty in pastel pink, yellow, blue, and purple, so it had to taste good! But Momma wouldn't buy it for me. I couldn't understand why, so I kept asking her. Eventually, one day, she gave me cotton candy. I tried to bite it, but it disappeared as it melted and hardly had any taste. I was so disappointed and angry that I threw the cotton candy down on the ground. Crying, I yelled at Momma. She must have known me better than I did—otherwise she usually gave me what I wanted.

Afterward, we went to our grandmother who we lovingly called Mother Dear's and my father's gravesites at the cemetery. Mother Dear passed away in 2017 at 106 years old. I didn't cry much because I was truly blessed to have had her in my life until past the age of myself being the age of a grandmother. My father's grave was in the military section. He served in the Korean War. I don't know where Momma is buried.

CHAPTER 10: MOMMA REAPPEARS

April 2020. Today is Momma's Earth Day. I thought of her throughout the day. As I wrote in my journal, Momma's spirit reminded me of the lovely-smelling lilac powder she gave me for my eleventh birthday. The powder was in a large, light purple round container with a powder puff inside. I loved the smell and dabbed it generously on my neck and chest. When I was younger, in Philadelphia, I loved the beauty and the smell of lilac flowers, especially after it rained. I don't know how Momma survived emotionally. I was homesick for the lilacs, honeysuckle, fireflies, and Fairmont Park that we left behind.

The jonquils that I saw on my way to the grocery store in Chicago also reminded me of Momma, who then reminded me of the lilacs. In the fourth grade, we painted pictures of lilacs. The teacher also had us make jonquils out of yellow and green paper for the spring season, and later roses out of layers of soft, pink facial tissue for Mother's Day. Momma was acknowledging receipt of those gifts I brought home to her. These memories from Momma are a precious gift to me this morning. She let me know that although she was quiet and didn't seem to take notice of us back when I was nine or ten years old, she *was* aware and *cared* about us. In spite of stepfather being so abusive that Momma was depressed, and he didn't allow her to be a mother to us.

I also received a precious letter from Kani, in which she mentioned Momma being resurrected by God on Resurrection Day so that we could be together again. I opened her letter on Momma's birthday! Kani hadn't written a letter to me before. The letter was dated April 17, and it took a couple of days for the postal service to deliver out-of-state mail. Also, because of the coronavirus crisis, I only left my apartment once a week to go to the grocery store and check my mailbox. That's how come I read it on Momma's birthday. To my surprise, Kani mentioned Momma, which she rarely did, even in phone conversations.

The next day, I called our brother Emin the day after Momma's birthday, after I realized that Momma had given me a message with the images of jonquils and the memory of the lilac powder. Curious, I asked him, "Did anything happened to you yesterday since it was Momma's birthday?"

"I never knew when Momma's birthday was. I don't remember much of Momma, except that she read me stories," he said. It is for my brothers and younger sisters that I got brave enough to write this book. So they can get to know Momma.

Chapter 11: Healing Assignments from Momma

The first year of a clinical psychology doctoral program is challenging, of course, but I had some additional anxieties. There were three teachers that took off points for grammar and punctuation errors and graded accordingly. Why wasn't emphasis placed instead on whether students understood the lectures, reading assignments, and could apply the principles of clinical psychology? In addition, a teacher made me repeat a course. Over time, my anxiety level increased, until two weeks into the summer semester, I was so anxious and restless that whenever I started to think about doing even a minor writing assignment for any class, I could not sit still. My mind went blank. In order to avoid the anxiety, which felt like painful muscle tension all over my body, I would get up and do another activity for distraction. Days went by as I tried to relax enough to start my writing assignments. Worry kept me awake all night, and my appetite decreased due to a nervous stomach. I had automatic thoughts that the teachers would give me a bad grade. 'I can't do this now. This is too much. Nothing I ever do is good enough. I'll never be able to find every mistake.'

Both of my grandmothers in Philadelphia insisted that we speak proper English and often corrected our pronunciation. They didn't allow "ain't" or "y'all" or "yeah," so I actually did very well with spelling and reading. When I was in the first grade, an older white teacher kept putting me back in the lowest reading group because I "read too fast." Of course I read fast! My mother read

CHAPTER 11: HEALING ASSIGNMENTS FROM MOMMA

to us daily, so I already knew how to read by the time I got to first grade. Really read, beyond "See Spot run!" Later, when I was in the fifth grade, another white teacher told my stepfather that I was very good at art and reading but I didn't know my multiplication tables and long division. My stepfather beat me. Neither the teacher nor my parents tutored me to help me understand how to do the math. I had to teach myself from the pictures and examples in the math book.

Both my stepfather and foster father frequently physically and verbally punished me for trivial reasons without an explanation and told me I was bad, dumb, and stupid. Although I worked extra hard and took pride in my work, they still criticized me, often making me do tasks over and over again. As a result, I often thought that I was dumb, and people would not be there for me. I had anxiety even thinking about asking my teachers or my advisor for help.

Instead, I just worked harder and longer, and when that strategy wasn't enough, I became afraid to even try and procrastinated in order to avoid anxiety. Until the doctoral program, I could usually push past my discomfort and do whatever needed to be done anyway. But the more I procrastinated, the more I handed in late or incomplete papers, and the more teachers gave me lower grades, increasing my anxiety and procrastination. I missed being with my family and community and participating in cultural activities due to the extra time it took me to do my schoolwork.

As part of the cognitive behavioral class, students were to choose a habit we wanted to change. I focused on reducing the distress of my anxiety symptoms and gradually reducing my fears around writing. My goal of no procrastinating was important enough for me to commit to during at least an hour of writing school assignments daily. This meant sitting at the computer in spite of the anxiety and doing deep breathing and relaxation exercises. Initially, it was only fifteen minutes, then more each day. I journaled about my procrastination feelings and behavior daily. In the process, I found shortcuts and assistive technology to help speed up typing.

In addition, Monica helped me with assertiveness and advocacy. We did role-play. She encouraged me to fit family, friends, and community activities into my schedule. She explained that we can have survivor guilt for having success beyond that of our significant others and fear of indirectly causing harm to the Black African American community. Hence, having the feeling of not belonging at a predominantly white institution, or at home, or in the Black African American community. She also explained "stereotype threat" as what happens when Black American students get lower scores on exams because they are too afraid of the white teachers judging them as inferior. Afterward, my writing flowed. I stopped worrying as much about teachers' personal biases, and I just wrote and learned what I could. Later in the doctoral program, I learned that, same as in first grade, some teachers did not want to let us know that we actually knew more than the white students.

Another source of unexpected fear was in the university classrooms, the young white women rarely spoke, even when teachers asked the class questions and expected answers. How boring and frustrating this silence must have been for the teachers too. I usually did speak up, having read the assignments. However, often being the only, or one of two, Black students in classes, I had silent terror, anxiety, and anger that were blocking me from asking for what I needed from the teachers and my advisor, things that were essential for my health and career. The memories of watching my mother and foster mother being emotionally abused had me too full of painful anxiety to ask for help.

A teacher gave me a C/C-, a failing grade, on my child development paper. This initially didn't bother me because we were told we were allowed to revise it for a higher grade. It was the consultation with the teacher on the telephone that was very upsetting. She yelled at me. "I don't know what to say to you. I repeated the instructions over and over in class. You had the worst grade in the class! Everyone else knew what to do but you! It shows you don't know how to do an observation."

I tried to explain. "I do know how to do observations. And I understand the theories. I just didn't know what you expected. The other problem is I never get to finish anything."

"Why is that? What takes you so long?"

"Writing."

"Well, if you know it takes you longer to write, why didn't you start earlier?"

I was silent.

"Are you there? Are you there?"

CHAPTER 11: HEALING ASSIGNMENTS FROM MOMMA

"Yes, I'm here. I'm usually a person who starts at the beginning of the semester setting up my assignments, and I am well organized."

"Why didn't you ask for help before now? You could've asked me or the TA."

Silence. Her intimidating, accusatory tone stopped me from saying anything more. I had talked to her at the beginning of the semester and showed her my ADA accommodations form.

"This says extended time for in-class assignments and exams," she said, and then refused to accept late papers and graded my papers harshly. She was even picky about commas, then wondered why my analysis papers seemed so disconnected! I was made to focus on the bugs on the individual leaves instead of the trees, let alone the forest! I rarely ever used my ADA accommodations, but I had to for her class because she was so picky that her class assignments took extra, extra time.

What was puzzling about all of this was that my other teacher said I had the highest grade in her integrative assessment class—90 percent on my midterm and 100 percent on my final exam! She took me aside and congratulated me. This class teaching us how to do integrative psychological reports was as complicated as the child development class or more so. I didn't say that I knew the other students divided up the parts of the exam between them. They didn't bother to ask me. I was glad I didn't join them in cheating. Some of the younger students told me they didn't bother to read the assigned journal articles or textbooks. They just googled the definitions. One student said she typed while the teacher explained the definitions, then went to the computer lab during break and printed them out to hand to the teacher as if she had studied at home. Instead, I diligently did my homework by myself. Why did it seem, for the other teacher, that the harder I worked on her assignments and the more effort I put in, the worse my grades were? Wouldn't you have been anxious and angry?

I've had to face my fears regarding the role of women and speaking up for my rights. I watched as my mother's generation was punished and humiliated for speaking up even a little bit. I think this mediumship message was also my mother's way of apologizing and letting go of her own guilt about the effects of the trauma from our stepfather and foster father.

***

Where Did This Anger Come From?

And so, my journey to heal from my Muslim experiences began. Young women being silent triggered memories of my Muslim mothers being silenced by abuse. Their Black American husbands were silenced by racism, discrimination, and abusive oppression before, during, and immediately after the civil rights movement. Stepfather, without education, hustled by selling incense and perfumes, being a roach exterminator, and whatever other self-employment he could do. He converted to Islam in adulthood, proudly took on the Muslim identity of wearing a long beard and kufi or Kenya cap, and learned Arabic. My foster father was well educated, brilliant in math and computers. He was often the lone Black man at his job. He was the son of parents who converted to Islam. He wore a business suit and drove a nice car. These men's only real, authoritative power was at home, over their wife and children, making sure whatever the man says goes. "You aren't supposed to think! I think for you!" He made sure he was the only person in the house allowed to get angry. Anger at the boss and the world was unleashed upon the family.

I thought I had healed from these childhood memories and my marriages during earlier therapy—until my own anger surfaced. Because of what I had witnessed from my fathers, I was afraid of my anger. It felt all-consuming, sometimes uncontrollable, with what slipped out of my mouth. I'd start talking and not be able to stop whenever anyone offered willing, compassionate ears, even if it was in the middle of a university hallway. The anger was incredibly painful, something I'd never consciously known before. It made all the muscles in my body painfully tight. The emotional pain sent me back to therapy.

Return to Therapy

Now the real therapy began. I had never told Monica about or felt I could trust her with my deep pain before. Now I really needed her. The emotional pain of anger is excruciating. There are no words for this pain. I sure tried talking and writing about it. The painful anxiety, procrastination, and anger. Yes, anger. An anger I never experienced before. I couldn't make it go away. It bubbled up, but I didn't act on it, just stayed miserable internally. Other Black students also complained of their anger from being insulted by teachers' comments, but I had nothing specific that I was angry about. It was the invisibility in the classroom and the curriculum that was the most painful, as if our culture didn't exist. Only negative information about Black African Americans was written in the textbooks.

Discrimination and exclusion had never felt as painful as now. So why now? Why at my age? At fifty-six years old, I had coped with far worse in life. Perhaps, as we neared the fiftieth anniversaries of the civil rights movement and the women's movement, I expected better. Studying at a predominantly white university was where I really, really felt racism, discrimination, and isolation. I was not only the only Black student in the classroom, but the only one in a wheelchair and the oldest. Sometimes there would be another Black student in a class, but again and again, we were both too shell-shocked to speak to each other.

I have an associate's degree from a community college that only allowed about twelve of us Black nursing students to graduate, went to an almost all-white art school, graduated with a bachelor's degree from a college in Vermont—where the whole state is 99 percent white—and later earned a master's degree from an almost all-white university. You would think I'd be used to it, resilient and toughened up. After a year of art school, I told myself that I would never go to another white college. I would rather go to Spelman or another historically black college. There is an old saying, "never say never." I guess I shouldn't have said never!

After attending the Today's Black Women's Conference in 2003 and a workshop by the authors of, *Shifting: The Double Lives of Black Women in America,* and reading the book at home, I went in search of a Black therapist. My goal was to heal my experience of being the only Black registered nurse in the department—and sometimes the whole hospital. In 1998 I'd read books about young Black people having a nervous breakdown soon after they graduated from college. As the first Black students in predominantly white colleges, they had Black community mentors to support them. None of this prepared them for being put in a back room somewhere at their first job and given tasks that had nothing to do with their college degree or training!

Since I had worked as a nurse's aide in a hospital emergency room for four years in the 1980s, I thought that after getting training on a medical surgical floor, I could learn how to work in the emergency room or intensive care unit. But I didn't get hired at hospitals. Nursing homes were more than happy to have me. Later I learned from other Black nurses who graduated with me that although there were full pages with multiple columns of hospital jobs advertised in the newspaper, we would only be hired for jobs that no other nurse would want. The jobs that required heavy lifting and cleaning up patients who had soiled their beds because they couldn't get up to go to the toilet. I thought it was because I wore a Muslim head scarf and modest pantsuits that they didn't hire me, especially at a hospital like Mt. Sinai.

I'd graduated from psychotherapy sessions, feeling like I didn't need them. Now I was back. My head down and my tail tucked, I came crawling back to therapy. The summer of 2013 was very intense for my healing. We got past my tendency to chat and tell my history while avoiding feeling the emotions. I wouldn't let Monica help me as much as she could have. After all, if my birth mother couldn't help me, how could I trust anyone? As an older Black therapist, she would of course, be most likely to physically remind me of my mother. I'd talk for most of the session, not letting her interrupt me to give me advice. Now I had to trust her enough to tell her about my real emotional pain and struggles. I still hadn't told her, after all those years, what really happened in the foster home with the sexual abuse. I hinted but didn't tell her.

What was I to do with this pain? How would my fathers have known what to do with this pain? I didn't yell, curse, or beat up on people during this time. I had been disciplined and socialized as a girl to just keep all that pain inside and not take it out on others, although others took out their anger on me!

Monica explained that often people are afraid of their anger, similar to sadness when the tears seem to keep flowing, at times uncontrollably. We wonder if the tears will ever stop! The tears do gradually decrease. The intensity of the anger also lessens with time. Her treatment naturally focused on how I really felt about my birth father not being around in my life. The first time I remember meeting him, I was twenty-five years old. Anger and resentment bubbled up as I blamed him for the abusive situations in my life, especially from my stepfather and then my foster father. I dealt with homesickness a few years earlier through therapy and a homeopathic remedy, Kali bichromicum. But this anger---angry at my father even when he came through in a spirit message at the church. If only he had been a father to us, then we wouldn't have had to have a stepfather and move away from our real family!

A few weeks later, the pastor's sermon at Church of the Spirit was about love and forgiveness. Some people say they've forgiven someone, but when they come in contact with them, their face scrunches up, and their gut tightens in anger. That means they really haven't forgiven yet. This can also happen with those who've passed on. You could say that they were too mean to forgive. Anger and not forgiving can weigh a person down with a heavy burden, making it difficult to move on.

This happened to me. I thought I had forgiven my father, instead I got the pain in my gut when he came through, apologizing through the church medium's spirit messages. The earlier therapy session opened me up to hearing the pastor's sermon. Over the next week, I gradually forgave him, which gave me more energy than I'd had in a while. Letting go of the past gave me the energy and clarity to start clearing the clutter from my home. Obsessed with cleaning, I worked long into the night, fearful for the effects on my health, but I couldn't stop. There was plenty more to be angry about—worse injustices and delays during the doctoral program—but I did not feel anger to the intensely painful level that I had in the first two years.

Momma Gives Firm Encouragement

"You're packing your bags. Not traveling yet. But getting ready to go someplace. I feel this has to do with your study in particular. Like you're getting ready for what's coming up. I feel like I'm writing and writing. Talking to an advisor or other people or something. But I feel like it's really taking off for you and that feels good.

I get your mom coming in for you. She's wearing that beautiful green color. So, she just comes in and wants you to know that she's with you. I feel like your attention will be going to green. When it does, you'll see green in the environment, then that's your mother just checking in. Just bringing your attention to that beautiful green color, wanting you to know that she's with you.

I get you being angry, because I feel like the first review wasn't really what you were hoping for. It's like, I did my best with this! Your mother says you're just gonna do it again. That's kind of her attitude about things. You got to do it again. She's showing me her shaping things, and it is turning out to be more and more in shape. Much more, proud of what that product is. There's also a spirit teacher that comes in to be with you—it feels like when you're doing your writing. Call on them for guidance, help, and inspiration. You just call on them, and they'll be there, and I say God bless you."

Meaning Momma is probably helping to clear out the obstacles or challenges and putting situations in good shape or in order for me. The medium didn't know that the teacher gave me a failing grade. I revised the final exam and passed the class.

More to Heal

2014. On my way home from a spirit circle class, it was dark outside, after nine. My eyes glanced over to the right-side window of the van, and through the large windows of a daycare center, I saw the beams of a backroom's light shining on a crib. In an instant, an image of a large crib with silver bars and frame flashed into my mind. I could feel my mother's presence and almost hear her soothing voice. I was reluctant to look any closer at the image of the large crib. I think she was encouraging me to look anyway.

In bed that night, the memories surfaced of why Momma wanted me to look. The crib in the window reminded me of the one I was put in at the hospital when I was ten years old after my mother accidentally hit me in the eye with a belt buckle. She hit me because I stole a pair of glasses from Goodwill, out of the Lions' Club donation box. My mother rarely ever spanked us and had not hit us since we moved to the Midwest. But since I broke one of her main rules, don't steal, she told Stepfather that she would be the one to punish me. She probably did not want him to beat me—really, really beat me—because this was a serious crime, although the store probably didn't miss the eyeglasses. Usually he whipped me for little mistakes, many times when I didn't do anything.

CHAPTER 11: HEALING ASSIGNMENTS FROM MOMMA

Momma hated to be the one to spank me. She especially didn't want to be the one to seriously hurt me.

A few days later, my eye was red and swollen. The school must have contacted my parents. My stepfather's mother took me to the hospital. It was an old hospital. I remember sitting and waiting for the doctor with my head and eye paining me so much I was miserable. I tried to sleep away the pain, while my stepfather's mother talked with the doctor. He said my eye was infected. She left me there. The doctor patched up both my eyes. Blind in the injured eye, I was not allowed to see out of the other eye. My stepfather visited me a couple of times at the hospital. He was actually nice to me. I was scared and alone, away from my family for ten days. This loneliness is what my mother wanted to acknowledge and apologize for. But her giving me the memory didn't initially bother me. I silently told my mother in spirit that I was okay, and I had forgiven her.

Monica asked me why I thought the memory came up. To my surprise, I started to cry as I connected my experiences over the past year at the university—feeling both neglected and abandoned by teachers—which reminded me of how I felt about my mother after she married my stepfather.

Why Didn't I Do It Too?

A colleague who is a therapist told me she has groups with adolescent African American girls who had been hospitalized. Some had histories of cutting themselves and were given the diagnoses of borderline personality disorder or bipolar disorder, although they were not adults. According to the *Diagnostic and Statistical Manual* (*DSM-IV-R*), patients can't be given a psychiatric diagnosis until they are eighteen years of age. My colleague was worried about these diagnoses and the resulting prescriptions. These girls were put on medications that made them feel worse and act out, sometimes violently. Ten years earlier, I saw a talk show about how Prozac and other new selective serotonin reuptake inhibitors (SSRI) could change people—especially adolescents—from suicidal to homicidal. Now a days, girls say that they cut themselves in order to feel something—anything at all instead of the emptiness. Or to feel connected to their self. To have a sense of self.

I became concerned for myself when, in graduate school, I read in the *DSM-IV* about the symptoms of borderline personality disorder, which included cutting. For years, when stressed especially with external situations where I felt unsafe---I had brief images of cutting or stabbing my arms whenever I saw knives or scissors, but I never did it. I asked my therapist, "Why is it that some people cut themselves, but others don't? What kept me from acting on it?" But an amazing thing happened to me. The urge to cut myself stopped immediately after I told my therapist.

Later she said, "Yes, just telling it usually makes it stop."

I had gotten used to managing these weird cutting urges but wouldn't dare tell anyone for fear of being labeled crazy. I could tell a homeopathic doctor because they welcome hearing about odd thoughts and behaviors along with the physical symptoms; it makes deciding on the best customized remedy for the patient easier. But all those years, I was too embarrassed to tell even my homeopathic doctor. After I talked to my therapist and the symptoms went away, I did get brave enough to whisper it to him in a phone call.

I think the cutting urges happened as a result of feeling trapped by the abuse, oppression, and discrimination that we are forbidden to speak about. The silence and depression that is accepted as normal for women and minorities. I think what kept me from acting out, in spite of intense emotional pain, was my use of alternative therapies along my healing journey.

Chapter 12: Spirit Messages from Other Relatives and Friends

The amazing variety of spirit messages kept me coming back to the Church of The Spirit. There I became part of a family and spiritual community. I arrived early on Sunday mornings to lead the 10:00 a.m. meditations. We meditated to raise the vibration and increase the love in the church sanctuary. I prayed that the congregation receive healing messages from their love ones and spirit guides. A longtime friend, Jen, donated a drum, giving it to me to play along with the hymns. Some of us would linger up front and sing, "Let there be Peace on Earth" together at the end of the service. Occasionally, I also helped with the energy healing at the back of the church during the message part of the service.

One Mother's Day service, Pastor Marrice acknowledged that some people's mothers died or weren't available to them during childhood. I was moved to get up and sing, "Sometimes I Feel Like a Motherless Child." The main words were, sometimes I feel like a motherless child, a long way from home. Surprised myself, as the sound of my voice came from deep inside me. People came up to me after church and thanked me, telling me that the song brought tears to their eyes. I had wanted to share a more uplifting song like "Summertime" that my mother also sang to me as a child. But "Sometimes I Feel Like a Motherless Child" is what I heard and felt. I was glad to for the opportunity and the healing experience.

Besides Momma, other spirit relatives and friends made sure their messages were heard too.

My Father

"Your father comes in, and hands you a flower, and says they are proud of you.

The medium called me "Hernitha." My father is the only one who said my name like that.

"Your father is here too, but at a distance. He might have died when you were at a young age. Anyway, they're showing me him at a distance. There are other loved ones here too."

My father died when I was thirty-five years old. He is standing at a distance because he was not in my life during my childhood. He came into my life when I was twenty-five, and after that, we had several honest, heart-to-heart talks. He would come on the Amtrak train to visit me, and I flew to Philadelphia to visit him during annual family reunions.

While lying in bed at five in that morning, I called out an open invitation for my loved ones to communicate with me from spirit. I heard my father's name. I said, "Oh, I haven't heard or thought of you in a while. Do you have a message or images for me?" Then I saw an open book held by someone sitting in a chair in the dark. I thought of a similar newspaper image that I saw in a reading last week. I saw it again. I asked my father if he had been giving me messages through the many books that fall open to random pages. I felt like he was saying, "Yes."

"You have a lot of spirit family around you. A lot of men this time. Roy is here and one of your father's brothers, an uncle. Lots of men from your father's side. Your mother is here too and says, "Um-hum!" The men used to do jobs that required a lot of heavy lifting. So now they are doing the heavy lifting for you. You'll feel the difference. Your mother, with her hands on her hips, says, "I'm still here."

Uncles

An uncle on your father's side here. A business-type man. He knows how to get things done. He is making changes for the better. Making things that are beyond your control better for you.

My father had three brothers and also lots of his own uncles. Mother Dear had three sisters and eight brothers. Therefore I don't know which of these uncles was a business person.

Father and Grandpa

"There is a man standing next to you who liked to tease. A father figure here. Your grandfather is here too."

My birth father liked to tease, but I was confused and didn't initially take what the medium said about my grandfather being there because I didn't know any of my grandfathers. I didn't remember meeting my mother's father or my father's father when I was little, while I was living in Philadelphia. This was disappointing for me. Later I remembered Mother Dear's second husband, a stepfather to my father. He also liked to tease. I remember him being attuned to my childhood imagination and fascination with the Christmas tree lights containing brightly colored liquid that went up and down the clear ornaments. It was hypnotic to a child like me, five or six at the time. Then there was the dollhouse in their backyard that he told me little people lived in. I believed him and played with the otherwise invisible family.

Grandpa played with me and disciplined me. He tried to scare me into not sucking my two fingers. He threatened to burn my fingers off on the stove—he only had half a thumb! Then there was the time that he and his teenage sons put live blue crabs on the hardwood dining room floor and let the crabs chase me. My little five-year-old feet didn't seem to go fast enough, running around and round the dining table.

Two days later, the significance of the medium reading became much more than just the memories of my grandfather. It was the awesome healing that unfolded as a result. The fact that other people are receptive to helping me is probably related to my new relaxed, positive attitude. My defenses are down. Perhaps this is because I am filled with the wonder of the love I did receive as that little girl. The message is that he still loves and looks out for me now. Instead of grieving a loss, as I've done with my parents and leaving Philadelphia, I am very grateful for the love I have received.

Mother Dear in Later Years

This is from a private sitting with the medium Rik in 2012.

"Any questions?"

"Well, in the first message you gave me a few weeks ago, and again last week, the pastor also spoke of a woman who sews."

"I don't remember," he said.

I nodded and continued. "I was wondering if it is my 101-year-old grandmother's spirit, because she keeps saying that she's the only one she knows who sews."

"No, that's not her," he said loudly. "Mentally and spiritually, she may be ready to cross over, but her body is not. She says she will be here another five years."

When I visited my grandmother, who we affectionately called Mother Dear, I slept in her room on a twin-size bed across from her bed. In the mornings, I would listen to her telling me stories or giving me advice. One morning, she asked, "Have you heard anything about your mother? I miss your mother."

"You say you miss my mother—what was she like?"

"She was quiet. She didn't talk much, but she could sing. She would sing around the house. She was good to have around. I liked her being there." She asked me, "Do you feel that your mother is still alive?"

I told Mother Dear what I remembered from what my younger sister Inara told me she found out about our mother in 2003. Since Inara is a librarian, she was able to do some detective work through ancestry and genealogy websites. All these years, we thought my mother was dead since no one had seen or heard about her after she went to Philadelphia for Thanksgiving in 1978. Inara was able to get our mother's death certificate, which had the name of the nursing home she died in. She called the nursing home and talked to staff, who said she

CHAPTER 12: SPIRIT MESSAGES FROM OTHER RELATIVES AND... 111

lived there for years and became blind from diabetes. Momma died of stomach cancer, which is common with chronic smokers.

On another visit, Mother Dear told me, "I received letters from your mother and the neighbor upstairs telling me you all were being beaten by your stepfather. I've felt guilty that I didn't do anything to help. But I couldn't at the time." Here was validation about the severity of the whippings, which went beyond the usual child discipline of my generation. Later my brother Emin told me that it was in our school records too.

"I always wondered why your mother was depressed. She was raised well by her aunt, who you called Grandma. She was given anything she wanted and went to good schools, including college. But your mother had a cleft palate, and she was always self-conscious about her speech, about how she talked." At the time Mother Dear told me this, I was in my thirties. I wondered if Momma had been sexually abused as we had been. Now, of course, I know how cruel children can be with bullying and the long-term effects of depression and anxiety in adults. It also had to have been emotionally difficult to be rejected by my father after he made three babies with her. Momma told us he married another woman and had four children after us. We were hurt and jealous, especially when she told us he took them to Disneyland.

Mother Dear's younger brother was outside shoveling snow when I called him. He was almost ninety years old, ten years younger than she was. We were discussing the great snowstorm of 2011, which closed down Lakeshore Drive in Chicago, with two hundred cars stranded in the snowdrifts.

"Schools and businesses were closed in Michigan too. But blizzards were worse when I was younger, often producing three and four feet of snow. Most people didn't have cars then. There weren't tall buildings to block the wind. There were no city snowplows or snowblowers then. We shoveled out by hand. We took trolleys, which weren't heated. They only had a woodstove that you tried to sit as near to as possible. You would time your walk to the trolley so as not to have to stand outside waiting too long for it."

Then he talked about Mother Dear. "The heart is like a battery that will eventually wear down. She keeps going and going and going and going. But eventually it will wear out and stop."

"Sometimes she and I have some very deep conversations, in which she pops out with things like 'I'd go if you go with me,'" I told him.

"A lot of people are afraid that they'll have to die alone. Maybe she doesn't want to die alone. She'd like someone there in the bed beside her."

"Well, that's what I thought I would be doing while I was visiting her during those eleven days in December," I said. "Being there beside her as she made her transition. But I think her strong will keeps her going. Her will keeps her heart going because she spends more time and energy in the preparation phase for dying, and perhaps that's why she has a poor memory."

I called Mother Dear, wondering how she was doing. She was alert and in her spiritual, contemplative mood. "At ninety-nine years old, it would be dangerous to complain," she said. A long pause followed. I waited patiently. I wanted to ask her to explain, but I didn't. She continued. "I've learned more in the past two years than in my whole life. I see and understand more than when I had to work and was too busy, if that makes sense."

I thought about what Mother Dear was saying. I could somewhat understand that from the ten years that I was unemployed while going to graduate school. The past two years had me gaining an accelerated wisdom and understanding from life experiences too. Her brother had also spoken about retirement being a time to do what one has always wanted to do. Mother Dear has been retired for decades, so I was surprised to hear her describe it as similar to when one stops working. Perhaps her declining health forced her to stop being so busy away from home and responsible for others. She was the matriarch of the family. She planned regular gatherings. She knew her grandchildren and their grandchildren and kept in contact with them. She went to weddings, baby showers, graduations, funerals.

As a Jehovah's Witness, she was very involved in duties such as visiting or calling the sick members of the church as well as caring for terminally ill family members. Well into her nineties, she climbed two or three flights of stairs to visit sick people in their homes, in spite of the degenerative arthritis in her back. Mother Dear told me that she would just say a prayer and somehow climb all those stairs! Perhaps it is from her that I get my determination and strong faith! She's outlived her friends, most of her siblings, and her own children. She frequently asked from 2008 to 2010, "Why am I still here? The bible says take care of your parents and you'll have a long life. I must've done a good job taking care of them."

As I was remembering this, she spoke. "I learned a lot from observing people who visit and their interactions with each other."

Another mediumship reading: "I immediately got an image of a rodeo, a cowboy hanging on a bucking horse with all his might. Amazingly, he hangs on. The horse gets tired and stops bucking. You are like the cowboy. Regardless of what comes your way, you are able to hang on. In the end, you will be the winner. As you sit on your horse, an older woman comes to give you a trophy. I want to say a grandmother. She is not heavy, but a little stocky. I want to call her downright strong physically and strong in personality. She is extremely proud of you. She watches out for you but often would have you do what she thinks is best for you rather than what you think is best. She has your best interest at heart but has a hard time because she has difficulty understanding things from your perspective. I think she loved chocolate—especially homemade fudge. Also, she was all about common sense. Never one to make rash decisions. Always conservative with choices. She is constantly sharing her opinions with you." (From the medium Debbie).

This is a great description of Mother Dear's personality! These are all the qualities that made her the matriarch of the family. I guess she is still in my life! She came through this medium approximately seven months after she died in 2017. Mother Dear did die five years later, at the age of 106, exactly as her spirit told Rik in 2012.

"Looks like a great-grandma. She's dressed like you are now. I am wearing a purple headwrap that looks like a hat. She has this wonderful hat on, with a big, white flower on the side. She's dressed in purple. She's absolutely beautiful. She is just beautiful. She is showing me your spirit, and it looks like this. I want to call it a flashlight, but it might be a mirror. There is just so much light. It's so bright it almost hurts the eyes. She is saying that you get that from her. That the two of you are very connected. There is a strong bridge to your ancestors. A strong bridge that goes all the way back down through the tiers of grandmothers to where you are now and where you are today. She says that you have such a deep spirituality and you are embracing it and using it. It's feeding you. Not only is it shining through you, but it is feeding you and your spirituality. As it reflects out into the world, it feeds and nourishes others, all the people around you, and even people that you don't know. She is saying to just continue to be who you are. Trust where you are at. Allow that light to shine. She says that you are an amazing presence in the world. An amazing light presence in the world and you may not realize it. But you carry the light from your ancestors. Especially your grandmothers. They are shining with you and through you. This is what she is telling you. So, I'm going to leave you with that. Continue to do what you are doing." (From another new medium).

Mother Dear loved hats and dressing up whenever she went out of the house, either in a suit or a pretty dress. She had a large hat collection. My uncle saved some of her hats to give to me after she died. The medium probably thought Mother Dear was my grandmother was my great-grandmother because grandmothers rarely live to a hundred years old.

"A woman comes up to you and gives you a flower. She then sits on the couch close to you. She looks a lot like you. She takes your hand and holds your hand in her hands. Then she leans her head on your shoulder. Tears came to my eyes as I listened to this medium student's message."

Mother Dear was letting me know that she remembered and appreciated me sitting next to her, hugging her, and putting my head on her shoulder. Family often commented how much I looked just like my grandmother. In her later years, when she had dementia, she often sat on the large couch by herself. By then she was hard of hearing and could hardly see. She looked so lonely on the couch, so I'd go and sit next to her. She was the matriarch of the family. All of her grandchildren would've been competing to be next to her and fighting for her attention and her ear. Now she sat stiffly next to me, expressionless, without eye contact, with a look of confusion. I didn't know if she wanted me close to her or not. Now, two years after her passing, she is telling me that she appreciated my hugs!

The Church of the Spirit invited visiting psychic medium Robin Hobson on Zoom call from England. In May 2021, he gave me the following evidential spirit message from Mother Dear. Usually mediums request that you only respond with short yes or no answers so as to not interrupt the flow of the spirit messages coming through.

"So Haneefa, I have got a lovely lady here. She's not very tall. She does feel particularly short because otherwise everyone feels short to me. (He chuckles since he is very tall). She lost a couple of inches as she got older because she's not very upright. I know she's a family relative because she feels very maternal. She's coming in very gentle with a gentle and loving energy. But I know that this belies a very strong lady. I know that she has an inner strength because if she had to she would tell you. Although she comes in as gentle, she's direct and to the point when she wants to be. But I know that there is a great deal of love and respect for you as she comes in. I know that it feels like you were very much . . . she's actually stopping me from saying that (He laughs). It feels like you were almost on the same wavelength. Would you understand that?"

"Yes."

"I know that you would have the same views as her, and she respects you for that! And that's not always the way with maternal links like this. Sometimes they have their own views and you have yours. But I know there is a real comparison between you and her. She's very traditional in her ways and traditional in her dress. Would you understand that please?"

"Yes."

"And I know that this lady loves color. I can see that. I've got vivid colors here and I love color. So I know this is important to her. She's telling me there's a picture of her in a particular top. Looks like she's got a scarf or something that goes over her top (blouse) here as I'm looking at her. It's all bright colors. She says there is a photograph with her in this (outfit) because it's her favorite piece. So you may have to look in the photograph box for that. Okay?"

"Yes."

"I'm trying to get more details from her but she's deflecting away from herself. It's almost like this would be part of her nature. So she doesn't want to talk about her. She wants to talk about you. And that's how she is. It's like her past and her upbringing is very much inside here. And she's not one to share it. I do know this lady went through difficulties as she was growing up. Would you understand that?

"Yes."

"I don't feel like life was very easy for her in her youth. And I'm trying to dig into the situation, and she won't let me. She's saying, "It's all in the past. I don't want to talk about that." It seems like that's a private part of her world. She wants to talk about you. And how you are in the world. Okay. I know nothing about you, but I know that you hold the respect of a lot of people because she's telling me so. Would you understand that?"

"Yes."

"You have values that other people have sought your advice or your interest in. Would you understand that please?

"Yes."

"Because it seems like you are an advisor to others. And she's very proud of the way you deal with things. Because it seems like you are sharing your process and how you got to how you got to be where you are in the world. Now don't be bashful because she's not being bashful about you. And she wants you to know how proud she is of who you are. Okay. Do you have items of jewelry that belongs to this lady please? Because she's just opened a little box. And I can see something gold colored in there that would have belonged to her. Would you understand this?"

"No. Not yet."

"Okay all right. She's opening this little box and let me tell you what it looks like. It's gold colored, maybe not gold gold. It's got little hangings on it. It looks very fancy. But it's got little hangings on it. This feels traditional. It doesn't feel like it's a modern piece. Feels like it's old. Now If you haven't got it, would you recognize it from her belongings? Because she's brought it and open this little box in front of me to show me. It's sort of like a triangle shape and it's got little medallions hanging on it. I can see the sun blinking on it, as she showing me. Understand that there's a necklace and it's got a piece across here where it's got something hanging on it. She's not showing me the chain, but she's showing me the bit that is here."

"I'll have to do some research on that."

"OK, that's fine. As I said, if you haven't got it, it certainly is belonging to her. I know it's here somewhere because they don't usually give it me if it's not here. If you don't have it, it may be somewhere else. But please ask about it because I know this is important to her. And do you know something? I don't even think it belonged to her. I think it belonged to her mother. It's something that's been passed down in the family. And I know it's here. Okay. So please ask. She is very

CHAPTER 12: SPIRIT MESSAGES FROM OTHER RELATIVES AND... 117

interested in . . . would you understand . . . you were planning something, but you had to hold off the plans at the moment. Do you understand this?"

"Yes."

"And she saying that you have really started to think about it again because it comes with a rush of excitement with her. Pick it up again because it will come to fruition. She wants you to put some energy into it. Okay? All right?"

"Yes."

So it is also you that is interested in the history of the family please?"

"Yes."

"Because she also referring to the history of the family that you're interested in. And it's almost like she's urging you to put your records down on paper or to record what do you know. Because when she passed there was an awful lot of information that wasn't passed on. Would you understand that?"

"Yes."

"Okay and I think this is certainly part of her nature as I said before, she's saying, 'that's private I'm not going there.' But I know that there is an interest in the past and the process that the family went through. Because, let me just say that as I get into that there seems like there was a big upheaval in the family. Big, big, big changes that happened within the family. And although she's proud of them, she doesn't want to talk about them. But I know you will. Okay?"

"Yes."

"She wants you to really investigate the family. Okay? Would you, as I'm talking to her, would you know a gentleman who is very slim is standing beside her. As I'm talking to her, I can sense him standing there with her. He's a little taller than her not very tall but he feels very slim. And I know they come in together because he's not moved the whole time that she's been here. And he's just standing there and being the strength that he always was. Okay. I know that this man exuded strength because he's just quietly standing here just letting her say her piece. Okay? I just had to bring his love to you because that's what I'm feeling as he comes in."

"Yes. (whispered through my tears, overwhelmed as I felt their love)

"He's saying, it may seem like a long time but it isn't really." Do you understand him saying that?"

"Yes."

"Because it feels like the separation feels like a long time. But he says it isn't really because he's always there. He wants you to know that."

"Yes." (Crying).

"Did you move a photograph of him please?"

I nodded.

"You either looked at the photograph or moved it or you moved it where the photographs are because he's talking about this. Because I know he was with you when you were looking at them."

"Yes."

"So I wanted to give you both of their love. Okay. Both very different in the way they offer that love. And there is a respect with the lady. And that's the way it comes forward. Very different. But nevertheless, it's given with love. And be who you are in the world. They want you to be proud of who you are in the world. And share what you know."

"Okay."

"Is there a September anniversary?"

I nodded.

"Because I want to say that by the September anniversary this project whatever it is that you're looking at doing, will be very much in presence. So there you are. Okay? And you have enthusiasm from them. So thank you for allowing me to work with you."

"Yes. And thank you for sharing!" (Sobbing).

This was an absolutely amazing, considering Robin Hobson was doing this mediumship reading from across the Atlantic Ocean in England. He has a British accent and named items differently than in the United States such as photograph box. He accurately described Mother Dear both by personality and physically. She was still walking with an upright posture at 106 years old, although her doctors told her, in her 90's, that her back pain was from natural arthritic degeneration of her spine. Some of her siblings had severe arthritis in their knees. She put away her cane and kept moving. Previously when Mother Dear was younger she saw in adults in their forties sit in rocking chairs on their porches and "rock themselves to death" she made a vow to herself to get up and out of the house somewhere everyday after she retired. Philadelphia has steep sidewalks to and from the bus stops that kept her legs limber as well as

CHAPTER 12: SPIRIT MESSAGES FROM OTHER RELATIVES AND... 119

her stretching before getting out bed in the morning. We adult children had to walk faster to keep up with her. Including me, although I too walked most everywhere before 1999 since I didn't ever have a car.

Mother Dear also told her grandchildren that there were secrets that she would carry to the grave with her. Obviously, now that she is on the other side, she is still keeping her commitment to not tell--especially in front of strangers. She was a private person, although sometimes when I would come to visit, she would sit me down at the kitchen table and begin what she was about to tell me with, "There are some skeletons in the closet that you need to know about." Usually it was some information about my birth father's addition to the family line. She did tell me a few things about herself. Mother Dear was one of thirteen children. She was a young adult during the Depression in the 1930s. Working as a domestic she had to protect herself from the man of the house and the various little critters such as mice and bedbugs.

It's interesting that Mother Dear said that she and I were on the same wavelength. She did offend us by being direct to the point especially when telling people, "You're too fat!" I would never do that, but I too can be too direct with the truth especially when it comes to injustices. Three strikes and you're out if you think you can keep taking advantage of my kindness. I divorced twice at a time when women pressured other women to stay in marriages even when there was abuse. Mother Dear to my surprise told us, "I don't see why young women get married these days. I stayed home with my children. I didn't work until my husband had a heart attack and couldn't work anymore."

I didn't know this because when I was little she was working as a licensed practical nurse (LPN) going to work in a little white cap, white dress, white stockings and white shoes. Later her youngest son would describe the family as being poor with not enough food to eat. By the time I came along they were living in a nice house. What we did have in common that we both worked hard to get an education to better our situations. She went to night classes to finish high school and then later to nurses training late in life. However she did tell me after I got my bachelor's degree to not go any further to graduate school because then no one would hire me. I would be overqualified. No one would want to pay me that much. Mother Dear was right of course. After I got my rehabilitation counseling degree employers were mostly hiring bachelor level counselors and the advertised job descriptions were the same! Hardly any university graduate counselors were hired. No matter what their specialty – marriage and family nor school nor community nor rehabilitation counselors. And none hired since then as the United States is still in the Great Recession.

Other people have been giving me complements, mostly through Spirit messages, about holding me in higher regard. I am shy about acknowledging my accomplishments. People do come to me for advice. And of course, I'm a counselor. But Mother Dear saw this years ago, in 1991 when she persuaded me to come to my father's funeral. She told me I was the calm one and a good mediator. Unfortunately I got to see what she was talking about as a couple of my siblings were fighting over our father's few barely valuable possessions.

The jewelry? I didn't really pay attention to Mother Dear's jewelry because basically I'm not really a jewelry person. And she would fuss at me, "At least wear some earrings." I didn't know if she had the necklace that Robin Hobson described. I will have to ask my cousin and my sister that were the closest to her while taking care of Mother Dear in her later years.

As I'm writing this book, I am attempting to "share my process and how I got to where I am now in the world." It seems that Mother Dear is giving me permission to tell mine and the family secrets! She wouldn't do it, but it's okay for me? "She wants you to really investigate the family." It's taken me a longer time to finish this book as I struggled with periods of intense fear of offending or embarrassing my relatives. I've left a lot of names and stories out. Plus I have had to "hold off plans at the moment" while waiting for my copyeditor. Getting feedback from my volunteer readers and editors, no lie is very painful especially when you're writing about topics and cultures that they are not familiar with. Therefore many writers often give up and tuck their potential books away for years or forever. Mother Dear's older brother, when he died at 94 years old, still hadn't published his book.

Family history? Well two things happened, first recently my older sister Kani asked me to facilitate a presentation of our family history during our family reunion that was postponed twice due to the COVID-19 shutdowns. Therefore over time I got busy and forgot about gathering and organizing the genealogy records that I have. It is odd that Mother Dear asked me because I did not do the genealogy research. I only have the separate booklets that my two cousins shared with the family almost twenty years ago. Why not ask my cousins? Probably because although my cousins did extensive research including photographs of official documents, they put her own opinions in their booklets, some of which wasn't true or was negative and offended some people. Second, unfortunately while Mother Dear was ill and had dementia in her later years, we didn't find out until after she died that some family members took the extensive family tree information that Mother Dear had researched all the way back to slavery on her mother's side of the family. She said her father's father was a freeman and never a slave. My birth father, Mother Dear's oldest son, also did an extensive family tree history that disappeared too.

Her photo albums are now almost empty. As grandchildren we were angry because all whoever did this had to do is make copies with their cellphones or at a copy center and at least return them. This is probably the "big upheaval and changes that happened within the family" after Mother Dear passed away. She may be sad since she organized and cooked for annual family reunions and regular get togethers to keep the family together no matter what. Mother Dear does know that I was interested in family history because I used to record her and her younger brothers' stories about their childhood, and typed transcripts. I planned to make audio CDs and share them with interested family members so they can hear her voice and get information straight from the original source. Emin made video CDs of her one-hundredth birthday and distributed them. On the front of his CD covers is a photo of Mother Dear with a colorful scarf around her neck.

The psychic medium also accurately described her younger brother, Dennis. He was very thin and short for a man. Shorter than I, and I'm five foot five and a half inches. Quiet, reserved he worked as a counselor with children. Dennis was my favorite great-uncle. He would drive six hours in spite of his arthritic knees and walking with two canes to visit their other sister Dorothy in a nursing home. Their youngest sibling, Pete, would come from Philadelphia with Mother Dear. They would stay for a weekend at Aunt Gussie's, their sisters-in-law's house, where I was living at the time. Sit around the kitchen table and talk for hours. Back then, Dennis would quietly allow Mother Dear to say her peace without arguing with her as she tried to persuade him to become Jehovah's Witness or at least a Christian like she and Pete were." Or to tell him what to do since she was ten years older than him. After Dorothy and Aunt Gussie died, Uncle Dennis no longer came to the Chicago area, but he phoned me regularly and sent me care packages with encouragement to finish graduate school. And I was recently looking at my photo album with pictures of Dennis, Dorothy, Pete, Mother Dear and Gussie posing together.

September anniversary? The end of September is when Mother Dear passed away and Dennis followed two weeks later. She held out because she didn't want her younger siblings to die before she did. And Dennis lived longer for similar reasons. When he died at 96 years old, they were all gone.

Feeling their incredible love, I was sobbing so hard by the end of Robin Hobson's spirit messages from my Mother Dear and Uncle Dennis that I couldn't even talk and answer his questions. Yes, I did very much understand what my grandmother was trying to tell me and her memories. Perhaps by the September 2021 anniversary this book will be launched and in print.

Great-grandmother

"I have an ancestress here. Someone along your mother's line. She might be a great grandmother. She's tall. She's elegant. She's so beautiful. Oh, my gosh! She's absolutely glowing. She's like an angel in your vibration. She is smiling down on you. She is saying, "Congratulations." She's throwing a party, a celebratory party. Not just for the graduation, although that was a tremendous accomplishment. She is also throwing you a party for your health challenges that you managed to meet. In your own way, you have overcome them. She is saying, "So much of that is in your past." She shows you walking through the cloud, and out of the cloud, and out of the fog. The light is getting stronger and stronger, brighter and brighter. She's showing me that she is throwing the party for both of these goals that you have met in your own way, in your own style, and you have not allowed anyone else to get in the way. That's what she's saying is the most important. She's encouraging you to think about, now that you have graduated and might have a little more time, to think about unfolding your gift. Your spiritual gifts. She says you have really strong energies around you that you could master easily in whatever that means to you. Whether that means coming to the church class via Zoom, finding other teachers online. Whatever resonates with you. Maybe reading books and studying that way. Finding a group that you can practice with. But she wants to really encourage that as part of your path moving forward. I leave you with that. She is so proud of you!" (From a mediumship student).

I'm not sure who this relative is. I don't remember any tall women in our family other than Kani and an aunt, both of whom are still living. It could be my mother's grandmother, who is very light-skinned and Irish. Kani was born with strawberry-blond hair, light skin, and blue eyes that she inherited from our Irish great-grandmother.

Grandma

"Your mother and grandmother are here. They bring warm compresses for your knees and thighs. These need extra attention. They're showing me they're cooking up carrots and parsnips. Something you enjoyed as a child."

This is the aunt who raised my mother. We called her Grandma. I loved the sweet mashed carrots mixed with what I thought were white potatoes. They might have been parsnips. If so, she cleverly disguised them!

Foster Mother

"There's a mother vibration here. She had problems with forgiveness, and she wants you to help her. You can help those who have trouble forgiving her. You have a forgiving heart. Show people what it means to forgive."

Again, I think this was probably my foster mother, who did have resentments and guilt that she held on to up until she died.

April 2020. This afternoon I called a friend from Church of the Spirit, and she told me that because of the COVID-19 crisis, the Sunday service had been moved to Saturday evenings at six fifteen on Zoom. It was good to see familiar faces, even though it was on Zoom. I was glad I decided to join the Zoom service because there was a new young woman who gave me a mediumship reading, which was a blessing because most of the readings given to the other people were encouragement for coping with the coronavirus shelter-in-place orders all across the country. It was no surprise that my mother came through and gave me a clear message.

"As I'm coming into your space, I'm getting a mothering energy. Not your ancestors, but your immediate family that you grew up with. So, I'm seeing a picture of you as a little girl. You're all cooking together. So, this is you, an older girl, so it feels like an older sister, your mother, and either her sister or her mother, who was a little bit younger and had your mother young, so she is close in age to your mother. They are all cooking in the same room. They are here to say that you were cooking today. You are cooking in a pot on a stove. They said that it reminds them of when you used to be little and they would all joke around and tell the same stories every time. You all would laugh just as hard as if it were the first time that they told you the story. So, they are here to say that this is a great time for you, meaning that you are in a good place mentally and spiritually. You are finding your spiritual side, stronger than ever. This is a time when you are going to be very grounded and helpful for others. Maybe perhaps look into spiritual service in the future as some sort of religious pastor or something like that. Some sort of inspiring person. So, keep studying your spirituality. All the women in your family are with you as you cook. And I'm going to leave you with that." (From the medium Janyce).

It is possible that the "older girl" is my foster mother. My foster mother was gentle and kind with her discipline and teaching. She is the one who taught me how to cook when I was a teenager. When I'm in my kitchen at home, I often think of her and thank her, especially for teaching me how to make yeast bread and my famous holiday dinner rolls. Although I am allergic to the gluten in wheat, I still love to knead the dough and smell the aroma of the yeast as the dough is rising, while the rolls are baking, and of course fresh out of the oven!

Big Granny

"I have a woman here. People called her Granny. But she's not related to you by blood. She's showing me flowers—lilacs. It is more about the smell of the lilacs. Not to worry about having to decorate with flowers around the house. But the smell of the lilacs is important and healing for you. Will help with your sleeping problems. She wants you to enjoy the loveliness of life's smells."

CHAPTER 12: SPIRIT MESSAGES FROM OTHER RELATIVES AND... 125

Big Granny's name came through earlier with my morning meditation prayer and I greeted her. She is my foster father's grandmother.

Husband

"There is a man here who worked on cars, maybe as a hobby. I see you're up walking. He will work on your spine." (From the medium Rik).

The man who worked on cars was Roy. The man who fixed cars was my ex-husband. He loved fixing cars so that's why it might've been described as a hobby, but actually he had a job as an auto mechanic at a Mobil station. He also fixed his own cars and other people's in his free time. Imagine waking up to find a car's transmission on your kitchen table! A dirty, greasy transmission that stayed there a week until he got it fixed. I hadn't seen my husband in 30 years. Then, he caught up with my brother and exchanged phone numbers. He was awfully thin when I saw him a few years ago when he came to Chicago for a family reunion. I didn't even know he had family in Chicago. The next year we went out of town to a funeral together. I've worried about him because for a couple of years he hadn't answered my calls. Now his phone is disconnected, and his emails don't go through, so I don't know if he's alive on this side or the Other Side.

"Things are opening up for you now. A thin man here. I don't know his name. Roy or Leroy. He's dancing. He's dancing because he's happy for you, for all you've accomplished. Get out in the sunshine more. He says, "You didn't have children this lifetime because you were here to work on you." But he wants you to know that you would have been a wonderful mother."

The bright sunshine Roy showed the medium, was of course, his way of calling me "Sunshine."

"I get a male spirit coming in. He says, "You are my sunshine," right away. He does like this. The medium gestures. The sun just comes out and kind of halos around you. So, "You are my sunshine" is what I hear right away. He's saying things didn't go the way you wanted them. But it's going the right way. Right now, you are not seeing it, though. She laughs. You're not seeing it. He's saying, "It's going the right way." Always remember, Haneefa, what he is telling me to tell you is that everything is in divine order. That is all you need to know. Then he is doing like this. That is all you need to know. Everything is in divine order. So, even though I want this, and I want that to go this way or XYZ, know that it is going the way that it should go. If it is something that is still in your heart, continue to move forward toward it, because it is there in your vibration. Just because you did not grasp it the first time, it is okay. If it is in your heart, go forward and remain steady, is what I'm hearing. I will leave you with that. God bless you." (From the medium Audrey).

This second medium was new and would not have known Roy's nickname for me was Sunshine. She wouldn't have known that there were still obstacles and hoops to jump through before I could complete my clinical internship and graduate from the doctoral program. The university I attended for eight years, like other for-profit psychology schools went bankrupt and abruptly closed. I had to transfer to another university. The COVID-19 crisis added to the already slow communication from my new university. We had to quickly learn how to do therapy with clients using video calls. Everything seemed beyond my control for when I would graduate.

This is part of a private medium consultation by Cher on the phone.

"Is it Ray or Roy? I want to say Roy."

"It is."

"So Roy comes in to be around you. He just wants you to know that he is with you. He has a big smile on his face as well. Was he in a wheelchair when he passed?"

"I have no idea. I still don't have any official notice that he passed, other than that the another medium brought him through in 2013. Then you started bringing him through. When a student and I did weekly phone mediumship practice, he really took advantage of that time. He was glad that he found a way to reconnect with me. But I have not received any official word of his death. People described him as skinny. The last time that I saw him, he was slim, but he wasn't *that* skinny, so I don't know."

"Well, he comes in, and he looks like he's in a wheelchair, but then he stands up. So, I'm just going to say that whatever ailments or illness that he had, he's now showing me that he's just really full of life right now. He smiles real broad as well. He's showing me a white uniform."

"Yeah."

"I know that you cooked. Right? Did he cook with you?"

"Yes!"

"I feel like this is a dress uniform. So, he's coming in and just making himself about to be something. That is what it comes down to."

I laugh with joy! "He's beating his own chest."

The medium laughs. "Yes, kind of. We are talking about stepping out and showing our best self. He is showing me his best self. So, like he's in a dress uniform, whole, healthy and just a happy, happy man. He shows strength. He's got a lot, lotta strength. He brings strength through."

"Wow! There was a student in the spirit circle who also brought Roy through. All of this is evidential stuff. She also said he was dressed in white."

"Um-humm."

"That's because we were both cooks in the Air Force. Our uniform was white. That's where I met him, and that's how we ended up getting married."

"Great!"

"In regard to the dress uniform, I think it is his acknowledgment of the confidence that I've gained. He is letting me know that it's okay to be proud of it."

"Yeah, we also need to recognize our accomplishments and to take pride in whatever we've been able to do. There is nothing wrong with that at all. I think that is like the fuel to help us do more. Whatever that might be."

Father-in-law

"A man here playing the tambourine. He had right hand withered with his arm pulled to the back on his side when he was on this plane. Lots of beauty and love on the spirits' side of life. Be happy this week. There will be schedule changes this week. Take a big deep breath because if you weren't on a higher level you would be angry. But you will go with the flow and see where it goes."

My father-in-law had a stroke in his later years and was paralyzed on one side. He was a gentle, quiet person with great humor.

***

Friends Pop In

From my first private reading with the medium Rik:

"Any more questions?"

"Who sent me the 'Lost without You, Babe' song? It's been stuck in my head."

"It's a young man named Joseph, or maybe Joseph is his middle name. He loved you very much. He died suddenly of an accident or illness in 1984 or 1986. It was a sudden illness. He's around you and sends you ice cream. He loved ice cream." (From the medium Rik).

"That's funny." I started laughing. "I've been craving and eating ice cream. But I didn't like ice cream before because I don't like to be cold. Plus I'm allergic to milk, however I found at the store some delicious, irresistible, coconut milk, almond, chocolate-covered popsicles last month."

Four days later I remembered who Joseph was. We called him Joe. He was Roy's friend who always seemed to know what time we ate dinner—any meal, actually—and would join us for food, conversation, and jokes. He was quiet. That was from 1977 to 1979.

"There is a man here with cotton, white cotton. Someone from down south. I'm seeing a lot of cotton, which means a lot is about to happen for you. You're up walking. Will work on your spine." (From the medium Rik).

That's Joe again. Roy used to tease his friend and call him "Cotton Picker" because he was originally from down south and had a southern accent.

"A man here who says you and he used to talk a lot together. He uses a lot of big words." (From the medium Rik).

James was a neighbor in my apartment building that I used to visit. He was old enough to be my father. This message came a few weeks after he died. He did use a lot of long words—you would need a dictionary to understand him! While he was incarcerated, he taught himself how to read and memorized dictionaries to increase his vocabulary. He introduced me to video games that were mysteries, that required problem-solving to get to the next level. He taught me the card game Pitty Pat at a Thanksgiving dinner. James had an amazing memory. He told me about Alexandre Dumas, a Black French playwright and author of *The Three Musketeers* and *The Count of Monte Cristo* and over two hundred other publications. Everyone assumed he was white. Another book he shared was *They Came before Columbus.* He could be very serious. James did not slack off or evade issues, and he didn't let me do it either. He always asked deep questions of everyone. Somehow, he did this with a smile.

"You know who is here. He's been with you for a week. You have your armor on, which would have been okay for arrows, but not bullets! You need a different type of protection. But even that is not enough for where you're at. You can help the people who come there, but you will have to leave the rest."

James too wore armor when he was around other people, but he went after what he wanted—no matter what. In this spirit message, he was advising me that at my clinical training site, not even my armor, problem-solving skills, ambition, and toughness would be enough for the excessive burdens that others were piling on me. James also saw the troubles that I have not been able to talk to others about. It's better that I reach out for help instead of doing too much alone. He was the only man who would step in and do what needed to be done for me. I wasn't used to that. James was letting me know that he was still with me and I was not alone. This is what others at the church, everywhere, need to know for their own lives.

James went into the hospital for unbearable back pain, which his doctors initially said was back spasms. In the ER, and during the following week, they found much more wrong with him. "They opened Pandora's box," is how James described it. There was arthritis in his back, diabetes, kidney problems, and pneumonia, and his left leg kept going out from under him, with extreme pain, so that he couldn't stand or walk. He was transferred to a physical rehabilitation center. But he went back into the hospital almost every other week. The doctors put a feeding tube into his stomach when they discovered he had problems swallowing because liquids and food were going down into his lungs.

Not being able to eat or even drink water was frustrating for James. He told me he began having visions that were so real of a woman holding out food to him. He would be reaching for it when he became alert, it would disappear. She offered him other items and other visions prior to the food visions. This upset him so much that he even asked to see a psychiatrist!

"Your visions are probably normal," I told him. "Similar to when someone is lost and thirsty in the desert begins seeing an oasis with palm trees, water, and people everywhere, yet the real oasis is still many miles away."

His stories reminded me of when he was very ill in the ER. I came as soon as I could. He was looking at spirits in the room and turning to them, answering their questions, while still carrying on a conversation with me! I didn't see the spirits. I observed that he responded to them as if they were as real as I was in the flesh. He told me a few days later that he had seen the bright light twice and they had come to him a couple of times with a boat. But he fought them and refused to go. Since I had had a near-death experience, I told him about heaven and how spirit loved ones and guardian angels often come to greet you.

The food visions were also possibly spirits communicating with James and comforting him. I thought perhaps he would die in a few days and told his son when he called the ER that he needed to come and spend time with his father. This happened in April. In July James ended up in the intensive care unit with kidney failure. He improved and went to a hospital room, where he required less care. However, when I arrived to visit him, I noticed that he had had a stroke. One side of his face drooped, and he complained about not being able to move his arm or his leg. I did not mention the possible stroke to him or that the end was probably near. It was as if he were in denial for months. He was still talking about going back to the rehabilitation center to learn how to walk so that he could take care of himself at home! I encouraged him to have a heart-to-heart conversation with his son, and they did.

The next day, I received a call from the doctor urging me to come quickly. When I arrived, his son was standing next to the bed, smiling. I couldn't help but smile too because of the look of pure joy frozen on James's face. His arm reaching upward. A few days prior, he told me he didn't want to die because he didn't want to leave me yet, because of the love he hadn't had before with any other woman. Now the room was filled with love. His son told me that on the way to the hospital, he couldn't cry because he too felt the love at the moment that his father died.

James took my ability to love to a higher level than I believed was possible. The true love he gave was unconditional, and I did the same for him. We weren't affectionate or sexually intimate with each other. We were just very good friends. He was, however, a very romantic, old-time gentleman in the way he cared about my needs. His love and romance continued after his death. The songs that came into my head, "One in a Million U" and "No One in This World," I know came from James because I'd never experienced that kind of love before. Therefore, it was a one-in-a-million kind of love. A love that I am eternally grateful for and share with the world to let people know what's possible.

Thank You from the Other Side

"A male spirit is here. He wants to thank you for helping. For helping his wife and someone else he loved. Several spirits on the other side are thanking you for taking the time to help others. You need to develop your listening. You already listen but could read books about more ways to listen." (From the medium Rik).

This was a friend's father who had recently collapsed on the sidewalk and died. I'd been comforting my friend Sarah and her mother. At his memorial service at their house, I felt him hug me in his own unique way, a hug that made me giggle briefly in surprise.

"There's a woman here named Jackie or Jacqueline who had a lot of problems with her stomach and her lungs. She's been in spirit for maybe three years. She wants to thank you for helping her. As you may know, Haneefa, you tend to help and remember those nameless spirits. To look out for those who seem to be forgotten." (From the medium Rik).

This was a classmate in college who was blind and used a wheelchair because of muscular dystrophy. I helped her with algebra, and we talked on the phone. I didn't know she had passed.

"Lots of family around you, and they're proud of you. They're really proud of you, and I think it has to do with you developing your mediumship. They are glad you've been able to bring them and others through." (From the medium Cher).

Thank-you's from deceased acquaintances and friends are reminders that we can make a significant difference in other people's lives even in the brief time that we know them.

Birds as Spirit Messengers

The red-winged blackbirds rarely came around after those first few years in the 1990s. Back then, I found in a book at the library about red-winged blackbirds and meadowlarks—that these birds are capable of human speech. Occasionally, while traveling on the highway, I've seen the red-winged blackbirds as they fly up out of the reeds. Otherwise, I have to purposely seek them out in parks near water and during migration season. I can hear them but can't see them because the tree branches are up too high. Occasionally, I see the red-winged blackbirds flying low, busy with their own tasks and not paying attention to me.

Other birds nowadays surprise me and tickle my insides with joy. Soon after my foster mother passed away in 2010, I started seeing cardinals. One of my younger foster sisters also started seeing several cardinals a day—they would tap on her large deck window. The cardinal's song is one I can recognize anywhere. They would get my attention initially up in trees, then on bushes close by, or even where there was no greenery, like on buildings and lampposts in busy city areas. While I'm waiting for a bus, a cardinal will come close, although there may be a few other people waiting too or walking by.

Of course, robins are a sign that the warm days of springtime are arriving. Most people are happy to notice the first robin of the season. Usually I see robins at a distance across green lawns, pulling up worms, or in a nest in a tree. But one day, as I was going down the sidewalk, in front of me was a robin. It didn't fly away. I slowed and stopped. The bird appeared to dance. In my head, I heard the song "Rockin' Robin." A little later, as I continued on my way, I remembered that was my husband Roy's favorite song. He used to sing and dance to it.

In fall 2020, soon after my dear friend Ruth died, she sent birds to her family and friends. To each person, she sent a different bird. She sent me a bird early in the morning, when I'm usually awake anyway, writing. I didn't know what kind of bird because it was dark outside. It was a bird that I hadn't heard before, with a very distinct soft chirping sound.

Chapter 13: Apologies

Besides my mother's apologies, other apologies also came through the mediums from the people who hurt me the most.

"Haneefa, I have someone here that wants to talk to you. I got a man here from spirit who is hanging his head. He is hanging his head because he feels so ashamed and remorseful. This is a man who hurt you, he said a long, long, long time ago. He's here to just say he was very young and he was out of his head or something, and he says that he didn't know what he was doing. But now that he is in spirit, he is like a wise man. He is saying that you have evolved so much as a human being, that you are such a spirit now, that you don't even think about it anymore. But he is saying if you just let go of that and actually see that he was just young and out of his mind. Let loose of that. You do that, and you will be more able to forget it.

You don't have to forgive him. It's not about that. It's just that he wants to say that he acknowledges what he did. He takes responsibility. The last thing he wanted to say is you are a real healing soul. You should use all the experiences that happened to you to help heal children and women. Because there is a lot of suffering in the world. You have been spending time by yourself with the shelter-in-place. Obviously we all have. But he says get ready because the women and the children need you. Like the ones who have been hurt the most could benefit from how you are so trustworthy. All this has made you a sterling soul. So, he says thank you for your grace. I will leave you with that." (From the medium Janyce).

This man in spirit was my second husband Sameen apologizing to me. With new understanding, I accepted his explanation and apology. That was a long, long time ago, thirty-one years. I hadn't seen him since then. A couple of years after we divorced, I forgave him, but mostly to relieve my own suffering, to not be tormented by constant thoughts, fear, and memories of what he had done to me. He probably doesn't know when I forgave him because I never told him. No one told me to forgive him, it just occurred to me, perhaps through spirit, that I should release the hurt by internally forgiving him. Later I actually thanked Allah for Sameen because, without him, I probably would not have gone to therapy. Now l am no longer a zombie. I now feel alive, and I know joy.

"A man is in spirit here who used to be mean to you. He is asking you to forgive him. He was not a nice man. You probably have forgiven him already. But he still feels guilty and wants you to forgive him. You don't have to, you know. He wants you to know that he's seeing how far you've come. He wants you to continue to share your ideas here and with others and to know that he hears you. They are helping him to heal." (From the medium Rik).

"A father is coming in. He identifies as having lived in the Midwest. There is a distance between you. He said that he wouldn't have thought he would be saying this to you. But he says he's proud of you."

I cried a little. I was surprised at the tears and that I was happy that my stepfather had finally come through.

Seeing my face, the medium continued, "Remember, the door for reformation is never closed." (From the medium Cher).

However, a couple of days later, as I thought about the medium's reading in a therapy session, I was surprised that I was again feeling tears, but I was also feeling angry. Hearing that Stepfather said he was proud of me, I thought initially that he meant he saw how much healing I had done with a lot of spiritual and emotional growth. So I wasn't prepared for the tightness around my heart. The sadness and the hurt. He was proud of what? That I'm strong? What does "strong" mean? That I didn't break like he broke my mother? I really felt angry. He destroyed my mother and took her away from us. If that is what being proud of me means, then I don't want it!

As what often happens with the process of forgiveness, when later reminders and hurts surfaced, I realized that I couldn't fully except these men's apologies yet. Not knowing then, that in the future, I would have to learn and understand about Islam first.

Art in Therapy

On August 3, 2020, Momma's spirit surprised me while I was looking for something else by having me pull out a sketchbook that would usually be on my living room art bookshelf, not on my bedroom bookshelf. I had completely forgotten about the pictures that my therapist asked me to draw of my childhood in 2006. Sure enough, I found not just one journal from 2006 but five other writing journals! I began to understand that Momma wanted me to add therapy to her book, to explain how I got better. How I recovered from the childhood abuse and later domestic violence. How other women could heal too—it was all to be included in this book.

Monica specializes in treating children and adolescent patients. She only had a few adult patients like me. Usually our sessions were talk therapy. After she learned that I liked art, she asked me to do drawings about my childhood. Over the weekend, at home, I started to feel different as soon as I decided to do the drawings. I silently thanked my therapist for asking me to do them. Otherwise, I would have put them off indefinitely because it had been difficult for me to draw anything. Worried that I'd get overwhelmed with memories and feelings, I procrastinated by watching TV and cleaning the house. Cleaning house is what I usually do when I'm unconsciously afraid and anxious. But I decided to jump right in and do it. Somehow, I knew that in order to get unstuck and move forward in my life, I had to do the drawings.

I started drawing a picture of my empty refrigerator at 11:00 PM and kept drawing until midnight. How's that for procrastination? I'd waited until the end of the day. But I was determined to do it. I didn't have many feelings, I just concentrated on not putting in too many details and getting it done quickly. I wondered what my therapist would say about an empty refrigerator. I drew it first because it gave me practice drawing and was less emotionally charged than the childhood drawings. I would finish in the morning. I hoped my therapist wouldn't ask me too many questions about my empty refrigerator picture. I feared she would focus on my eating and then we wouldn't discuss the more important pictures.

When I woke up the next morning, I started drawing a picture of me sitting at a desk in a second- or third-grade classroom at the primary school in the Midwest. Anxious, I sketched anyway, telling myself to just keep doing it. I reminded myself to not worry about details. I drew a picture of myself first, then the students in the desks in front of and to the side of me. The students were looking at and laughing at me. It was a challenge drawing the boy behind me reaching to pull my scarf off. I was surprised that I did this without a lot of emotions. I was also amazed by how the little children, desks, and chairs took shape before my eyes. Encouraged, I kept drawing.

After lunch and changing pencils, sharpening them, and finding a better eraser, I returned to drawing. Looking at the picture that afternoon, I realized that the desk and little Haneefa were much too large. I looked like an adult in comparison to the other children. I made the desk, and then me, and the boy behind me smaller. I got tired as I added more students and details, so I stopped. I wanted to do other pictures instead, but a lot of anxiety surfaced as I began to draw a picture of us sitting on the prayer rug while our stepfather read the Quran aloud. I decided to wait until the next morning to draw the picture of me decorating the Christmas tree at school and the beating I received from my stepfather as a punishment.

In the morning, I started drawing the picture of my stepfather cutting my hair off. It was very difficult emotionally. I was too anxious and angry to draw my stepfather. All I could draw were his arms and hands holding the scissors and my hair. I packed up the drawings and got ready to leave. For the therapy session, I put on a pretty dress to celebrate my achievement of being able to draw the pictures from my childhood and, hopefully, the healing from doing the work.

Outside, the trees were beautiful. I felt a little of my inner child's wonder, openness, and innocence.

"Are you taking it all in?" my therapist asked.

"Yes! I'm taking it all in. I'm enjoying being outside. But it was still a little scary doing the drawings. I had to keep telling myself, 'Just do it!' Actually, the drawings were easier to do than I thought they would be, maybe because most of the memories and feelings came up last week and as I thought of what I would draw. I was more absorbed in the process of drawing the pictures. But I had a lot of anxiety and difficulty drawing my stepfather."

"That's all right. Did you draw any part of him?"

"Yes, his hands," I said.

She paused. In that instant, I thought his penis, but shook it out of my head. I didn't remember that. "Did you feel in control while you were drawing this?"

"No, only in control by not putting in too many details."

"When I look at the drawing of the refrigerator, I see that the door is open," she said. "Could mean open to opportunities. Open to receive. You could have drawn it closed and then said it was empty. You cleaned out the refrigerator, threw out the old stuff. So you can now put new stuff in it. It could also mean that you were exposed. What's that look?"

I turned my face away. Ooooh, I felt that. "Yes, all right, exposed is a good word. Just that the process of being exposed is very uncomfortable."

She continued. "I like how you drew the butter compartment and put the temperature knob and the word 'Frigidaire.' What do you feel with this picture of school?"

"I don't feel much now," I said. "I did when I was drawing it. That's me. I'm dressed different. I was teased for dressing differently."

"The children are staring at you," she commented.

"My mother and grandmother were involved in school activities before I moved to the Midwest. Remember the March of Dimes fundraiser?"

"Oh, I remember that—and the green stamps."

"Yes, the green stamps and postage stamps, savings bonds, and plastic recorder flute lessons. My sister took flute lessons. I wanted to take flute lessons too."

Just then, a man went by, ringing the noisy bells on his ice cream pushcart. "You remember those from when you were little?" she asked.

"No, I remember the big ice cream trucks. Maybe because I lived on the East Coast. There were also trucks with big, hot soft pretzels with mustard. A truck with a Ferris wheel. And another with a merry-go-round. Some people called it a carousel."

She was surprised. "You had those?"

"Yes, in Philadelphia."

We returned to looking at the pictures of the classroom. My therapist asked, "What about this little girl here? She looks a lot like you." I didn't answer. She continued. "She has a pencil in her hand, and she's not smiling."

"Except she doesn't have pants on."

"Yes, but she is like you, if you were to use juxtaposition."

"I will have to look up the word 'juxtaposition,'" I said.

"It's like a mirror reflection."

I nodded. I was too stunned at her intuition to know what to say. I too was drawn to the drawing of the girl as soon as I finished drawing her—that she could be me. But that was never my intention when I drew her.

"Such details. Look at this under here," my therapist said.

Looking at the picture later at home, I really thought the pencil was just a line and not really in her fingers. How did she know it was a pencil? The mark on the paper was very tiny. "I didn't know where to put the teacher. I thought maybe I should have her writing on the chalkboard with her back turned. I wrote 'third grade.' The teacher saw students do things to me, but she didn't do anything. She might have even joined in. My stepfather went up to the school."

"What about the boy?"

"It's not finished. It was a lot of work. I got tired. I just wanted to go on to the other pictures so I could tell you my story. I didn't want to spend too much time on him."

"I'd like for you to finish the picture," she said. "How come you didn't go to a Muslim school?"

I got upset, probably because I was repulsed by the whole idea of having to be a Muslim back then. My therapist kept talking about how there must have been Muslim schools, but I was silent.

"No? Maybe another time."

"Well, at least I would not have had to be an outcast."

Later I remembered there were Sister Clara Mohammed schools. I don't know if there were Muslim schools in the Midwest, or anywhere, when I was little. In addition, we were poor and probably couldn't have afforded the tuition.

We turned the page to the picture of me putting ornaments on a Christmas tree with a teacher standing next to me, guiding and encouraging me. "She's nurturing you," the therapist said. I quietly nodded. Next to it was a picture of my stepfather beating me when he found out about it. "You can tell that's an extension cord."

CHAPTER 13: APOLOGIES

I didn't say anything, but I felt it, because what she said was true. I didn't think of this while I was drawing it. I don't know why I was chosen to help decorate the tree, just me and the teacher. Maybe one other student was also in the big school entrance hallway. The school principal came by later and helped. It never occurred to me that it was bad to do.

She turned the page to the picture of us children sitting on the prayer rug. "Tell me about this picture. Where are you?"

I pointed. "My mother, sister, and I are sitting in the back."

"Your brother and stepfather are up front because they are males?"

"Yes, because they're males."

"I went to hear Farrakhan speak," she said. "What's that big event called? Savior's Day?"

"I'm not sure. I was a different kind of Muslim."

"I wore a long, white skirt with a split on the side. They made me pin it closed with safety pins." We laughed.

"My stepfather would make us get up at four in the morning to make Fajar prayer. We were just little kids! During Ramadan he would make us sit there on that prayer rug for hours as he read the Quran, first in Arabic, then in English. I didn't understand either language as a child. To this day, I hate the sight of oriental prayer rugs. Even the recent mention of a cousin of mine that collects oriental rugs makes me shudder."

"He spoke Arabic?"

"No, he was Black American! He just took some Arabic classes to learn to read and write the Quran. You mentioned last session that I have choices now, as to which religion I want or what holidays I want to celebrate. I've made plenty of choices. I chose not to have a religion when I first became an adult on my own. My first husband, who wasn't a Muslim, became interested in Islam and brought me back to the mosque. Later he left because he didn't like the power struggles among the men. But I stayed six years. We divorced. Then I married my second husband, who was also a Muslim and a religious fanatic like my stepfather."

"He came into your life so you could heal this." She pointed to my pictures.

I nodded but didn't know what she meant. "After my near-death experience, I began exploring other religions and spirituality because I wanted to find out how to have that incredible love and peace of heaven in my everyday life. There's a difference between religion and spirituality."

"You are spiritual," she said.

"Yes, I'm more spiritual. So recently it isn't so much about making choices about which religion but the need to grieve what Stepfather did to me in the name of religion. This brings me to the topic of going to Easter services. A friend invited me. I didn't know it was going to bring up such strong emotions." My voice got gruff. I hesitated as I felt strong feelings, and I wondered if I could safely express my beliefs about religion.

"I know." She used a soothing voice. This gave me the okay to continue.

"The Easter service was at a huge church. Over eight thousand people were there. If each gave a dollar, that's a lot of money. The church stated part of its mission is ministering to the miseries of humanity. It is a large church. What is it doing to improve the lives of people? Most of the service was praising God instead of praying together for solutions to society's problems. Blaming it on the devil instead of taking responsibility. All of this brought up my own issues, how religion is used as an excuse to abuse people. Even as a child, I wondered how there could be such a thing as holy wars."

"Muslims and Catholics seem to attract this type of people."

"Yes, but it's not just Islam or any religion. People use money or the lack of it to abuse others. It occurs in sports, on jobs, and when teachers give grades in school."

"You want to talk about the other picture now or wait until next week?"

"Now," I said, thinking, I did the work, so let's just get it over with.

"He's cutting your hair? Tell me what's going on here."

"My mother always braided my hair. I took some of the braids down and styled it at school from under my scarf. When my stepfather found out, he punished me by cutting off most of my hair."

"Why did you take down your hair?"

"Because I wanted to be like the other girls. I was eleven years old. Him cutting my hair hurt my mother very deeply. She refused to comb my hair after that. Neither did she talk about it." There was silence in the therapy room for a while.

CHAPTER 13: APOLOGIES

"That shows you fought back. That ability that you had as little Haneefa you still have now as an adult."

"I knew even as an eight-year-old that he was wrong. That what he was saying and doing wasn't right.

I wanted to tell you that the last time I let go of a big chunk of healing concerning my stepfather, the loneliness and emptiness was so awful that I had a strong urge to drive my wheelchair through my living room window."

"What kept you from doing it?"

"I thought about the people I would leave behind. I thought of how I made it through the two other times I felt similar strong feelings and urges."

Monica didn't question me about what I meant or about the other two situations.

"At that time, I thought about all the supportive people who had helped and watched me come so far. So why give up now? "But I don't want to be so strong all the time."

She was quiet for a while. I couldn't tell why from her face or body language. Maybe because I turned my head away. We were sitting close so that we could look at my drawings together. I wasn't aware that I had turned my head away completely. Usually I looked straight ahead when I was uncomfortable, but she could still see my face and comment on my expressions. I didn't know why I still spoke into the air instead of making eye contact with her when I was upset. Did I do it with other people too? For years I spoke very softly. Later I realized it was because I felt that no one really listened to me anyway. Was turning my head away because of a similar reason or habit? I asked myself these questions silently.

"There is therapy where the client is rebirthed out of wounds. Then there's therapy that does a combination of this and cognitive therapy. I've tried to do a little bit of both. I take into consideration your health. Drawing helps give you some control. You have to be able to separate the strong emotions of what's coming from childhood and what's happening in the present."

"What have you learned from doing these pictures?" she asked me.

"Well, first, I'm excited that I can still draw people." She nodded. "I was amazed as I watched the pictures appear before my eyes. It flowed. I did this in the morning and in the evening." She nodded again. "I took the risk to jump right in and draw the pictures. It was very hard to get started, but I knew I had to do it. Something inside of me knew that my being stuck now is related to what happened to me as a child. I can't go forward without going back to that. Now I actually feel better, more alive yesterday and today for doing the drawings. When you first asked me to talk about school, I thought, fine, there isn't much that happened at school when I was a little girl. I liked school. The only thing that I missed was my mother's participation and support of my education when we lived in the Midwest." She nodded. "I wasn't thinking that all of this had bothered me so much."

"Perhaps you've done so well, in spite of the traumas in your life, because you had a strong, loving foundation before the age of seven, during the formative years of your development."

Memories had come up the night before as I decided which pictures to draw. I felt them, but it was more like watching a movie. Having my mind focused on the goal of drawing the pictures may have decreased the intensity too. There were strong emotions as I drew the pictures. However, the amazement and excitement of how the little children and details appeared on the paper kept me from getting scared. I didn't realize how strong these emotions were until my therapist asked me how I felt as I was drawing the pictures and only a few words came out. Words that didn't even begin to describe the experience. Maybe there was still some fear of telling what happened to little Haneefa to another adult. I was able to better connect to my therapist by letting the pictures tell the story for me. I was still partially mute and guarded with Monica, unable to say what else was going through my mind while I was alone drawing the pictures. I still wondered what she meant by saying, "You have more control by drawing or journaling."

Soon after the therapy session I saw a man with a beard and wore a Kenya cap on his head like my stepfather used to wear. I told myself, "But he doesn't actually look anything like my stepfather." I deep breathed. Since I had processed some of the stepfather memories earlier today, I felt relieved I did not have a flashback. I would be all right.

Always Loved

Gradually I have been healed by the messages I received at the Church of the Spirit. At first the messages didn't seem to apply to me, but later, the messages from my parents were the most healing. I used to wonder why the mediums didn't give me psychic readings like they gave most of the rest of the congregation about jobs, projects, or the need to slow down, or take risks, or change one's attitude.

Instead, my messages were mostly about a lot of spirits being around me who loved me. Sometimes they described or named people that were unfamiliar to me because I was separated from my extended family when I was a child. Most have passed on by now. But finally, the main message sank in. I was loved, and I'd always been loved and taken care of. They did not abandon me when they were incapable of caring for me on the Earth plane, leaving a big hole in my heart and a feeling of never seeming to know love or to ever feel close to anyone until last year. I started keeping phone and voice mail recordings of family and friends just to remind me that they were dear to me because I didn't feel physically close to them and I was always terrified of losing my loved ones. Now I'm starting to understand, and most important, I am relaxed now, realizing as I write this that the intense fear of losing my family hasn't been there for a while. My friends and relatives help me experience that I am always loved.

Chapter 14: Forgiveness

"I have someone here. Your mother, or someone like a mother to you. She used to do your hair, and you used to give her a hard time, squirming and moving when she used to do your hair or give you a bath. She loves you and will always be with you. She said she's proud of you."

From as far back as I can remember, my mother washed, combed, braided, and sometimes straightened my hair. The only time my mother was ever mean to me was when she combed my hair. Momma whacked my hand with the comb if I put my hand up to my head to try to stop her from yanking it through my hair or pulling my hair too tight as she braided. It seemed that no matter what I did, I could never be good enough with whatever happened to my hair. She would yell at me because my stocking cap came off during the night. Or when my braids came undone. Or when the curlers made out of small pieces of twisted brown paper bags fell out. She would yell at me because it was hard for me to sit still and just take the pain. I cried and cried. The top of my head hurt the worst. Momma told me, "You are too tender-headed!"

At the beauty shop, the hot comb or curling iron sent hot, melted grease down to burn our tender little scalps, and the beautician trying to get down to all the naps meant burning our ears, forehead, and necks. My knuckles were burned too if I tried to protect myself from the hot comb or the curling iron. Thankfully, the edges were cut off close to the scalp to hide the hair that was too short to straighten with the hot comb. Having to watch little girls with long, wavy, "good hair" sitting under the dryer be praised and *ooh*ed and *ahh*ed over sent those of us with nappy hair the unspoken message that we were ugly and bad. Sometimes Momma would give us touchups at home with the straightening hot comb, heated on the gas burner on the stove. The awful smell of burned hair! I wished I could get all my hair cut off like my brother!

Grandma would bring Emin home from the barbershop, carrying him in her arms while hugging and kissing him and smelling the cologne on his little head, and tell him, "You are such a good boy!"

I could never be good enough to sit still while getting my hair done! Otherwise, in the rest of my life, my mother was very encouraging, fun, and compassionate, rarely ever even spanking us. After we moved to live with our stepfather, I don't remember struggling with my mother as she combed my hair, especially as I got older. Rather I welcomed her touch.

When she had time, she would creatively braid a design into it. Sometimes she would put my initial, H, on the back of my head or my favorite, a heart shape. I would beg her, "Momma, may I have a heart, please?" Whatever design she chose, I was proud of it. Otherwise, Momma put in three boring cornrows, evenly spaced, from the front of my head to the back.

I didn't think of combing my own hair until I was eleven years old. Kani, who was now going to junior high school far away from the elementary school that my brother and I were attending, was possibly doing her own hair then. One day, I decided to let my hair down so that it would show from under the back of my scarf. I reached under my scarf and gradually unbraided my braids in class.

When I arrived home, my mother wasn't pleased that I had taken her handiwork apart. She might have told my stepfather, but neither she nor I was prepared for what he did next. I was expecting a beating. Instead, Stepfather cut my hair very short. Momma yelled and pleaded with him not to do it. Then she grew silent. I could see the pain in her eyes.

"This will teach you to keep your scarf on!" This definitely meant that I kept my scarf on! Humiliated and ashamed, I also felt guilty for adding to my mother's hurt. She said, "I will never comb your hair again!" And she didn't. I had to learn to comb and style my own hair.

While Momma's, Kani's, and my hair had been natural since we left Philadelphia, all I knew was that to have long, straight hair was beautiful. Since I was a little girl, I was ashamed of my black skin and nappy hair. If we didn't have naturally straight hair, at least we had long braids. Our long hair was my mother's pride and joy.

In the midst of the constant chaos in our home, I don't think I thought much about my hair while we were living in the Midwest. Getting my hair done for Sundays and special holidays like Easter was just another family tradition taken away by my stepfather. Yet how could I miss getting my hair straightened? I hated the hot straightening comb and the hot curling iron burning my scalp, forehead, ears, and neck. I vowed never to get my hair straightened again, if I ever had a choice. I used to envy my brother going to the barbershop and having most of his hair cut off. But now with my hair cut short would people think that I was a boy instead of a girl?

What I didn't know at the time was that the natural look had come into style. The natural was initially hair cut short on "negros'" heads. In the early sixties, the natural grew and expanded to become the afro—a symbol of Black beauty and pride by the late sixties. In 1966 the afro became part of the Black Is Beautiful and Black Power movements. That year, Kani and I worked at a small Muslim-owned boutique selling Dashiki tops, African robes, and jewelry to earn the money to buy these African pride items *and* flowered bell bottoms.

Thoughts on Black Hair

Recently, I was looking for what I wrote in my journal about hair, the two heartfelt, expressive writings including a poem for a presentation for the Chicago Chapter of the Association of Black Psychologists. As an adult, I didn't consciously have intense feelings about it. Five decades later, when I shared my story about how I hated getting my hair done, other women said their mother, or grandmother, or auntie did the same. So it wasn't only my mother!

But why? I could understand that Momma and many other Black women back then didn't know how to care for our extra curly, *nappy* hair. But getting angry at me, a child, because of my hair? Did my mother in spirit believe I still had healing to do, so she was making me write my memories and feelings over again?

Since I have a Black therapist, we can talk about such things as feeling invisible with all the racism in our country and communities that has not allowed Black people to talk about or even acknowledge the pain within ourselves. Why and how do we feel invisible? Well, the answer is similar to why Black people have always had to hide their hair. If you want to be accepted, then you hide your hair. Even to be accepted in the Black community, you have to hide your hair. Black people are the worst in terms of being the hair police, having to constantly question if every hair is in its correct position. It's guaranteed that no matter how we style our hair, someone is going to criticize it, even if it's the straightest of straight. Any amount of nappy hair is done away with. Even little boys' hair is shaved off every week or two, while girls' hair is braided, or straightened, or covered with a weave to hide the naps. Our other good attributes are hidden away too—yes, due to others' judgment and criticism. Trying to hide our skin color, hair texture, culture, language, feelings, intelligence, and natural talents becomes automatic.

Older Black women have told me that when their hair was being combed when they were little girls, their mothers hit their little knuckles too! I had never really talked to other girls or women about it before, so I thought it was just my mother who was rough with my hair. But back in the day, few knew how to take care of our hair. Mothers didn't know that you should start combing from the ends of the hair and gently work your way down to the scalp. Or to comb the hair while it's wet and not tangle it up by rubbing it roughly with a towel to dry it. Or to not put our hair directly under a dryer before combing. Instead, it's best to detangle it and braid or twist it first to prevent it from curling up tightly again under the dryer. They didn't know how to put water on it to make it easier to comb. Back then there were no "Afro combs." To this day, I chuckle at the three-inch, fine-tooth combs that the nurses give us in the hospitals and at school. No wonder we couldn't get a comb through our hair!

When these women were younger, before the "I'm Black and I'm Proud" movement, little girls were tortured while having their hair combed. For boys the sounds and nicks from the clippers were torture too, but they still had it easier because they could go a couple of weeks or a month before having to go to the barber again. The psychological effects of what is done to our Black hair—teaching us to endure abuse. Having our hair straightened for Sundays and Easter! What message is that? That even God doesn't accept us as we are?

I wrote the following poem to express my thoughts and feelings about our hair experiences.

Hair As a Metaphor

As Black people
    We've had to hide our hair
    Like we've had to hide our souls.
    Men at a young age
    And as boys have it shaved off
    Shorter than a white boy's
    Crew cut
    Not done only
    In military basic training
    To show who is in control.
    Forced to shave off his beard
    The biological manifestation of manhood
    And Sansom's strength in the bible story.
    History removed from the textbooks.
    For women the assault
    Goes much deeper
    As we hide our hair
    And who we are
    In so many different ways.
    Not allowed to cut our hair
    Or be accused
    Of looking like a man.
    We straighten it
    By any means necessary.
    Starting with the hot comb
    And curling iron as a little girl.
    The hot iron and grease burning
    Our hair, scalp, ears, neck, and face.
    To get to the very edges.

CHAPTER 14: FORGIVENESS

We learn to endure
To have "good" hair just like her.
Straight hair
the only image
On TV, in movies and books
The only look.
We try so hard
To be good
To be just like her too.
Good for our fathers
Who threatened to
Straighten us out.
We endured the tight plaits
That didn't let us sleep,
Scratch, smile, or frown.
Just so our naps
Won't show.
Then along came the perms.
Straight lasted for weeks.
A sigh of relief.
But then while we slept
pillows covered with hair.
Hair down the drains
Along with who we are.
They offered us theirs.
We took it on.
We are willing
To pay the high price
Of letting go of our greatness
Which is priceless.

***

Freedom

Discriminated against because I have a dark complexion when I'm with white people, discriminated against by everyone when I use a wheelchair, and I can't be a Muslim because I'm Black even if I were from Africa, and especially since my parents were converted by Ahmadiyyah Muslims from Pakistan. Can't attend many mosques and participate because I'm a woman. I don't belong anywhere! So why should I have to hide who I am?

Starting in 2017 I just allow my hair to be. I still don't straighten my hair. I made a vow when I was thirteen years old to never straighten my hair again. No hot comb. No perms. No hair dye. An appreciation of the beauty of God's creativity. As my grandmother told us when we were very young, "God don't make ugly!" Yes, my hair is kinky, tightly curled, after I shampoo it. I oil it and braid it right away so it doesn't tangle. But my hair does straighten out naturally from the dry air in the wintertime. I'm too tender headed to "wash and wear" my hair like young Black women do these days, or as white women regularly do. No dreads or twists, either, because my scalp itches, even with small braids. Therefore I feel I have to be able to comb and brush down to my scalp.

In the winter, when I let my hair down occasionally, a white person will comment, "You look pretty." The first time this happened, it was a white male colleague. It suddenly occurred to me that he hadn't seemed to notice or pay me any attention, or even have much conversation with me before then.

I yelled at him, "Does that mean I was ugly before now?"

This still happens—someone who previously had not said anything to me before will say, "You look pretty today." I guess I was invisible the other days. Is my hair only pretty when it's straight? By now I'm used to it, so I quietly smile. I wish I could record these events so others would understand and believe me.

More recently, although I'd attended events there for years, I went to a summer workshop with my hair down. One of the white women came up to me. She was too shocked to know what to say. She stuttered, "Your hair. Your hair. Don't you usually have your hair braided or something?" She continued to stare at me.

"It's my hair," I said. "It's just my hair." I shrugged my shoulders and walked away. By then I'd had enough experience of freedom that I didn't even think about my hair anymore. I style it and wear it as it is. People tend to compliment me more on the hairstyles I quickly put together as I hurry to get out the door. Sorry, folks, I can never reproduce that style again on purpose!

PART THREE

TOUGH ASSIGNMENT FROM ALL MY MOMMAS

Chapter 15: Unexpected Tasks

Private Consultation with the Medium Cher at Spirit Fest 2015

"Do you have a question for me?"

"They wake me at night with a partially recurrent message. It's usually a problem to be pondered or solved. Last night, it was something about the number twelve. I got the impression it was about extending my concerns past myself to show compassion for others. For their struggles. A warning or something. It's hard to explain."

She nodded as if she understood. "Your prayers are good, and they are heard. They want you to go beyond prayers for yourself and those close to you, to global prayers. You have another question?"

"Yes, about my mediumship. I had a dream with me in a glass cubicle inside the lobby of a building. In the book, <u>How to Interpret Your Dreams and Discover Your Life Purpose</u>, it says glass can symbolize being a medium. I prayed and made my commitment to my mediumship."

"Was the cubicle open?"

"It was open in the front, partially—like a doorway without a door."

"But could people hear you? And you them?"

"Yes, people could come in. They could hear me, although I have a soft voice. I guess I could yell out to them."

"At least they can hear you. I've had dreams where there were no openings. Where no one could hear me. Although it's made of glass, it's still walls. The walls we build around ourselves.

Your mother and your grandmother are here. They are pleased with what you've done. You have done more than what they could back then. The women in your family say you have to work on changing some issues, some habits that they passed on to you."

"I've done that work already. I had more father issues than mother issues. In therapy I've worked on my father issues."

She shook her head. "No. Your mother and grandma say it was not what the men forced on them. Your grandmother said that that is not the way she thought. She said she could have done more. We could have chosen to do differently."

"Many women's and other national concerns were brought to my attention over the past couple of weeks." She nodded. "But there are so many rules that keep the oppression going. I've been asking to be shown better ways of doing."

Afterwards, I wondered what my mommas meant by "The women in your family say you have to work on changing some issues, some habits that they passed on to you." I was willing to work on it. But what could my mothers have done differently? And what am I to do different myself?

Muslim Sisters

While I was in California, at an Association of Black Psychologists convention, my younger sister Inara came to visit me. She took me to Friday Jumah prayer first. On the women's side of the mosque, there were mostly Pakistani Americans. Inara and I were the only Black Americans there. I was wearing a long, colorful, beautiful, two-piece African dress with a matching head wrap. I didn't think about how fitted my dress was until I got to the mosque. The women wore loose, neutral-colored clothes. Little girls kept looking at me. Perhaps they were dazzled by my dress's bright colors. The Kutbah sermon was in Urdu and then English, but mostly Urdu. Inara introduced me as her sister. Many of the older women came over to greet me.

Inara and I went looking for a Whole Foods that sold homeopathic medicine. We drove around for several miles because many of those stores were newly

CHAPTER 15: UNEXPECTED TASKS

remodeled and smaller, so they no longer sold the homeopathic medicines. While we drove from small town to small town, we talked. We did eventually find the homeopathic remedy that I was looking for and then stopped and ate at a restaurant. Inara told me what was going on in her life. Although we'd phoned and texted off and on for the past fifteen years, we hadn't seen each other since the 1970s, when she was a teenager. Her father kept her and her older brother Obadiah and younger sister Marzia away from me, Kani and Emin. Inara looks a lot like Momma, with the same body build, smile, and dimples. Her darker complexion, eyebrows, and mannerisms are like her father's. Yet the tone of her voice is soft and loving. She told me that she inherited Momma's passion for sweets. She cooks Pakistani-style food, which is very, very spicy.

The next day, Inara told me that she'd arrived home after midnight since it took her six hours to get home. I was really touched and overwhelmed with gratitude that she had traveled that far to be with me. The mosque and the shopping center were also far away, and she had to drive me back to the hotel in Oakland before heading home.

After I returned home, Inara sent me YouTube videos of imams' sermons that were mostly in Arabic and Urdu. Sometimes the videos from Africa had translations in English. Young Muslim women were being rewarded for graduating with university degrees in other videos.

A month later, Inara and the women's leader of the Midwest Muslim Women's region invited me to go to the local mosque. They said there would be women there who had known me and our family since we were children. I went to the mosque on the South Side of the city for Friday Jumah prayer. I was shocked as a Pakistani brother opened the door for me and then again when I saw there were two older Pakistani men inside. I had hoped the members would be predominantly Black Americans, the same as when I was growing up. No women were there yet.

After the greetings, "Assalamu'alaikum" and "Walaikum salaam," I introduced myself and asked, "Where is the bathroom?"

The man walked me over to the women's section and pointed to a long hallway and doorways on the far side of the prayer room. "You can drive your cart inside."

"No, I will get the prayer rug dirty."

"That is all right," he said.

Piously, I said, "I'll leave my wheelchair parked here for now."

However, as I slowly walked sideways, barefoot, across the prayer rug, I discovered that it was a long, long way to the bathroom entrance, through the room with the sinks for wudu ablution, and even further to get to the room with the toilet! I made it there and back by holding on to the walls. Inside the prayer room, there were pillars between the walls that were spaced barely two arms' lengths apart. I had to stretch my arms out to reach the next pillar. Then the chairs seemed so far away, at the very back of the room. Since I was the only one in the women's section, there was no one to ask to bring me a chair to sit on. I should have listened to the brother and used my wheelchair.

The Muslim sisters came from out of town to the mosque especially to meet and hug me. My fear showed in my voice, or should I say my lack of voice, as I was either silent or spoke very softly when the Muslim women asked me questions. I still cringed when I heard the Arabic and Urdu, but I wasn't triggered into flashbacks and trauma memories. However, intense emotional feelings were triggered by the memory of being forcefully immersed in these foreign languages and cultures in a new city at seven years old. The brief sermon alternated between English and Urdu. The imam used broken English for a simple message that I barely remembered soon after. The Eid-ul-Adha holiday had started the day before, and its observances and festivities usually lasted three days, so part of the sermon was about the sacrifices that Abraham made for Allah. The other part was about having kindness for everyone, including within our homes.

After the short sermon on the faith of Abraham, I thought of the meaning of my name, Haneefa. A few years ago, an elderly blind man dressed in white became very excited when he heard the driver of the paratransit van say my name. He was the fourth person to tell me that Haneefa means "holy." In 1997 a Palestinian student was the first. Later a group of Pakistani students also told me. When I was a little girl, my mother told me that it meant "inclined to righteousness." Later, as a teenager, I saw in a name book that Haneefa means "true believer." Perhaps this is why, although I knew men who had the name Haneef, I didn't meet any other women with the name Haneefa until I was twenty-five years old. As if only men could be holy and leaders.

CHAPTER 15: UNEXPECTED TASKS

More recently, a taxi driver from the Middle East was at a loss for words as he tried to explain that the Arabic word "haneef" had to do with the story of the strong faith of Abraham, to obediently almost sacrifice his only son. "Do you know what your name means? Where did you get your name from? Where are you from? Where are your parents from?"

I interrupted him. "If you tell me the meaning of my name first, then I will tell you where I got it from. People have told me different meanings."

He paused and stuttered, paused again, as he raised his arms out to the sides and arched them. "The name Hanif is so big it is hard to explain." He paused. "Do you know the story of Abraham in the bible?"

"Yes, although I don't know much about the bible. I learned the story from the Quran."

"But you know what Abraham did? His faith was so huge. What he did for God, that is what 'hanif' means." He was silent for a while, not explaining more.

"Okay," I said. "My mother told me Haneefa means 'inclined to righteousness.' Name books and the internet say it means 'true believer.' That goes along with the Abraham story. Abraham had to really believe and to have a lot of faith to be willing to sacrifice his only son for God. A classmate from Saudi Arabia told me that the word 'hanif' means 'to straighten out what is crooked, to make it right.'"

The taxi driver said, "Then she must know."

"This is similar to what a Cuban woman told me about my destiny. 'Your life will be like a double-edged sword. Your spiritual path will always be cleared, because anything or anyone that does not belong on your path will have to go away.' I cried when she told me this because it explained why I had so many losses in my life. I had become hurt and bitter. It was a big relief to have this explanation and meaning. Now I could I stop blaming myself and others, to open to forgiveness."

He said, "That makes sense."

"Men from Pakistan, Israel, and Palestine have told me Haneefa means 'holy.' I didn't meet another Haneefa until I was twenty-five years old. I met her at the Islamic Center. She's from Pakistan. Where are you from?"

"Iraq."

"Are there many women named Haneefa there?"

"No, I don't know of any." He shook his head. "There were mostly men with the name Haneef when I was growing up."

"Where do you go to the masjid?" I asked.

"I go to a masjid not too far from here. But I go there to pray to God. I don't go there to socialize and to have a lot of friends!"

I smiled and remembered he'd seen me hugging people as I was leaving the Church of the Spirit, including some of the men. Hardly appropriate for a Muslim woman!

"What kind of church is that? I mean, you do have a Muslim name," the driver said.

Then I understood that he was trying to figure out how I got from being a Muslim to going to a church. I was somewhat dressed like a Muslim, in a long, white dress with white sweatpants underneath it to stay warm. He was probably feeling really confused. If he knew what kind of church he was taking me to, from the white church on the North Side to the African church on the South Side, he probably would have thought I was all mixed up!

I did try to tell him briefly how I got from being a Muslim child to here. I told him about the typical near-death experience of going to be with the bright light of huge energy that fills you with love and peace and total acceptance.

"All religions worship God," he said. "Muslims believe in all the prophets and that no prophet is better than another prophet. It is not possible for a man to be God because people die and God doesn't."

I said, "No one has seen God, except for a few people who have had near-death experiences or visions. They say that God does not have a human form."

The taxi driver interrupted. "Moses saw God."

I nodded. "Yes. After my near death experience I wanted to explore the spirituality that people had way before there were religions."

"The religions that were there thousands of years ago, with Moses and Noah?"

His only references were the Quran and the bible. I quietly nodded again. I didn't tell him about the abuse from so-called Muslims or that one elderly Muslim taxi driver told me I was going to hell because I'd stopped being a practicing Muslim. "Born a Muslim," he'd said, "always a Muslim!"

My angry retort at that time was, "That is only if you men are actually living the beauty of Islam!"

I do have strong faith and did in every religion or organization I have belonged to in the past. But I have cautioned young women who have wanted to name their babies after me to make sure that's what they want for their child because having the name Haneefa means the child's faith will be repeatedly tested throughout her life. My love for God is very strong because of the miracles I experienced.

That evening, Inara called. "Well, how did you like it?"

"I liked the warm hugs and kisses on both cheeks from the Black and African American sisters at the mosque, same as we had growing up. Only a few of the Pakistani women hugged me."

"I know. Pakistani women can be kind of lazy with hugs, but they are wonderful in other ways."

Sister Circle

A few weeks later, they invited me to a Muslim women's weekend retreat at the mosque's community center. I was not triggered at the Muslim women's retreat. I felt comforted sitting shoulder to shoulder with the older women on a bench. In the Sister Circle, the facilitator tried to get us to open up and tell why most of us didn't come to the mosque anymore. It was like pulling teeth. She showed us a chart of data of the differences between the generations in attendance over the years. But eventually, oh, my God, we went there! Young women spoke up. We began telling the truth about the physical and sexual abuse we endured during childhood and then later domestic violence as adults. How the men recently put up a curtain between them and the women in the prayer room. They don't let the women speak, not even to give educational workshops, claiming even the sound of our female voices is too much for them. We are to cover our faces too, when speaking in public. Yet we know that at their jobs and in their neighborhoods, the men speak freely and respectfully to other women. Some women said that they have not been abused by other men whether wearing the hijab or not; they have only been abused by Muslim men in their families. We talked about how Muslim women criticize and judge each other with our silent looks and expressions, but this is not what any of us want.

Afterward, the women asked me if I could help lead Muslim women's healing groups in the future, please, please? The facilitators said that I helped open the door to the conversation—getting the discussion going.

I answered, "Sure I'd love to. I'm in training leading diversity groups at the university now."

Chapter 16: Being Muslim

Private Medium Consultation with Cher September 2018

"Did you ever wear the headdress? What's it called? I don't know how to pronounce it. Is it a hijab?"

"Yes."

"Did your mother wear one?"

"Yes."

"Did you wear one too?"

"Yes."

"Okay. Well, she's coming in, and she's placing it back on you. It feels like it's just for a sense of being more connected with her. I don't know if this is something that is common. We kind of move away from parents at some point, and then we come back to them and move away again. So, she comes in with that [hijab] for you and places it very gently on your head. But it just feels like it's a reminder or a connection. She brings it to you. I don't feel like you are going to wear this. Physically, you are not going to wear it. It may be metaphorically. But even if it's metaphorically, I don't feel like you keep this on. It's like, 'That's not who I am.' So, there's a lot going on here with identity. It's okay. I feel like it's okay with her. But it's kind of like a reminder, maybe, of where you came from. I do get them being very happy with your spiritual work and your own journey. It is certainly different from what theirs was. But I do get your mothers being very proud of you.

I'm going to use the word 'accepting.' Accepting of your spiritual path and your spiritual exploration. This is not something she would have done. I feel like there was no allowance for her, in this regard. But she just encourages you to continue to be your own person. I don't know how much she had of that. I feel like there was a lot of oppression around her. This may have to do with the stepfather in particular. But that was her journey. That's all it was. That was her journey. So, she's very proud of you and what you are doing on your journey. That feels really, really good to me."

It is a great relief and consolation for me that my mothers now approve of my spiritual choice and career. I remember Mother Dear telling me on the phone, "Your sister Kani is more spiritual than you. She's a Jehovah's Witness. I wish you were like her."

This made me feel sad, and it hurt. But I didn't argue with Mother Dear. Kani is more religious than I am. She follows the rules and interprets the bible scriptures literally, word for word.

But I am actually more spiritual than Kani, especially since I had my near-death experience. I feel like I have a closer relationship to God. Most people who have had a near-death experience become less religious and may avoid religion altogether because they have experienced God as loving and accepting them just the way they are. A loving god. Not a mean and vengeful god. This God doesn't care about all those impossible religious rules and sins, only judges us by how much we have loved each other. This makes us strive even harder to please God in learning to love.

It has also really hurt me that Kani, being strict with the Jehovah's Witness rules, has been afraid of me, avoids me, and of course didn't want her children around me. Jehovah's Witnesses don't believe in afterlife communication with ancestors. She started avoiding me twenty years ago when I attended an African spirituality church. She would travel out of her home state to city events and museums and go shopping near where I live and then call and tell me the next day. I'd say, "You were so close—why didn't you come visit me?"

"Oh, I didn't have time. I had to get back home."

Yet she has time to go to all fifty United States, to almost all the discount shopping centers across the country, and even other countries on multiple cruises, and be with hundreds of strangers whose beliefs or religious affiliations—or if they are atheists—she doesn't know.

Conversely, Mother Dear, who is also a Jehovah's Witness, has maintained family ties, perhaps out of maturity and wisdom. She once took me aside and said, "I hope I didn't offend you by talking to you and asking you Jehovah's Witness questions we would ask any Muslim and that's why you don't come around. It doesn't matter to me. Family is more important."

This was back in 1990, when I was angry at my father for telling me that I should've come to him for advice before I decided to marry my husbands. I was angry at my father for not being in my life until I was twenty-five years old. Like, maybe if he had been my father, I wouldn't have had a cruel, abusive stepfather and foster father.

In another conversation with Mother Dear, she said, "I'm worried about not leaving a legacy."

"What do you mean by legacy, Mother Dear?"

"I've done bible study with my children and grandchildren, who are now adults, for years and years. But I still haven't been able to convert any more than two people to be Jehovah's Witnesses."

I was confused and tried to understand. "But you already have a legacy by the way you live and as a role model. I almost thought about becoming a Jehovah's Witness a few years after you first became one because I liked how peaceful and kind you were."

"But I still want to convert more people before I die."

I am a more practical person, believing that it doesn't matter what religion or beliefs a person has. Our behavior and how we live are more important than how well we know scripture. Mother Dear's younger brother, my favorite great-uncle, is an atheist, yet kind, loving, generous, and wise. He said that he's been an atheist since he was a child. He never bought into "the bible story."

The Interview

On November 9, 2018, a Sunday, I was surprised by a call on my cell phone at 5:50 p.m. It was the clinical director from the Muslim clinic. He was inviting me for an interview. I was so surprised and excited that when he asked where I lived and if I could come out to the suburbs, I said, "Sure." All while calculating in my head that it had to be either a Wednesday or Friday in order to allow me to schedule rides with the paratransit service. I chose Wednesday and completely forgot that I had been advised by the university disability office and my disability mentor to only have phone interviews! I realized this as soon as I got off the phone. The call was so brief I even forgot his name. It was possible that he was a professor at the university and remembered me, since he paused after asking me if I would be able to travel. I decided it was too late to change the scheduled appointment. Therefore, I was going to the interview in person.

After two years of trying, it was difficult for me to feel optimistic about the internship application process. But I was getting interviews, so this let me know that getting an internship was possible. My cover letter to the Muslim clinic had been very heartfelt—honest and to the point. My heart beat excitedly during the phone call. Could this be real?

When I arrived for the interview, the young receptionist wore a niqab covering her face, with only her eyes visible. She greeted me with, "Hi," so I didn't know whether to say "Assalamu'alaikum or not. She said, "I will let him know that you are here. You can wait here in the waiting room."

The waiting room was decorated beautifully. I squeezed my wheelchair into an uncarpeted section since Muslims usually remove their shoes as soon as they enter. While I waited, I read a brochure on the table called "No Need to Hide Our Faces." It was about the Rohingya Muslim girls and women in Myanmar being gang-raped by the military, similar to what was done in Bosnia. They watched their family members being killed in front of them before they were raped. The military men were young, in their twenties and thirties. Rape, unfortunately, can be used as a weapon of war to force women to produce their enemies' offspring. That is totally disgusting!

The clinical director came and got me and gave me a brief tour of the second floor first. He showed me the prayer room and the side of the hall for women therapists and clients. It was not until almost the end of the interview that I realized he was wearing baggy blue jeans with a neat striped shirt. And here I sat in a long dress with a turtleneck, trousers, and thermal leggings underneath, plus a scarf and a hat! I was glad it was cool in the building. Another woman there were in full hijab with colorful scarves and accessories. I didn't ask what the dress code was, perhaps because I didn't want to know. Already I knew that I was not going to be wearing all of that! I don't even know why I kept my scarf and hat on.

Heaven gave me a sign when my scarf ripped as I was pulling it down to cover the hair on the back of my head. A big, long rip! I guess looking at the fully covered receptionist influenced me to leave it on. But I was getting hot. What else would I feel pressured to do as easily? The stark contrast between the freedom of the men and the women, as illustrated by the differences in the clothes they wore, was worrisome. However, the interviewer was as relaxed as his clothes. I felt comfortable speaking with him. I could be myself, straight forward and direct.

Match Day

My cell phone chimed. It was eight thirty, time to take my medicine, eat my breakfast, and then bravely check my emails. Scared of receiving the bad news that I didn't match any internships, like last year, I breathed deeply and said a long prayer. I asked for all my spirit guides, loved ones, Great Mama, and guardian angels to come and stay close to me, to infuse me with love, comfort, and guidance. Then I breathed some more and meditated briefly.

I opened my inbox. In bold, blue letters:

"Congratulations, you have matched! You have matched to:

Training site: Consortium.

Program: Muslim Clinic

Program code: 1234567

The internship will send you an appointment agreement postmarked or emailed within seven days of the release of the Phase 1 APPIC match results."

I screamed! I sobbed and talked loudly as I thanked all my spirit guides, loved ones, Great Mama, and all my mommas. I asked them all to still stay present and close to me throughout the day.

Then I got on the phone. I decided to do personal calls instead of sending texts to announce that I matched. Celebration time! I was really surprised to receive a text before I got started with my calls: "Congratulations!" It was from my past therapy practicum supervisor! How did she know so soon? It was only

9:32. She texted further: "I was so happy to see your name. That internship site seems like a great match! You'll have a few Friday trainings here at our clinic too."

I didn't need to pinch myself quite so hard—her text confirmed that it was real!

When I signed the contract at the beginning of my internship, I agreed to be a practicing Muslim for a year and to wear the hijab while working in the clinic locations and outside while representing the organization. So for a year, I wore the hijab everywhere I went. My earrings, bracelets, and necklaces stayed in my jewelry boxes. I personally committed to fully practice being a Muslim to the best of my ability. This meant making the five prayers daily, fasting during Ramadan, and reading the Quran. I really wanted to know the beauty that my mother had found in Islam.

During the spring and summer, I enjoyed designing modest long blouses, suit jackets, and loose pants, pulling out my old sewing patterns and going to fabric stores to select lightweight, colorful fabrics to sew. Since I can feel sick when I'm overheated, I looked for fabric made of cotton and other natural fibers. They sure don't make things like they used to. The fabrics are very thin and see-through these days! I had to improvise, choosing prints and layering.

To prepare for working at the Muslim clinic, I also read a lot of books about Muslims' personal stories regarding dilemmas that are rarely talked about but which bring them to therapy. I also watched YouTube videos. I was very happy to find Black Muslim mental health videos.

Well, starting in fall 2018, the medium's spirit message about wearing a hijab came true. Truer than true because I did actually have to physically, not symbolically, wear a hijab.

Immersed in Muslim Culture

The didactic classes for the internship were different from any clinical classes I'd had anywhere. The classes were in the prayer room, with men on one side and women on the other. We mostly learned about Islamic beliefs and some of the spiritual and behavioral problems that Muslim clients might have.

CHAPTER 16: BEING MUSLIM

To my delight, we were also learning about Sufism! For a few years prior, I'd been curious about it after one of my classmates at the university showed a video of a Sufi dervish. It reminded me of African rituals in which dancing helps people go into a meditative trance. I didn't know Muslims did that type of dancing. The books I bought at that time about Sufism were mostly Quran and hadith quotes. There was just a little mention of the ecstasy, bliss, and connection to Allah that Sufi Muslims and saints have from praying. The internship classes weren't about dervishes, but I was pleased anyway because the book the teacher used was titled, *The Way of Sufi Chivalry*. The class and the book showed me another side of Islam. It brought tears of joy to my eyes, and I felt closer to the beauty that my mother saw in Islam.

Some of the teachings I already believed, and I tried to live my life by them daily. Seeing these beliefs and words brought me comfort. Sufi chivalry refers to how we should be as a community (ummah) toward each other. By putting faith in Allah (God) first, especially having faith that your substance is guaranteed by Allah, you are then able to be generous. It is knowing you have the love of Allah and that Allah will love you more when you love others. Sufi chivalry is loving others before oneself, giving everything, if needed—even one's life—for one's community, caring for your neighbors, sharing whatever you have, inviting others into your home for hospitality and food. It is, of course, treating others how you would want to be treated. Ignoring other's mistakes, even when they are mean and irritable, and instead being kind and compassionate. Sharing joy and humor. These teachings remind me of the African Kemetic principles of Ma'at. I saw people living this way in the villages in Zimbabwe, but they were not Muslims. The people were very poor, but they shared what little they had, and they rarely ever criticized anyone.

We also had non-Muslim therapy clients from the surrounding neighborhood, several of whom were immigrants whose children spoke English. So, besides the different Muslim cultures, I was always learning about other cultures as well. Some days, I worked at the Islamic schools. Being there with both teachers and students, wearing the full hijab, brought back memories and emotions of me being the only child in the third-grade classroom dressed in a hijab when I went to a public school. My brother at five years old, was the only child wearing a cap. We were the only obvious Muslims in the whole school.

As an adult, I had mixed emotions bubbling up. In one way, it was healing for little Haneefa to be with other Muslims. (Thank you, Momma). But I was still the only African American. There were a few African immigrants, along with others from Muslim countries or the children of immigrants. All spoke another language fluently except me. I couldn't bring myself to wear the full hijab. I did try a couple of times, but it just wasn't me. Covered modestly, instead, I wore my head scarf tied to the side in a fancy style similar to African head wraps, with a turtleneck to cover up my neck.

Perhaps I couldn't bear to wear the traditional hijab because I couldn't ignore the fact that other Muslims can be prejudiced against African American Muslims. Unfortunately, they believe the negative stereotypes and do not consider us Muslims, even though Mali, Senegal, Mauritania, Ethiopia, and other countries had mosques and Islamic schools, and their people read and copied the Quran in Arabic long before some of these more recent Muslim countries existed. Since most of the clinic's classes were in Arabic or Urdu, if I hadn't been reading in English about Ahmadou Bambu, I wouldn't have understood what we were learning. A very devoted Sufi Muslim, Bambu brought education and equality to his disciples and the region. When the French colonizers came into Senegal, they and some of the local chiefs and kings who preferred hierarchies based on wealth and servants resented Bambu and eventually exiled him to a wilderness. But his prayers still brought miracles for himself and the people.

There were times in the internship that were very challenging. Working with families that had domestic violence was the hardest. I've worked with families with all different complexions and backgrounds, so it's not just Muslims. Other orthodox religions try to hide the shame of domestic violence too. Of course, it was also hard for me because my mothers were survivors of domestic violence, and hearing clients' stories brought up my own memories, emotions, and frustrations. It was not until the end of my internship that I realized that one of my clients was a lot like my mother, who collapsed mentally under the weight of my stepfather's 24/7 emotional and physical abuse. Momma suffered possible postpartum depression and later psychosis after he left her, divorced her, married a white woman who had recently converted to Islam, and took Momma's three babies away. It reminded me of my own experience with domestic violence from my second husband and how he gradually took away

CHAPTER 16: BEING MUSLIM

everything that mattered to me. When the cupboards and my bank account were bare, he went away for longer periods of time. But I knew that it was only to Allah that my soul belonged. Therefore, I made a vow that I was not going to give up my soul to anyone. That's when I had the courage to leave.

Helping women to get a spark of her true self, her soul restored, and what she really wants was very tough. Although I expected this to take months or years, like it took me to get free and to heal, I saw women rally and find their strength. Our mothers from heaven were helping out, healing themselves, me, my clients, and others in the process.

In the middle of my internship, in March 2020, the COVID-19 pandemic officially arrived in the United States. The holy month of Ramadan had begun and increased Muslim introspection and anxiety about the afterlife, of course, with the possibility of relatives, friends, or oneself dying. Clients questioned themselves and asked me, "Have we prayed enough for those that died? Have we been kind enough to others? Have we forgiven everyone?" Hospitality and caring for others are a big part of Muslim culture, so there was some guilt over not being able to fulfill those obligations. Were they good enough to their parents, and what responsibilities should they have if parents were abusive to them? There were sadness and confusion about how to do Ramadan during a shutdown. They couldn't go to the mosque or gather together to break the fast (iftar) and read the Quran together at the end of the day. I continued therapy with my clients online from our homes. This resulted in me having more long-term clients who were stressed yet serious about feeling better and having a better life.

Chapter 17: Not Done Yet

Earlier in the spring, I saw an advertisement for a Women in Islam class at an Islamic college. I wanted to enroll in the summer course but not enough students applied therefore the class was cancelled. During the fall semester the professor at an Islamic college emailed me two days before the class was to start: "Dear Haneefa. Salam alaykum. I thought of you when I was preparing for teaching my Gender and Islam course this fall. It is the only course on gender and Islam taught at an Islamic college."

Reluctantly, I replied. "I will go on and register. Initially, I was interested in the two-week summer intensive course. Fourteen weeks seems like a long time. However, the topic of women and Islam is important to me because I am a therapist who has Muslim women clients. Many are in domestic violence situations or young women hesitant to get married. I like how you represent different perspectives in your book."

Plus, I thought later, it would help me in writing this book to learn more about women's rights in Islam, especially concerning domestic violence. I groaned aloud as it occurred to me that my mothers were giving me yet another assignment!

From modern scholars, I learned the Quran and hadiths were written during a time when wealth and slavery influenced everything. For Christians, Jews, and idol worshipers too, this was the norm. All women were basically "slaves" and considered property. The only difference was that if a woman was married to a wealthy man, she had more status than if she were a concubine or a slave. Men could have multiple wives and no limit on the number of concubines and slaves he could own and have sex with. Therefore, all women were subjected to being taken advantage of as a man's given right. With the marriage contract and the acceptance of the nikkah dowry payment, the wife was agreeing to be sexually available at all times, even performing sex on the back of a camel. However, the nikkah contract did not mention true love, romance, choice based on spouse's character, or future children.

I don't know if Momma had a nikkah ceremony or if Stepfather gave her a dowry, but he did strictly follow the other cultural "rules" concerning women. These "Islamic" rules about sexuality and women having to cover their bodies had nothing to do with religious morality. It was about wealthy men maintaining their social status and distinguishing their wives from other women.

As a new convert to Islam, Stepfather was zealously following the Islamic rules and enforcing his interpretation of the Quran and hadiths on us. I wasn't aware these rules even existed until 2020! That's why my Muslim mother and foster mother led me in spirit back to Islam. They wanted me to get a different perspective and understand why our Muslim fathers, stepfathers, and husbands did what they did. Maybe they were hoping for some forgiveness, perhaps some empowerment, and for me to know about choice and free will. Most important, they wanted me to know the truth.

Genesis Story

In the Gender and Islam class, we studied what the Quran really says about Adam and "Eve." There is no woman mentioned in most of the Quran stories about the garden. Only Adam is in the garden, and he alone makes the mistake of eating the forbidden fruit. Over the centuries, through oral tradition, historians, and later scholars, the story was embellished and exaggerated by adding a snake and a woman. Adam's rib became Eve's crooked rib, she intoxicated him with wine (wait a minute, Muslims don't drink alcohol), then changed to a camel instead of a snake that misled Adam, and unbelievably, more. Yet people do believe these stories, especially men. They interpret these symbols to mean that Eve and all women are weak, deceitful, ignorant, stupid, too emotional, and compassionate, while men are rational. Rationality is somehow considered superior to women's compassion. Because of Eve's disobedience in the garden, all women were cursed with monthly bleeding and painful, sometimes deadly, childbirth! Women like pain, but men don't! Totally outrageous. Perhaps it is women's true intuition and spiritual power that men are really afraid of and not this fear of falling for the sexual attraction of her physical beauty.

In the year before my foster mother died, although she was Muslim, she frequently talked about the bible's genesis story. She believed that women were meant to be martyrs. At that time, I just thought she was obsessed with this belief because of the abuse that she had experienced for decades in her marriage, and perhaps guilt over being forced to take part in some of the abuse of her children. I did not know that Muslims also believed the bible genesis story.

Recently, because of the COVID-19 pandemic, Kani has been sending me bible verses from the book of Genesis. She sent me these scriptures to comfort me and to help me cope.

"Adam and Eve Rejected God's Sovereignty: Genesis 3:1. Now the serpent was the most cautious of all the wild animals at the field that Jehovah God had made. So it said to the woman: "Did God really say that you must not eat from every tree of the garden?" At this the woman said to the serpent: "We may eat of the fruit of the trees of the garden. But God has said about the fruit of the tree that is in the middle of the garden: 'You must not eat from it, no, you must not touch it; otherwise you'll die.'" At this the serpent said to the woman: "You certainly will not die. For God knows that in the very day you eat from it, your eyes will be open and you will be like that, knowing good and bad."

Notice, in contrast to other bibles and the Quran, Adam is not mentioned. Only "the woman," and still the woman doesn't have a name.

This scripture is meant to provide comfort to Jehovah's Witnesses, who believe that believers will be brought back to life and live forever. Kani began her letter by writing, "I have to apologize. I didn't realize we hadn't talked about the possibility of seeing our mother again in the resurrection. This scripture shows what Jehovah and Jesus will do for us in the new system, including resurrection of our dead loved ones, like our mom."

Kani doesn't understand that I probably believe more than she does that, yes, we were meant to live forever and will be resurrected and that there will be a Judgment Day. I believe it more because, of course, Momma already comes

CHAPTER 17: NOT DONE YET

to me and shows that she is alive. And probably comes to all of her children they're just not aware of signs of her presence. Most everyone who has had a near-death experience during their life review judged their own behavior soon after dying. Saw and experienced the effects of their behavior on other people. Therefore were already judged before the dreaded group Judgment Day. They were resurrected, their heartbeat restored in the hospital or at the accident scene, and sent back to Earth to be with their families who were still living, but mostly to finish whatever personal life lessons were needed. Given a second chance to come back and get it right.

Some people argue that after experiencing the awesome love, peace, and acceptance of God, being sent back to Earth is hell, not being sentenced to an eternal fire. In the stories I read about people who have had near-death experiences, some people temporarily go to a place that they describe as hell, which is not fire but being with souls expressing similar behaviors, for example being so depressed that you don't notice other souls around you or God and God's love or being with other mean, cruel, violent people and creatures. But after these scary experiences, most everyone ends up meeting with God in a heavenly place. Therefore, God is most merciful and most forgiving.

But then Kani wanted to know about the argument between Allah and Iblis (Satan) and the other original angels in the Quran, which she remembered from childhood. I texted her the following:

Quran Chapter 2, Verses 34-39:

34. And behold, we said to the Angels: bow down to Adam and they bowed down. Not so Iblis. He refused and was haughty. He was of those who reject faith.

35. We said, Oh Adam! Dwell thou and Thy in the garden and eat of the wealth of the bountiful things therein as (where and when) ye will but approach not this tree or ye run into harm and transgression.

36. Then did Satan make them slip from the garden and get them out of the state of (felicity) in which they had been. We said, Get you down, all (ye people), with enmity between yourselves. On earth will be your dwelling place and your means of livelihood for time.

37. Then learnt Adam from his Lord words of inspiration, and his Lord turned towards him, for He is Oft-Returning, Most Merciful.

38. We said, get you down all from here and if, as it sure, there comes to your guidance from me, who so ever follows my guidance, on them shall be no fear, nor shall they grieve.

39. But those who reject faith and disbelieve our signs they shall be Companions of the fire. they shall abide therein."

Here again, there is no mention of a woman in the garden.

As the translations of the Quran's garden story became more and more outrageous, I began to wonder what was really the difference between each culture's creation myths and the Quran and bible. Many Indigenous cultures use animals to explain how the world came into being. Another thought that occurred to me was, oh, my goodness, if men believe that women are that bad, stupid, and weak, no wonder there is so much domestic violence! If you consider that many people are illiterate and Arabic is not their first language or their country's official language, then surely, both men and women believe the stories that have been passed down from generation to generation.

The idea that Haw'wa (Eve) got Adam drunk is really far-fetched since a Muslim shouldn't have wine so easily available! Since all babies come out at birth with exposed genitals, then what is so terrible about being naked? When we die, we will be naked again as our clothes dissolve away in our graves. Most mammals, including humans, use sex to reproduce, so the pseudo-Darwinian theory of a man having to coerce a woman in order for the human species to survive does not make sense either, unless, of course, the man has a history of abusing the woman and not protecting her.

Quran Chapter 4, Verse 34 Wife Beating?

"Men are the protectors and maintainers of women, because Allah has given one more (strength) than the other, and because they support them from their means. Therefore, the righteous women are devoutly obedient, and guard in (the husband's) absence what Allah would have them regard. As to those women on whose part ye fear disloyalty and ill-conduct, admonish them (first), (Next), refused to share their beds, (and last) beat them (lightly); but if they return to obedience, seek not against them means (of annoyance): For Allah

CHAPTER 17: NOT DONE YET

is Most High, great (above you all)." <u>The Holy Quran.</u> Yusuf Ali English translation.

As a new convert to Islam, Stepfather was zealously following his understanding of the Islamic rules. Decades later, somebody told me that children could also be beaten for not learning the Quran and saying their prayers. I've since searched the Quran for these rules but only found some passages from hadiths. Basically, parents are to make their children learn the five daily prayers (salats) starting at seven years old, when a child should know the difference between right and wrong, and also the gender differences between a man and a woman. At the age of ten, the child can be punished for not saying their prayers. This is why our stepfather, although a few years younger than our mother, beat her and us. Foster father did similar. As an adult I got away from this Islam.

My first husband brought me back to Islam. Excitedly, he told me he had gone down to the masjid. I didn't know what a masjid was. He liked what he heard and invited me. When we arrived, I saw that the inside of the large brick building was a mosque. It felt familiar, similar to the Islam that I grew up with, but the people were more easy-going. I knew the prayers already in Arabic. However, I vowed to read and recite my prayers in English so I could pray to God from my heart. Warith Deen Mohammed was the leader. I liked being at the masjid. We all prayed in the same room, with the women seated or praying in rows behind the men. Women also mingled with the men and talked with the imam. I enjoyed participating in social activities and fundraisers, which were often led by the older women. Later, the principal of the Sister Clara Mohammad school asked me to teach math. This was a year after my ectopic pregnancy. There was a Muslim woman who was going through infertility treatments at the time, and we became close friends. I regularly attended this masjid for six years.

Decades later, I learned that these were Sunni Muslims. I don't know what kind of Muslim my second husband was. Although I met him through a Muslim married couple that attended my masjid, he took me only once to a mosque, on the far south side of the city, for our wedding ceremony. There were mostly men in attendance, except for Kani and her little daughters. The men barely spoke English. I don't even know what countries they emigrated from. My husband, Kani, her children, and I were the only dark-skinned people there.

All I know is that whatever kind of Muslim he was, my husband was mean and cruel, criticizing everything about me and also abusing me while telling me, "You are a pious Muslim woman. You're also a nurse, so you should understand and be compassionate with me and my children." He quoted and showed me Quran verses to justify his behavior. He was so abusive I thought he was making the quotes up!

What Is the Truth? Culture versus Islamic Law

In our modern lives, it's not even possible to live out any of the traditional fundamentalist religions. Colonialism, capitalism, and obsolete industrialism took the ability—and choice—to provide for one's family away. Corporations now decide who will be employed and at what salary. Therefore the men's role as sole provider and the women's sole role as stay-at-home mother are questionable. Children's roles are changed too, as they are taken away from their families for eight hours a day, five days a week or more for education in schools that are often miles away from home. The children are not even home for the mother to care for them. Add to this time away from home—the long commutes, academic assignments, and sports and other extracurricular activities. Everyone is too exhausted to do anything together, even prayers or other religious practices. We are really lying to ourselves that we are still living in the ancient ways!

Regarding all the elaborate ramifications of the Adam and Eve stories, if men did not treat women so badly, women probably would have easier pregnancies and childbirths. They would be surrounded by other compassionate women in a loving village where everyone pledges a commitment to share in the care of the new child. Instead, women are in a cold hospital room, where male obstetricians and administrators want the birth process to be as efficient and cost-effective as possible. Then the mother goes home to care for the new baby and other children alone.

It is men that make life harder as they add on more and more responsibilities on the job and at home. It seems that anything men do to cause trouble they blame on a woman, as if she's the one who's doing it instead of him! In psychology, we call this projection. More men get into substance abuse than women, then it is the woman that usually tries to save the man from self-destruction, get him sober, and be a comfort to him regardless. Most women are not whores, especially after the first or second baby, she's not in a hurry to make another one. Without social support, why would she? In the nine months that a woman is pregnant, the man is the one who can go out there and have all the sex and make more babies. So how can a man's transgressions be blamed on a woman's "seduction"? Yet he wants more and more and more and more! It is only common sense that a woman should be able to provide for herself and children if need be. Women can. It is now obvious women are strong enough physically and mentally. But why should a woman's natural survival abilities be a threat to men? Even what I am writing here, which everybody already knows is the truth and observes everyday be considered a threat?

The Quran gives guidance on ways to protect and nurture women and children during marriage, pregnancy, childbirth, breastfeeding, and if they are widowed or orphaned. It specifies ways that the men are provided for too.

Chapter 4 Verse 22

Commentary 528. Another trick, to distract from the freedom of married women was to treat them badly and force them to sue for a Khul'a a divorce (see 2.229, and 258) or its equivalent in pre-Islamic custom, when the dower could be claimed back. This is also forbidden. Or the harshness may be exercised in another way: a divorced woman may be prevented by those who have control of her, from remarrying unless she remits her dower. All kinds of harshness are forbidden. (Yusuf Ali translation, page 185)

Quran Chapter 4 Verse 34

Commentary: In case of family jars four steps are mentioned, to be taken in that order: (1) perhaps verbal advice or admonition may be sufficient; (2) if not, sex relations may be suspended; (3) if this is not sufficient , some slight physical correction may be administered; but Imam Shafi considers this inadvisable, though permissible, and all authorities are unanimous in deprecating any sort of cruelty, even of the nagging kind, as mentioned in the next clause; (4) if all this fails, a family council is recommended in 4.35 below:

"548. Temper, nagging, sarcasm, speaking at each other in other people's presence, reverting to past faults which should be forgiven and forgotten— all of this is forbidden. And the reason given is characteristic of Islam. You must live all of your life in the presence of God, Who is high above us, but Who watches over us. How petty and contemptible will our little squabbles appear in His presence!" (Yusuf Ali English translation, page 190)

Can we now use the good advice in the Quran and our everyday truths to choose to have true love, appreciation, peace, and harmony with whole, healthy families in communities and the world?

Note: there are many English and other language translations of the Quran. I have a few different Quran myself. I chose the Yusuf Ali English translation here, because it has a commentary and is easier for me to understand.

Chapter 18: Ancestor Worship

The idea of ancestor worship bothered me at first too. Wouldn't that be shirk, the Arabic word for worshiping something or somebody other than God? The first time I heard about ancestor altars was when I met some Yoruba people from West Africa. My father had died the previous week. The Yoruba priest told me to wear blue and get a piece of my father's hair or clothing. At the wake, in the funeral home viewing room, Mother Dear, who is a Jehovah's Witness, was standing there beside the casket with me, so I didn't try to get a piece of his hair. Plus I was scared of the whole idea, afraid of voodoo stuff that I really knew nothing about.

Months later, at a class, I was given a handout on how to set up an altar on a small table for my ancestors. The instructions were to add photos of my parents along with items that they liked, even their vices—their bad habits, such as their favorite brands of alcoholic beverages, cigarettes, or cigars. When I ate, I was to place a plate of food on the altar for my ancestors too. Remembering to feed our ancestors helps us to remember them, especially on their birthdays and holidays. Back in 1991, I shuddered at the idea of setting up an altar table, and after a week or two, I removed the little round table with a dinner plate and photos. Besides, I didn't have a private place to put an altar. I couldn't explain the purpose for it when visitors asked. Also, I personally didn't believe in it. To me, maintaining an altar was just another religious ritual without meaning.

In some parts of Africa and Asia, it is taught that bad things will happen to you if you forget your ancestors. There will be calamities and curses. When these misfortunes happen, you must hurry and make a sacrifice after paying a lot of money to someone to appease your ancestors. This is what I've read and been told, but it didn't make sense to me. Over the years, I forgot about all of this. For years afterward, I didn't even think of ancestor worship except for brief moments when I read in college multicultural psychology textbooks that some East Asians and Latino cultures practice ancestor worship. Mexicans celebrate the Day of the Dead with beautiful, elaborate altars and shrines for the ancestors, both in public and at home. Ancestor worship, to me, was a form of religious ritual that people did in foreign countries. Therefore, it was a foreign idea to me.

There are many books about the West African Yoruba religion, but most are not written in a way that is easy to understand. It's like trying to understand the Quran, hadith, or Sunnah without adequate translation from Arabic. The same happens when reading the bible and Torah. We did not live back in the prophets' times. It is similar to reading a neurobiology book with a lot of big, scientific words the authors acquired after many years of study. Some Native American spiritual books are similar, not because of foreign language terminology but because if you didn't live in that culture or country from birth, then you wouldn't understand. It's the same with trying to understand descriptions of spiritual experiences such as deep meditation, visions, and astral (out-of-body) traveling.

Having had a near death experience myself, gone to heaven, and met with God, I know God is a glowing energy of pure love without any shape or form, just pure love with total acceptance of you and is incredible peace. Many people who had a near-death experience in which they died temporarily and went to heaven returned to life telling stories about how their deceased relatives, friends, and even pets came to greet them upon arrival in heaven. Some of their loved ones led them over to God. Therefore, it became less difficult for me to believe that my family and friends might occasionally communicate with me from heaven.

But in 2012 I began wondering and praying about ancestor worship. Several months later, I found the Church of the Spirit. When I first attended, and for a few weeks afterward, I didn't even know or understand what a medium was. But gradually I began to wonder if mediumship could be a form of ancestor worship. The Church of the Spirit is a spiritualist church—spiritualism is simply the understanding that a physical body has died but the spirit and personality live on. The Spiritualist Declaration of Principles includes the following beliefs:

We affirm that the existence and personal identity of the individual continue after the change called death.

We affirm that communication with the so-called dead is a fact, scientifically proven by the phenomena of Spiritualism.

We affirm that the doorway to reformation is never closed against any soul here or hereafter.

We affirm that the Precepts of Prophecy and Healing are divine attributes proven through Mediumship.

In 2020, as a result of the COVID-19 pandemic, African American healing groups began sharing information about cultural traditions and spirituality that were helping them cope emotionally with stress. The importance of ancestor worship was mentioned. But again, what did that mean, besides setting up an ancestor altar? Finally, I got my answer! A women's workshop facilitator explained that having an ancestor altar reminds you to remember your ancestors every day. It helps you remember to speak to your relatives daily, the same way you would have when they were still living. Because they are still alive. You and your relative still love each other. Yes, they can continue to guide, nurture, and protect you from heaven or the Other Side. The Other Side is separated by a thin, invisible veil, which is why you can feel your loved one's presence next to you, in, or behind you, feel a hug, and smell their favorite perfume.

In an earlier African spirituality class, we were told that our immediate family members that passed recently were not developed enough to be our spirit guides and give us higher spiritual or moral advice. Some regions of Africa have ceremonies to purposely invite deceased loved ones to return after a year to continue caring for and giving guidance to those who are still living on Earth. My experience with my mother and other relatives on the Other Side has shown me differently. To my surprise, in *Spirited: Connect to the Guides All around You*, the author describes when her deceased grandmother became her teacher and healer. Her grandmother helped break the cycle of debilitating depression in the family. Apparently, my mothers and grandmothers are also helping to break the cycle of domestic violence in my family and for everyone.

It may seem like a curse when we forget to acknowledge our ancestors, but it's more about facing the consequences of not paying attention to what is happening around you, spirit predictions, and warnings of upcoming events. Yes, you may still have to go through trials, but it's much easier to go through trials and challenges when you're being guided along the way. Hurricane Katrina is an example of people denying the warning signs, including the meteorologists' warnings. People said, "Oh, we've been through plenty of hurricanes before." But by paying attention to changes in the way they felt physically and mentally and observing their dreams, the animals, and the skies for themselves, people would've known a bad storm was coming weeks, even months ahead and made preparations.

Is Communication after Death Haram (a Sin) in Islam?

In, *Book of the Spirit: Kitab Al-Ruh,* Iman Ibn Al-Qayyim writes, "When a human being dies, all of his actions come to an end, except in one of three ways: continuing act of charity, a useful contribution to knowledge or a God-fearing, beautiful child who prays for him."

This means to me that our loved ones who have passed over into the afterlife continue to assist Allah in providing abundance, guidance, and knowledge to those of us who remember them, and by following divine guidance, we can be more moral and compassionate.

Jinn

Belief in the "unseen" is frequently mentioned in the Quran.

Quran Chapter 2, Verses 1–6:

A. L. M.

2. This is the Book; in it is guidance sure, without doubt, to those who fear Allah.

3. Who believe in the unseen, are steadfast in prayer, and spend out of what We have provided for them;

CHAPTER 18: ANCESTOR WORSHIP

4. And who believe in the Revelation sent today, and sent before that time, and (in their hearts) have the assurance of the Hereafter.

5. They are on (true) guidance, from their Lord, and it is these who will prosper.

6. As to those who reject faith, it is the same to them whether they're warning them or do not warn them; they will not believe. *The Holy Quran.* Yusuf Ali English translation.

A very important question is who is the capitalized "We" frequently used in the verses of the Quran. Are they the unseen beings in heaven? Are they Allah, our guardian angels, spirit guides, and loved ones who have passed over?

Quran Chapter 11, Verse 49:

49. Such are some of the stories of the unseen, which We have revealed unto thee: before this, neither thou nor thy people know them. So, persevere patiently: for the end is for those who are righteous. *The Holy Quran.* Yusuf Ali English translation.

The Arabic word *jinn* simply means, "hidden from sight."

Quran Chapter 72 Verses 1 and 2: Surah Al-Jinn, or The Spirits

1. Say: it has been revealed to me that a company of jinns listened (to the Qur'an). They said, 'We have really heard a wonderful recital!

2. It gives guidance to the right, and we have believed therein: we shall not join (in worship) any (gods) with our Lord. *The Holy Quran.* Yusuf Ali English translation.

I contemplated what these Quran verses meant. In a phone discussion with my younger sister Naimah about jinn, she explained her understanding of what a soul is. She described it as "similar to air and the breath, essential, important, necessary—quintessential. I'm not even sure what quintessential means." We were both shocked as I read Merriam-Webster's history of the word. I summarized the information as the ancient philosophers and scientists and those in the European Middle Ages believed the Earth and its atmosphere were made of the four basic elements of earth, air, fire, and water. Aristotle was credited with adding a fifth element ether. Ether is an invisible matter that fills the space in between, an invisible light or fire. It is interesting that the jinn is described as both invisible and fire in the Quran. The word "quintessential" comes from quinta essentia, which means "fifth element." However, otherwise it is used to describe something that is so perfect that it surpasses the limits of the Earth.

I sought books to learn what fire spirits are. In *Legends of the Fire Spirits,* the author, through his own research, explains that jinn are not ghosts or the deceased. They can be male or female, good or bad. They are like humans but have extra powers, such as magical abilities and flight. They can shape-shift to appear as items, people, or animals. Mostly they are transparent or invisible. They work and have families. They have their own beliefs and religions. The concept of jinn existed before Islam and was part of Judeo-Christian belief. Some jinn are considered evil, like the devil. In the United States, we think of jinn as genies who are fun, do magic, and grant wishes or, perhaps in science fiction movies, as aliens.

Another book, *The World of the Unseen*, made me think of removing the topic of jinn from my book entirely. Angry, disappointed, and filled with a sudden fear, I was about to back away from further research on jinn. I didn't even want to read any more about them. But then, a couple of hours later, I realized that was the reason I was writing this book, to clear up misunderstandings about our loved ones who have passed over. Laughing, remembered that although those who live in the United States are supposedly educated, we also allow television shows and movies to scare us, as the picture gets dark and the music gets creepy, about ghosts, psychic children, and mediums. It's not just in Muslim countries that people are afraid of ghosts, but here in the United States too!

The author of *The World of the Unseen,* seems to be afraid of jinn, believing that they are always from the devil, Satan, and that anything humans do that God can do is influenced by them. If someone is able to know information that is "unseen," without being educated by another human or human technology, then this is because of jinn. The same, apparently, of knowing the future or being able to communicate with deceased loved ones. Any psychological distress or addiction is attributed to jinn. The person is possessed by jinn and needs to be exorcised! To me, the belief that anything humans can do that is special is attributed to jinn instead of God is shirk, or idol worship.

If our souls leave our bodies at night while we are asleep and dreaming and actually go to be with God, is it not possible that God shares wisdom with us then? *The Soul's Journey*, states that our souls travel out of our bodies while we sleep and go to be with Allah and other souls of both living and deceased people to exchange knowledge and information about the unseen. Deceased relatives often come to the living in dreams, to see and know how we are doing. This book also mentions that the unseen jinn live on Earth together with humans.

Those that have had near death experiences say that God answered any question they asked and explained the knowledge of the whole universe while they were in heaven. People who had seizures or spiritual revelations during prayer, fasting, or meditation often return to consciousness as geniuses. All of a sudden, they know more than they did before the incident.

I think we have to take into consideration the fact that ancient scriptures were written before we were able to communicate and share information globally. Perhaps that is why the Prophet Mohammed was commanded to "Read!" Then he had scribes write the revelations that he received. Women were allowed to be educated too. But education isn't only about reading books, we now have television, phones, podcasts, and YouTube videos, which provide information faster than books. We can now share information with each other. We have the opportunity to know what's true and what's not.

Children frequently communicate with the unseen, which we adults call their "imaginary friends." They remember God's true love and brilliance. Then we send the children to school, churches, mosques, and other places of worship—to tell them that their love for God and their guardian angels and the grandparents that protect and rescue them is not real. If we cut ourselves off from guidance from God, angels, our guardians, spirit guides, and the souls of our deceased loved ones, then, yes, calamities befall us. Without these unseen, we also cut ourselves off from the energy of true love, peace, and joy! We lose faith and a purpose for living. Then we tend to do mean and horrible things to other people and avoid taking responsibility for our behavior by blaming it on the devil.

More and more people are having near-death experiences because they were "saved" medically from premature birth, heart attack, cancer, accidents, natural disasters, wars, gun violence, and domestic violence. The survivors have met with God, angels, and their loved ones—including pets. They return with the truth of what they saw.

Perhaps the Prophet Muhammad is the last prophet because a multitude of people now know the truth. We have experienced the revelations for ourselves, or others close to us have stories to tell about the magnificence of heaven and the hell that is often of our own making. Hell is the absence of true love and our refusal to believe in both the seen and the unseen. The sexual abuse treatment group, rebirthing, massage, holotropic breathwork (although mostly done by healers and therapists who identified as Caucasian or white), led me to my Native American culture, and in turn to my African Indigenous culture. It opened me up to accepting the concept of spirit communication. When my massage/holotropic therapist moved out west, I found a Black American holotropic breathwork practitioner in the Yellow Pages. She is the one who introduced me to a Black massage therapist, who then introduced me to a traditional African religion group. So, as the Native American medicine man recommended, I began to explore my African Indigenous culture. They have healing rituals in which the priests and priestess receive and give spirit messages while in trance.

Previously, as a Muslim, I would not have believed any of it. I remember going to hear an interfaith panel discussion that had, of course, a priest, a rabbi, an imam, and a babalawo—an African Yoruba priest. I remember saying afterward that everything the African priest said was wrong. I don't know where I got such strong opinions from, because I don't remember any Muslims saying anything against African religion directly. It was probably from television and movies showing us that Africans are bad, pagan, and primitive. Perhaps it was also because the concepts were so different from the little of Christianity and Islam that I knew.

My momma gave me yet another assignment just when I thought this book was almost done. I had not planned to research the Muslim perspective on jinn and dreams. It was like she was asking me to carry on from where she left off. She wanted me to thoroughly heal the misunderstandings from my childhood to learn about the beauty of Islam and her love for it.

Jehovah's Witnesses insist that when people are dead, they are dead. Buried six feet under, or placed six feet up, or their ashes scattered. But what happens when your deceased mother and other friends and relatives make their presence known? Religions deny the existence of deceased ancestors and even our guardian angels because then the faithful wouldn't listen to tyrannical authoritarian leaders. People would be prepared for events such as famine and other disasters if they paid attention to dreams, their ancestors' guidance, and young people like Joseph in the bible and the Quran. They would know who their enemies were and who to trust. They would not listen to lies because they would know the truth, and experience that they were truly provided for, abundantly, by heaven. "Ask and you shall receive" is true.

Dreams

Muslim, African American, and Native American cultures used to put a lot of emphasis on interpreting and reporting dreams. The dreamer and the community then followed the guidance given in the dreams. Islamic cultural interpretation of dreams provided personal insights into behaviors and morals that needed correction or reward. According to, *Dreams and Visions*, students of Islam said that they learned more from their shaykhs—their teachers—after they were dead than when they were alive. Most were encouraged by scenes of the afterlife and Day of Resurrection in visions and dreams of what awaited them after death. The natural, ecstatic bliss of Allah's love, peace, and beautiful scenes of paradise is similar to what people describe from their near-death experiences. After this blissful experience, they also have the aftereffects of increased miracles and wisdom. Sufis developed theories and theological approaches for actively producing dreams and dream analysis. However, many other groups in Muslim countries also had folk traditions of dream interpretation.

My mother used to ask us our dreams every morning. As a young child, I didn't know that my dreams foretold the future. They were like watching a movie, and then the next day, the activities, people, and events would be exactly as I'd seen them in my dreams! It wasn't until she married my stepfather that I became aware that my dreams came true the next day. Somewhat like déjà vu, I saw where we were going, who was there, and what activities we would do when we got there. This was amazing considering that in those days, African American parents didn't discuss their plans with her children. "Get your clothes on. Get your shoes on. Let's go!" But after Stepfather's anger and threats for Momma to not tell him any more of my dreams, my vivid predictive dreams stopped. To this day, I have not had such movie like dreams. Probably because in a dream when I was nine years old, I saw him going to Mecca on pilgrimage and something happening. Approximately twenty years later, in 1987, he did go to Mecca and died there. I was angry when a Muslim friend told me that because he had died at Mecca, all his sins were forgiven. I thought, That's not fair at all! All the pain and suffering he caused us.

In my thirties, my dream life was more active. I was connected to friends and family through my dreams. Tossing and turning during the night, I'd realize one of my friends was awake worrying. I'd call the friend, we'd talk about whatever was bothering her, and then we both were able to sleep! Some nights I dreamed about my brother and then called him up to say, "Whatever you're about to do, don't do it!" We would have a conversation, and then I'd roll over and go back to sleep. He would thank me. Other times, I waited until the next day to call him. A friend and I twice dreamed the exact same dream! Of course, we didn't know this until we talked the next day.

Deceased friends and relatives gave me personal advice through dreams. My stepfather, and foster father although he was still alive and suffering from Alzheimer's came twice. Perhaps that was the only way I could tolerate seeing them. In the dreams, I accepted their advice. Perhaps it was their way of apologizing, because they haven't come again. A dear friend, who called herself my adopted mother since I didn't have family in the city, came to me in a dream and told me, "You should be more understanding toward the men in your relationships. Don't be so hard on them or expect so much." In life she was very critical of her husband and sons. Another dear acquaintance who was a priestess Queen Mother was often in my dreams, but I didn't know until two years later that she had died.

After a while, I gradually became less aware of my dreams or whether they directly showed me the future. There were some déjà vu experiences as an adult, where I knew everything that was happening in new situations and faraway locations and even saw people that I could not have possibly met. I recorded my dreams in journals for twenty years. But none, that I know of, showed me like a movie what would happen the next day in the way they did when I was a little girl. Recently I have been dreaming more vividly, but the memories fade as soon as I turn over in bed to reach for my notebook. Yet I just know, without knowing how I know. During the night, it feels like I'm being shown and given assignments way above my level of daytime understanding. Turning over in bed, pulling the covers up, I frequently yell, "I get it. I understand now. Just please let me sleep!" They show me calculus formulas and PowerPoint slides with the same concepts gradually repeated throughout the night, giving me the main point or answer just before I wake up in the morning. Then I promptly forget.

Spirits and ghosts do come in the darkness of the night and in our sleep. They frequently bring us answers to problems. Ideas for inventions such as the sewing machine, science and math theories (atoms, molecules, the periodic table, analytical geometry), and great stories, poems, and songs all came from dreams. If it were not for visioning and dreaming into being, we would not have most of the modern conveniences that we now take for granted. So why is it these days we are afraid to sleep? If we knew the truth of the chaotic environment around us and admitted to a sense of constant fear and lack of control over it, we would then have answers and have to do something to change it. Perhaps that's why we unconsciously and consciously avoid sleep.

Spirits Communicate through Mediums

Mediumship is contacting spirits, usually of ancestors, saints, spiritual mentors, or God. This is done in several ways: long prayers, meditation, fasting, getting the Holy Ghost, speaking in tongues, and rituals with ecstatic dancing, such as what dervishes do. A medium is the person who can go into a mild trance and say the spirit's message. In Indigenous and ancient cultures, the purpose of mediumship was for community and personal transformation, growth, and positive human evolution. Because of colonization and religious conquest, most of these traditions were lost or hidden, so much that only pieces of the initial rituals survive. Mediumship was not for entertainment or solely for comforting. Neither was it for fortune-telling or a sinful source of income from scaring people who sought counsel. Today, in spiritual places (churches, temples, synagogues, mosques), leaders should not be content merely to have a large congregation that comes regularly. What is more important is making sure that the people and the community are improving. Meetings should always begin with prayers and intentions for only positive, wise guidance. The place where mediumship occurs should be clean, purified, and considered sacred. People who attend should also be clean in mind, spirit, and lifestyle. Everyone listens and allows the healing energy and wisdom to come into them and also learns from all the other spirit messages they hear during the service or rituals. In the United States, spiritualist churches openly include mediumship in their weekly religious services.

Chapter 19: Medical Intuitive

A friend at Chicago IANDS suggested in 2020, that I go and see a medical intuitive to get answers for my increasing health problems that medical doctors were slow to diagnose and treat after I started having problems with my legs. I didn't know what a medical intuitive was. The medical intuitive explained that she has X-ray vision, the ability to look inside my body and see what's wrong. However, before she told me what she saw, she said, "Your health problems began with something that happened when you were between the ages of seven and eleven."

She didn't tell me what it was. She didn't have to. Immediately I burst out sobbing. Seven years old was when my mother married my stepfather. At age twelve, he started being absent from our home. The medical intuitive continued, "Your skeleton is underdeveloped and probably stopped progressing at the normal rate of growth beginning when you were five years old." This was also possibly true because when I was five years old, I had complications from measles that developed into double pneumonia and difficulty digesting my food.

"I'm also concerned about the condition of your heart," the medical intuitive said. "Your heart is in such bad shape that you need to decide whether you want to stay on this side or cross over to the Other Side. Either way, you will have help." I quietly considered what she said. "You don't have to decide now. I can do healing on your heart, if you'd like."

"Okay," I said. She had me lay down flat on the couch. With her hands gesturing but never touching me, she performed psychic surgery on my chest and heart. I felt some of what she was doing, mostly a pulling sensation and tightness.

When she finished, she said, "You've done a lot already for the benefit of the evolution of humankind. You've done enough. Now you can rest. It's important that you not do much of anything at this time. Just rest." Near the end of the session, she went on. "You will be probably be diagnosed with something like multiple sclerosis (MS) first, but then the doctor will change that diagnosis to something else. Then you will get the services that you need. You are a hero for taking on MS. MS is actually a blessing. You can rest now." I didn't understand what she meant about the spiritual aspects of MS being a blessing or about benefiting human evolution.

Two days later, I telephoned her, complaining of chest discomfort. She did remote psychic healing. It felt as if she were removing stitches one by one. My chest felt a whole lot better! I had also decided during the evening after the consultation that yes, I did want to live on this side—on Earth.

The medical intuitive had told my friend Calvin who was with me at the session that he needed to listen to me and allow me to release my anger—anger that I was not aware I had at the time. Weeks later, I did become very angry because of his unreasonable jealousy. Having had enough problems with men, why would I want to be bothered with even one man, let alone adding on more men? He accused me of looking at other men one day after we returned from shopping. His fears didn't make sense to me, especially on that day. I had just heard that one of my girlfriends died suddenly from undiagnosed diabetes, and I was scheduled for a surgical procedure early the next morning. My mind was definitely not on whatever men were walking down the street!

I went back to the medical intuitive for another consultation a few years later. She was really surprised by how much I had improved after taking some of the supplements and making the dietary changes that she suggested. "You're going to be a mover and shaker one day," she said. I didn't know what she meant. Other than doing my creative watercolor painting at home, I was still resting, like she'd told me to.

The Medical Intuitive's Predictions Come True

In 2003 the fourth neurologist that I visited finally gave me a diagnosis. He said, "I am so sorry that you went through what you did with the other doctors. I knew as soon as I saw you that you have a neuromuscular condition. I can tell by the way you talk. Your speech is what we call 'iambic pentameter.' This means that you split your words into syllables when you talk. It gives a Shakespearean, poetic rhythm to your voice. Neurologically, we call it scanning speech. Based on how quickly you went from walking, to walking with a walker, to using a wheelchair within four years, you probably have primary progressive multiple sclerosis. Again, I'm really sorry how other doctors were with you. Primary progressive multiple sclerosis is rare, so even an experienced doctor perhaps would only see one or two cases in twenty years of practice."

A month after the new neurologist sent me for new MRIs and other tests, he told me, "You have spinocerebellar degeneration, or maybe olivopontocerebellar ataxia." He showed me on the MRI scans that the upper spinal cord was thinning at the base of my skull, where it meets the top of my neck. He explained that the cerebellum is nearby and helps with balance and coordination. "Ataxia" is another word for problems with balance and coordination. "Your other symptoms will be similar to MS."

This is what the medical intuitive predicted the diagnosis would be. By this time, I had completely forgotten about the medical intuitive mentioning MS! I really didn't know much about MS. As a nurse, I had one patient in a nursing home that had it. She used a wheelchair and required help with most of her functioning. The neurologist did not mention, of course, that when doctors don't know what is wrong with a patient, they routinely send them, especially women, to psychiatrists. In regards to MS and health disparities, although women get autoimmune diseases such as lupus, rheumatoid arthritis, sclera derma more often than men, it often takes up to seven years to get a diagnosis. Today, doctors still believe MS is a white peoples' disease affecting mostly Europeans who live further north away from the equator. So with African-American patients doctors don't even think of MS. It is the same with women's heart disease because for a long time it was thought that heart attacks were a man's disease.

Later I read that the severe form of spinocerebellar degeneration is usually hereditary and begins in childhood. Rarely it can present first with heart problems, because the heart is also a muscle. The medical intuitive had already told me that my heart condition probably wouldn't show up on tests because it is more a problem of the muscle of the heart being weak. I had severe chest pains even at rest while sitting or lying down, and it was worse with exertion especially with climbing steep stairs. I could hardly breathe by the time I got near the top and my legs felt like lead.

While it took four years for a neurologist to notice that the MRIs showed the spinocerebellar degeneration, it actually took twelve years to find a cardiologist who specialized in women's heart problems to give me a diagnosis and treatment. She looked at all my past heart tests from way back in 1995, when my chest pains began. She angrily said with each test report, "They didn't do anything! And they didn't do anything! And they didn't do anything!"

Previously my primary care doctors sent me to famous male cardiologists that told me I was too young and didn't have high blood pressure therefore my heart was fine. Disregarding that my tests showed ischemia—meaning blood wasn't getting throughout my heart.

After I had an echocardiogram, mobile electrocardiograms, and another stress test, she told me, "You have diastolic dysfunction. But I don't understand why. Diastolic dysfunction usually happens because of high blood pressure and diabetes. Your blood pressure is usually too low, and you don't have diabetes. I will put you on a blood pressure medicine that helps to take the strain off of the heart. Nitroglycerin for the chest pains. You will have to be careful with your fluid intake. You need to make sure that you drink enough water, but not too much. So only drink between thirty-two and forty-eight ounces of liquids a day."

By then, I had gotten used to my symptoms not showing up on standard medical tests. Even when there were significant test results, the doctors still did not believe me. Although later when they finally gave me a diagnosis and I researched it, I saw I did have the classic textbook symptoms. Now I don't get upset anymore. Honestly, I was surprised the cardiologist believed me after all these years. I stopped going to doctors. From experience I learned to wait until I was really, really, seriously ill. Even then, doctors would send me home in twenty-four to forty-eight hours. I don't know what would have happened to me if the medical intuitive had not done the heart surgery back in 2000 and if I hadn't known to choose life.

It was difficult to go from walking miles to being totally exhausted after walking two blocks. Other than taking a bus for long distances, I previously walked almost everywhere because I never had a car. In Zimbabwe I walked two hours over rough terrain, up and down hills, at a regular pace to and two hours from villages. Approximately six months after I returned to the United States, I began having difficulty walking up curb cuts and up the humps in the streets that allowed for water drainage. Huh? you are probably thinking. Well, I never noticed those inclines and declines before neither. A man observing me one day said, "You look like you're trying to climb a mountain." To my legs, it did feel like I was trying to climb a steep mountain. Soon after, climbing stairs became almost impossible and then impossible.

Used to doing at least twenty activities a day, I learned to be grateful for accomplishing only one or two tasks a day. This was very humbling. However, it was terrifying for me to have to begin to depend on others for my physical needs. My parents and husbands were not there for me because of domestic violence, so I learned from childhood to take care of myself. Doctors' misdiagnoses almost let me die several times. My worst fear was to ever have to depend on anyone for anything. After all, who could I trust? I would wake up in cold sweats from nightmare scenes of being taken to the emergency room unconscious, unable to tell the doctors my unusual symptoms or advocate for my needs. Eventually I had to learn to depend on others because I had difficulty talking, eating, dressing, bathing, even turning myself over in bed. My legs would collapse without warning. With reluctance, after reading an article about a medical doctor who gave in and started using a wheelchair, I too discovered that with the wheelchair, I had less exhaustion and pain. Using an electric power wheelchair also gave me my independence back.

Other people's reactions to the wheelchair were different. Housing case manager wanted to put me in a nursing home as soon as I got a wheelchair. I tried to explain that I could now do more—not less. Equipped for Equality lawyers wrote a letter to the housing program and she stopped pestering me. Although my aunt begged me to move in with her, in her one level ranch style home where she had a contractor quickly build a ramp to the backdoor, she yelled at me telling the rest of the family that I was being lazy for using a wheelchair. I tried to explain that because I had ataxia, my legs were uncoordinated with partial paralysis and my not been able to feel my legs made my back hurt terribly as my back was jerked and twisted with each step. Walking was also very exhausting. The rooms in her home were huge, especially the kitchen where the stove was on the front wall, a long way from the refrigerator by the window, and the pantry was on the opposite side. Finally I told my aunt, "I don't sleep at night because of the awful pain from too much walking during the day. Then I'm irritable and angry with you. I'd rather that on Judgment Day that God writes in my Book that I was kind to people and not mean. Therefore, I'm going to use my wheelchair in the house!"

When I was much younger, in my 20s, I worked in nursing homes as an aide and later as a registered nurse. I told myself then that I'd rather die than have to wait and wait and wait for someone to rudely come to care for me. But this was decades before there were rolling walkers with seats, power wheelchairs, portable ventilators, and other assistive devices to help people speak, write, and feed themselves. Plus there is a natural survival mode that kicked in that kept me busy and mentally occupied with making it through each day, and going forward.

Until I became ill, I was a bit too passive. Having a physical disability taught me that I had to really fight for my life, not just be glad to be breathing, but fight for a better quality of life. That's why I now make each day better than the day before. Make the most out of each day because we don't know if it will be our last day. Our health could be snatched away at any time, even if we don't die. I learned to appreciate life and share with others. And as important, I learned not to go to extremes with diet or in any other area of my life!

In 2014, while I was doing research for a doctoral biopsychology classroom presentation, I learned that I most likely had subacute combined degeneration of the spinal cord, not the diagnosis the neurologist gave me in 2003. The myelin sheath is damaged similar to what happens with MS. These diagnoses are similar, as subacute combined degeneration of the spinal cord is also usually located in the cervical (neck) region but the cause is due to vitamin B12 deficiency. When my blood test results in 1999 came back showing that I had megaloblastic red blood cells, I, of course, went to the library to find out what "megaloblastic" meant. One of the reasons for megaloblastic, or enlarged, red blood cells is vitamin B12 deficiency. In 1988 I started getting stomach pains, whenever I ate meat, that lasted forty-eight hours or more, so severe that I couldn't eat any food at all. So, I naturally stopped eating meat.

Unfortunately, I was introduced to a spiritual group that promoted being vegan. While this was great in terms of having socializing activities and learning to cook tasty vegetarian meals, they also taught that salt, sugar, dairy, eggs, and any other animal foods were bad. Thinking that I was eating healthy all these years based on what I read and following what I learned from nutrition classes, I thought I was getting enough vitamins, protein, and minerals. In addition, I was taking B12 pills that went under my tongue. But B12 supplements were expensive, so I didn't take them as regularly as I should have. You could only get enough vitamin B12 from animal products. Otherwise, you would have to do like the Total breakfast cereal television commercial and eat ten to twenty bowls of beans, nuts, and green vegetables daily in order to get enough vitamin B12 in your body. To my horror, I read that vitamin B12 deficiency can cause permanent nerve damage within six months! I had been on a strict vegan diet for ten years already!

The burning pain started in my feet and moved up my shins in 1993. I would look down at my legs, expecting the lower part of my pants to be on fire. That is how intense the burning pain was, especially at night. By 1999, when my legs started giving out from under me, my hands and lower arms were also burning at night. I started eating fish in 1998 because no matter how much food I ate in a day, I didn't have any energy. But it was too late! The nerve damage was done. Because I had been eating fish for a year, my B12 blood levels were in the normal range. Therefore, the doctors didn't prescribe any treatment. Although I told doctors all this in 1999, they ignored me. My wheelchair was delivered to my door a week before Christmas 2001.

The diagnosis of subacute combined degeneration of the spinal cord better explains why my neuromuscular disease got better and did not decline further. I eat meat now in moderation. When I shared medical journal articles with this information with my neurologist in 2014, he said, "I just happened to have several middle-aged patients come in with similar symptoms to yours.

I discovered they had B12 deficiency because they had been taking antacid proton pump inhibitors for years, which prevented the absorption of B12." He thanked me and scanned copies of the journal articles into my chart.

Having a disability taught me a lot. It helped me think outside the box because I had to compensate and solve problems and do things in a completely different way than I had learned coming up or from how most people did them. If I didn't, I would be a lot like many of my friends with disabilities that mostly stayed in their homes. And I was determined to be in a nursing home. The reason that I can walk at all is because I walk sideways like a crab. I walk from my hips because I cannot lift my knees up to pull up the rest of my legs. For me to walk forward means that I trip over my feet, almost falling. I catch myself, but jerking myself upright hurts my back. Walking devices, such as canes and walkers, are made for people to walk forward like everybody else. Well, I don't fit in like everyone else anyway, so that shouldn't be a surprise. The beautiful part, though, is that I did teach myself to walk. Even if it's walking sideways, it's walking! I can get across a small room very quickly, so quickly that people don't notice that I'm walking sideways. Walking backward is also easier than walking forward, and it gets me where I need to go. Therefore, in the rest of my life, I also learned to compensate, adapt, and do things very differently than other people. What does it matter how a task is done as long as the goal is accomplished?

All the medical and life predictions that the medical intuitive made back in the early 2000s came true, from initially advising that I should strictly rest to becoming an active mover and shaker. The medical intuitive also had a near-death experience which gave her psychic abilities.

Other Predictions That Came True

Several predictions and recommendations, such as the spirit message given to me in May 2018 through a medium, came true. At the time, neither the medium nor I knew these were predictions!

In this situation, we were both frustrated with Skype. This was her message:

"I think part of it is having enough of those experiences so that we become really comfortable with it, such as using technology like Skype. Practicing by having a friend that you can Skype with in a conversation and having three or four of those

CHAPTER 19: MEDICAL INTUITIVE

kinds of friends. Just to give you this experience could be really important. But this type of media is becoming almost the norm. We are going to have to get used to it and jump in at some point."

At the beginning of my internship, in August 2019, I was expected to quickly learn all of these technologies at the same time: Slack, Grasshopper, Tawk.to, several WhatsApp accounts, the agency's website patient portal, Practice Fusion—an electronic medical record platform—Google Voice, and the rest of the Google suite, which includes Google Drive, Google Docs—formatted and arranged very differently than Microsoft Word—and Google Sheets, which has many layers underneath the spreadsheet! In addition I needed to upgrade from my iPhone 6 since it was too old to put the clinic's apps on it. Apple completely changed its phones that year, getting rid of the thumb sign-on and changing to face recognition. I had to swipe up with just the right touch and at just the right angle to do anything. I was also learning how to use an iPad at the same time.

During the COVID-19 stay-at-home orders, working from home at the end of my internship, we had to quickly learn how to do video therapy sessions using Google Hangouts, Google Meet, Updox, and then, of course, Zoom. Who would have known that spirit's recommendation for me would become true for everyone across the world?

The following is more from the May 2018 spirit message:

"That has come up in rehabilitation counseling because people with disabilities can't always get out."

"Yes, absolutely. That sense of community that you had talked about comes in with this as well. So there could be something like doing group work and having conversations with people who can't get out."

"I hadn't thought of that. I do have friends that I keep up with that way."

"Well, that's what I'm hearing, and it feels like we need a little more effort with that, so that it becomes second nature."

Later during COVID-19 shutdown, only essential workers were allowed to leave home to go to work. The rest of us had to just jump in and learn new technology. After a while, it did become second nature.

Skype has not allowed me to log in since those two interviews back in 2018. Other people were having difficulties with logging in too. Very few companies use Skype anymore. It was easy to use before Microsoft took over. Previously when you heard the loud music, you simply clicked on the tiny picture of a video camera, and immediately you were seeing and hearing the other person.

On my end of the year evaluations, the supervisor wrote, "She will need to be more technology savvy as this is important for this day and age." Keep in mind that all my supervisors at the agency were in their thirties or younger. They were used to smartphones and computers. But thanks to my internship training, I am actually far ahead of my colleagues, young and old, in terms of using technology! I have added other apps to my devices and quickly used them with ease. So, over the year, I did master technology. At least for now, since technology is constantly changing and we are constantly learning. Microsoft and Apple are competing with each other, with frequent software updates, so even typing becomes complicated as the keyboard gets changed too.

***

Recently I woke up remembering that I'd been to a spiritualist church before! I went in search of the church in 1998 after reading *Company of Prophets*. An old man came up to me as I was leaving and told me about myself:

"Sometimes in life you have to go backward first in order to go forward. Keep your head up. Keep your head up high!"

Although I'd read the book, then I still didn't know what a psychic medium was. At the time I also didn't know that I was about to become homeless and have to work my way back up. Or that a neuromuscular disease was making my head feel so heavy that my neck struggled to hold it up. That I would have to go backward to heal childhood trauma first in order to heal physically and emotionally and go forward, and then, amazingly, graduate with a master's degree in counseling that allowed me to help other people.

Chapter 20: Mediumship Classes

Because I was comforted and benefited from spirit messages from my relatives, I wanted to learn how to help other people also experience the healing effects of having a medium connect them with their loved ones who have passed over, so I began taking mediumship development classes at the Church of the Spirit. There the classes are called spiritual unfoldment classes. We learned the history of Spiritualism, the different forms of mediumship and healing. It was only a year after attending the church that I asked and was given permission to be in the advanced class. The following are some examples of what it felt like for me while learning to bring a spirit message through.

The mediumship teacher gave me the assignment to see what I could pick up from spirit for a classmate's husband. The teacher started out by saying she saw his doctor and described him.

I added, "I see images of two young doctors standing side by side, shoulder to shoulder, wearing collared shirts and ties with white lab coats."

The teacher said, "Students?" She turned to the classmate. "Are medical students treating your husband too?"

I further described the young doctor. "He has a brown complexion, Middle Eastern, possibly of Indian or Pakistani descent. I feel a sharp headache on my forehead." I put my hand there. "I'm trying to describe an image of seeing the flesh of his thigh above his knee. Did he have problems with his knee or leg?"

The teacher said, "See an X-ray."

I closed my eyes briefly. "I see an X-ray of the whole leg. I am feeling pain in my left leg. But, wait a minute, the X-rays are of the other leg!" I suddenly remembered that X-rays are like looking at a mirror so that the right and left sides are reversed.

Classmate's response: "He was having pain in his left kidney, but then X-rays showed the problem was really with his right kidney! My husband had headaches. The kidneys were the problem, not his leg, but it's amazing how spirit pointed out that discrepancy of the wrong leg or wrong side!"

The teacher said, "You'd make a good medical intuitive. Did you know that? By being able to see the inside of the body. Maybe you should do that."

"Okay. When I was a child, I used to be able to tell what was physically wrong with someone, even name the disease. That was because I've always been observant and remembered people's symptoms. But I never looked inside anyone before! I don't know if I really want to know what's physically wrong with people!"

Phone Practice with a Classmate.

My message for a classmate: "I'm seeing huge flowers. I see a metal cup. It reminds me of the large brass cup used for the wine for holy communion. I hear the word 'chalice.'"

Classmate: "Goblet."

I continued, "I see a crystal glass with carved. I'm hearing the word 'facets.' Then a large brass bowl with a stem handle. Then a huge brass bowl. An open cardboard box with brown paper inside. But it's opened up, similar to a paper bag. Then I saw something round like a tan plate at the bottom of the box. Then a spinning circle came up out of the box. It's become larger and is now the only item in my field of vision. I'm seeing a large recliner, possibly leather—a smooth leather but well-padded in softness and thickness. Now a huge brass bell, and I'm viewing it from underneath. I am seeing a red car. Actually, I saw a car frame at the beginning, before I saw the car."

Classmate's response: "I was packing up some of my mother's crystal glasses last week! I wrapped them in brown paper. My father usually sat in the recliner. The bell, was it in a steeple? My family regularly attended a Catholic church.

The car frame usually represents my father because he worked in an automobile factory."

One way that I know my or other people's older relatives or spirit guides are communicating is the use of antiquated or intellectual words that are beyond my vocabulary. Plus, I don't know about the Catholic faith.

A classmate's message for me: "Your ex-husband Roy is here, and he's playing a violin. Now I'm seeing a man here who is possibly your great-uncle that you've talked about. He has dementia. An African woman here. She's very pretty, and she's wearing jewelry—bracelets and bangles. She's coming to get him. Then there's a woman here that looks like you. Your mother, perhaps, when she was younger. She's at a keyboard. Do you play a keyboard? You are sitting at a keyboard."

My response to my classmate: "My great-uncle is still in his right mind. He's very sharp and intelligent. So is my 105-year-old grandmother, and independently active until she was 100 years old. You were probably seeing my foster father. He has cancer, and I heard he now has dementia. He was a mean, stubborn person that pushed people away. The only one he trusted was his wife. She is probably coming to get him. He refused the chemo. But last week, I heard he was doing all right, as he decided to take the hormone treatment instead of chemo. But even so, people with dementia are in and out of their bodies. Either way, she may be coming to get him. Both my foster mother and my birth mother played the piano. I don't know how to play the piano. My foster mother played classical music from composers like Frédéric Chopin and Claude Debussy. She and Roy are probably acknowledging that they saw me at the Ravinia symphony concert yesterday."

My other message to my classmate: "I'm seeing some Mary Jane style shoes that are light colored, in a black-and-white background. Oh, now they are showing me pink, light orange, or salmon-colored shoes. I see the shoes hanging up. They are thin, like ballet slippers. I also see sausages. Long sausages hanging up from the ceiling, like in the old neighborhood butcher shops. This looks like inside a cabin. Perhaps a smokehouse for smoking meats." I mentally ask, Who is bringing me this message? "I am seeing a middle-aged man. Perhaps he is your grandpa." I heard "grandpa."

"He's wearing a wide, round-brim hat. He has white hair, with perhaps a white mustache. Wearing a blue-and-white plaid shirt. There are two men here. One clean shaven, with perhaps a hint of a mustache. The other man has a long, white mustache and long beard. Actually, the beard is getting longer and longer!"

"What emotion do you get?" my classmate asked.

"Well, fun. Fun, because he's making me laugh. I'm seeing a friend that we know, whose beard is actually getting longer and longer every time we see him. Now I am seeing archways, similar to the round archways between the living room and dining room in a bungalow-style house. Except there's a point in the center at the top of the arch, similar to the stained glass windows in a church."

Classmate's response: "When I was twelve, I took dancing lessons, and we wore ballet slippers. After dance class, I would get on the bus and go across town to the meat store and buy a lot of sausages for the family for lunches for the whole week. It was my mother who sent me for the sausages. She wanted me to be independent. It's a lot to have a twelve-year-old do. To have to get on a bus, then get off, and get on another bus to go across town. At the meat market, there were long lines. The women would always skip in front of me in the line because I was a child. But my mother would say, 'No, you tell them they can't get in front of you!' The man may have been my grandfather or my father. But I don't know any men with facial hair. My father used to dress up as Santa Claus. One day, when I was eight, I saw the elastic holding his beard on. But I didn't say anything because I wanted my Christmas presents! You were also right with the archways. But you changed it. You're good. The bungalow that I grew up with had the rounded archway between the living room and the dining room. We had two stained glass windows. Wow!"

"Wow, and your father kept showing me the long, white hair and beard separated like a wig!"

"Haneefa! Why did you do that? You know you're just supposed to say what you see!"

I had to laugh too, because everybody was telling our friend that he should be Santa Claus at Christmas time. Santa Claus was key to my classmate's father's message for her to remember how he used to play Santa Claus, but I hadn't made this connection while relaying these images to her.

CHAPTER 20: MEDIUMSHIP CLASSES

The teacher assigned the class a healing exercise where we sent love to a classmate seated in a chair halfway down the center aisle of the church. The classmate that I sent the love to told us that he felt the love in his heart. I had visualized a pink, loving feeling and healing in my heart reaching in a steady energy stream outward from my heart. The instruction for the person seated was to bring up a memory. When it was my turn to receive I started to cry as the pain of my fear of rejection resurfaced over the past three months through the internship application process. I called out to my mother. Soon I felt peaceful and light. A classmate said, "I saw your mother holding you as a baby. She was sad. She held and rocked you."

This felt very, very healing for me.

Rejections after multiple interviews for the required three years of clinical training practicums and now an internship were heartbreaking. It didn't matter that I work faster than my classmates and colleagues with better efficiency and clinical knowledge gained from life experience. Not slower as people assumed. People seemed to only see the wheelchair. Not the real me with plenty of talents and accomplishments. Others only saw me as an older Black American and since most internships were in the suburbs some supervisors worried about losing possible white clients who wouldn't want a black therapist.

I did eventually get my clinical training after often having to choose from the leftovers. There are advantages to being a therapist with a disability because people of all complexions and backgrounds tend to instinctively know that I understand their struggles since obviously each day—since I too have challenges, discrimination, and having to problem-solve. Supervisors discovered I worked very well independently meaning they could trust my competence and expertise with treating clients. They saw my clients make rapid improvements.

Mediumship Workshop

A Horse?

A middle-aged woman with beautiful, long, thick, gray hair was sitting across from me. It was my turn to give her a reading. "I'm hearing *cock-a-doodle-doo*. I'm seeing a carved, light-toned wooden rooster with a clock face. In my right ear, I hear a bell clanging. But it feels as if both my ears are clogged."

She asked me, "Is there someone associated with the rooster?"

"Yes, there is a man here holding a rooster on his right arm."

"What does he look like?"

"He's wearing a uniform, kind of denim colored, with a hat. But the hat keeps changing."

"That's okay—what was his build like?"

"He's just under six feet, slender, slim to average build, but he's not skinny. I hear Whitney Rogers."

"Do you see a dog?"

"No, but I see a big, muscular horse standing next to you. Beige, with long, blond hair."

"He, we, had a horse that died. But it was darker than what you described."

"Okay, that's why the other lady said it wasn't her horse. The horse was waiting for you! Wow! Now I'm seeing cymbals, like in an orchestra." I moved my arms as if clanging the cymbals together. "Perhaps he wants you to wake up and be more aware. Did he like to joke around?"

After the reading, she was excited. "That was my grandfather! He was tall and thin, and he had roosters. You also got my grandmother's last name right!"

Then she gave me a spirit reading. "I am seeing a man about five feet-ten inches, in a blue uniform. He's holding a little boy's hand. He says, 'I have our son.'" She paused and looked as if she would cry too as I began to sob. "I'm sorry, I didn't mean to make you cry. Wait," she said. "There's more. Let me tell you this real quick." The facilitator was instructing us to change partners. "He says you didn't do anything wrong. You didn't do anything wrong."

Shocked, I sobbed harder. "No, no, it's okay. Thank you. Thank you very much. I've been waiting years for this message."

I was crying because the little boy in heaven was the baby that I miscarried, which almost resulted in me dying. The man in the blue auto mechanic's uniform was my husband.

***

Spirit Circles

During the summer the spirit circle was usually in the cafeteria on the lower level. This time we met in the room at the back of the church where we usually have mediumship classes.

The facilitator brought through a message for me. "I'm going to break one of my own rules and ask you a question. Are you going to the Midwest this summer to visit your family? Not in the city, but in a suburb nearby?"

Surprised, I said, "I have several places I could travel to this summer, but travel has been difficult with school."

"There were some good times that happened in the Midwest that you should revisit. Like the times your family went to the park."

"I don't know if there is any family still living there in the Midwest. There was an elderly woman that we used to visit in a wooded area in a nearby suburb, when I was a little girl. But I don't remember her name."

"I am from that suburb!" the teacher said.

We stared at each other in shock. I started to say "Small world," but I didn't. For years, I'd forgotten the name of that suburb. I said, "I guess I have more healing to do. Just when I thought I was done."

"You're still here, aren't you?" another student said. Everyone laughed and made their own comments about ongoing healing and growth.

That is one assignment that, so far, I haven't done yet. I have not gone back to the midwestern neighborhood. I don't know what I may find there that will be healing for me and provide closure on a place from which I only have bad memories. But one day.

My Mediumship Abilities

My mediumship abilities are improving, but not like the mediums you see on television. I have to work hard at it. I'd also been out of practice for a couple of years because I was away for clinical practicum and internship training. I don't spontaneously see ghosts or hear spirits. No voices or conversations in my head. As with other mediums, messages are received by images, pictures, and thoughts that come into our minds and can be difficult to distinguish from everyday thoughts. It takes practice to be able to know the difference. Many mediums say it took them ten years or more of classes and practice. Most spirits are not able to bring their energy vibration down to a level slow enough to talk to humans, so spirit communicates using quick symbols, pictures, and brief words. While I may have had natural, innate psychic abilities, as most children do, it's going to take confidence to bring them back. I have had some success bringing through images of memories from other peoples' relatives, and I sometimes hear a word here and there, but more training and practice are needed before I'm able to smoothly interpret what I see.

Communication with my loved ones is usually easier and faster than getting messages for other people, probably because my loved ones' pictures, songs, and occasional words bring up memories to help connect the dots so that a story or message unfolds. These messages can be hilarious or full of such love that they bring me to tears. When reading for others, the pictures tend to be in black and white, blurred, and slow to materialize. The biggest problem is when I doubt and question what I see. Sometimes it's because what I see is so simple and common that it seems silly to say it. But then spirit will say the word that I was thinking again, and when I say it out loud, it's usually correct!

I do better when I ask spirit questions aloud. There are three main questions recommended by famous mediums: "Will you describe yourself? What's your relationship to the person here for the reading? And what message do you have for this person?" There are longer lists of questions in books, but these are the basics for a short reading. I've tried that, but spirits stubbornly refused to answer a long list of questions in the order that I asked. So I stopped asking! I do better with initiating a conversation aloud, as the author of the book, *The Last Frontier: Exploring the Afterlife and Transforming Our Fear of Death*, recommends that we do and just start talking. Repeat aloud what you see, hear, feel, understand, and don't stop talking! This has worked for me at home, in bed, usually in the wee hours of the morning while it's still dark outside. Although a few British mediums do talk out loud while they're giving a reading to the public, most mediums don't do this onstage in front of an audience.

Readings for strangers have better results when I'm using automatic writing or phone calls. Perhaps it's because of performance anxiety when standing on the platform in front of a full church or when there are too many people on

Zoom calls. Recently, much better in small breakout rooms on Zoom. Even spirit names are accurate!

My psychic sensitivity increased as I healed past memories and emotions, had quiet time during the COVID-19 shutdown and while writing this book. It is important to work on developing oneself by having a healthy body and mind, actively healing and clearing out old traumas and beliefs in order to know which thoughts are coming from spirits and which are coming from own head. I've gone to psychotherapy to heal childhood, domestic violence, and racism trauma off and on for years, so it makes sense that my mediumship has improved.

The accelerated pace of the universe has forced, or given an opportunity, for us all to let go of old emotional pains and habits by constantly shaking up the old routines in our lives during the two years leading up to the coronavirus pandemic. It prepared us for the 2020 stay-at-home orders, during which we've had extra time to reflect on our lives. Both inner personal and outer societal and governmental flaws were exposed. Addictions, overeating, substance abuse, domestic violence with beatings and sexual abuse of partners and children increased. Long-time government corruption and lying were exposed too. So were social injustices such as racism, sexism, classism, and health disparities. Food and other shortages at the grocery store—if you were lucky enough to have a grocery store nearby—shocked our sense of security. Businesses closed, although the government attempted to boost the economy with stimulus packages. Also, because of looting, other stores were forced to close. The uncertainty had us praying and wanting to know what to do next.

My sense of knowing has increased, just knowing without knowing how I know. So perhaps mediumship will now come easier for me. I consider myself a person with the ability to hold space for the spirit energies to come through other mediums. That is why I regularly attend the Church of the Spirit and the new Zoom meetings. I've recommitted myself because most of the new mediums there now are devoted to evidential mediumship. Therefore, although there are times when I am not in the mood or feeling physically well, I come anyway to take deep breaths, pray, and chant silently to provide energy to the spirits and the medium. For myself, I don't really need personal readings from the church because my loved ones communicate with me almost daily in many different ways. I often share the inspiration I've received from my loved ones with other people who are struggling.

The quality of a message given by a medium depends on your loved one's ability and style of communication from the other side. It helps for you to be relaxed and open to receive the message. Usually, if you are experiencing the initial intense emotional pain of grieving, your loved ones may wait a few months after their passing. Know that a medium has no control over which one of your deceased family or friends will decide to communicate with you. Very few mediums can say the correct names, so don't be disappointed or think the message is not for you. It also helps to be fully present, observant, and participating in your own everyday life in order to recognize the pictures and information that the medium is bringing through for you. Knowing some of your family history also helps.

Your loved ones in spirit will use other ways to show you that they still come around you at home. Their favorite songs may suddenly come on the radio. The phone rings with their number in the caller ID. Their photos appear on your phone. They leave coins in odd places, send you animals or ideas and inspiration to do activities that you previously enjoyed together, and in many other ways.

A Three-Way Call

Recently, I was pleasantly surprised by my mediumship abilities during everyday activities in the following phone call.

April 2020. In a dream, all night long, I kept seeing an image of a small, white bowl with a black rim. I wondered what it meant, but mostly I was getting annoyed. I gave up on trying to sleep. I was reaching for my notebook to journal about a request to do a spirituality presentation for the Association of Black Psychologists. I thought of how I was enjoying reading near-death experience stories again by authors explaining the wisdom gained during and after their experience. Because of the COVID-19 pandemic, I had a sense of urgency that my first book should be about my mother's reappearance via mediums ten years after she died. She found a way to nurture and guide me. The book could be comforting to others that were grieving. All these were projects that I could have gotten started on that morning. But I wasn't expecting what happened next.

I absentmindedly reached for the phone. I heard my younger sister's name, Naimah. I was questioning myself, why was I calling her? We talked yesterday and last night. Yet when Naimah answered, I said, "I keep seeing a bowl, a white bowl with a black rim. I'm not sure how to describe it. It has bumps on the outside, but it is small and smooth on the inside."

Naimah said, "Mom had a bowl like that."

"She did? The bumps are shaped like fruit."

I grabbed my tablet, opened a browser, and googled "white bowl with a black rim." Not helpful. The photos were of plain white bowls with a black rim. Then I heard "grapes with vines," so I typed in "white bowls with grapes and vines." There the bowls were! "Milk glass" also entered my mind just before I saw that some of the bowls were labeled as such. There were pictures of milk glass goblets too.

I said, "I remember the goblets."

"Mom had those too."

"I'm seeing more bowls. Why is she showing me bowls?"

"Because she used to collect bowls," Naimah said, "and I do too. I have the bowls that she used to let the bread rise in. Blue on the outside with white on the inside. I have her full stainless steel bowl set too, with all the different-sized bowls stacked inside each other."

"I'm seeing another white bowl. It has even bigger bumps, like a cantaloupe. No, like a muskmelon. Like the outside of a muskmelon, but it's white. I'm seeing stairs, with a bright light at the top of the stairs."

"At our first house, I used to almost fall down the stairs because I had vertigo," she replied.

"No, this is looking up the stairs. I'm seeing a post at the bottom of the stairs. A brown wooden post with a crystal ball shape on the top. It looks like a crystal ball, except it's painted with brown paint. But why was it painted?" My attention was drawn to the wood, the beautiful natural wood cabinets in the dining room.

Then back to the back stairs. I describe what I'm seeing. "So now I remember this is at the second house we lived in. There is a window on the landing halfway up the stairs. The light from the window is getting bigger and brighter. I now see the light from the open back door at the top of the stairs coming through the screen door. There is a coatrack, or at least coats hanging on a wooden rod, in an alcove in the dark hallway. The back door is closed now."

"I don't know. I don't remember the coatrack. I don't remember the back hallway."

"Underneath the bottom of the coats, near the floor is a hat," I said. "It's in the shadows. Did she wear hats? I think I remember one hat. Did she wear a hat when she was in the garden? My best times with her was when Mom was teaching me how to bake and the names of plants in the backyard garden. I still remember. She's showing me garden tools."

"I have her garden tools. I found the garden tools wrapped in paper after she died. I got them back. I made our sister give them back to me."

Then I realized that the phone call was like having a three-way conversation between me, Naimah, and her mother who was my foster mother, in spirit.

"Mom is still showing me the hat with cobwebs on it. It's in the shadows near the floor. Why is she still showing me the old hat with the cobwebs?"

"Because it's old hat. I know it already. I don't need to hold on to it anymore."

"Hummm. Sounds like you need to dust it off, clear the cobwebs, and come out of the shadows. Get back in the world garden and help it grow."

She started talking about something she found on Facebook about the coronavirus.

"No, no, no, no, no! She's saying, 'Naimah, stop it!' You're doing what Mom did before she passed over! Not eating, not sleeping. That's what the light at the top of the stairs is. The stairs were going up, not down! Going up into the light. Passing over."

"But I like my life. I like living. There's some who say that they didn't start living until they were in their seventies," Naimah said.

Huh? Mom died in her seventies. My mother died in her seventies. Doesn't make sense to finally get a taste of living late in life and then pass over!

This three-way call was an unexpected natural spirit communication. Naimah and I talk regularly on the phone, but it was halfway through the call that I realized that our mom was giving a message to Naimah through me. Mom used images, symbols, and metaphors to communicate. Understanding these added to my mediumship skills.

Chapter 21: Spirit Helps Write This Book

Encouragement to Write

Almost as soon as I started going to the Church of the Spirit in 2012, most of the medium messages from my deceased relatives and friends were for me to write, to share my experiences and tell my story. I did write, but I never told the mediums anything about it. This was because I was only writing in private composition books about my dreams, spiritual experiences, emotional events and my responses to my psychotherapist. Graduate school was so traumatic it forced me to continuously process my feelings in my journals as well as in assigned reflection papers. I prayed and asked for spirit experts in heaven, guardian angels, and spirit guides to help me write my research papers and exams. Thereafter, my school assignments flowed. I was able to relax and not be so stressed out. But I was too busy to even think of writing a book, plus I didn't think people would accept or understand my struggles or spiritual experiences.

Here are some of the mediums' messages:

8-19-2012. "Again, I feel a lot of energy." She gestures with her hands along the sides of her head. "That you've been hearing more auditory messages. You need to start writing some of this down."

Actually, at that time, I wasn't getting auditory messages. I didn't know what the medium was talking about. Later, during automatic writing, I did get telepathic thoughts that were messages.

10-27-2012. "I see paintings. Do you do a lot of painting?"

"Yes, sometimes." I shrug.

"Do you write poetry?"

"No."

"Well, you should. It's good to give what's inside to the outside. Everyone is different. Just like two people can look at the same thing and see something different, two artists will each paint something different. So it is with your writing. It will come from your inside and inspire others. You have the beauty around you and the sparkles in your eyes of an artist."

2-10-2013. "A woman is here with a quill pen with a feather. Do you write poems? She's showing me beautiful poetry and prayers. You're writing, and it's flowing, with the right syntax. She's using old-fashioned tools. She throws some kind of sand on the ink that will make the words permanent. They will be permanent because people will listen to what you write. Share your wisdom.

"You need to write your story down. Tell your story. It helps other people. Your words are powerful. When people hear your story, your story will be empowering. Please, if there is some way to publish it, we will help."

9-29-2013. "A man here who uses a lot of big words. So many words that I don't even know. He's telling you about the writing. You haven't felt like writing. Get the tape recorder out. Speak into it just three minutes every day. You meet up with a lot of interesting people. Write down some of these stories"

James must have seen me pick up a tape recorder once and then put it down that night. He may have even inspired me to think of it. After this message, I started using an old cassette tape recorder. It was emotionally and timewise much easier for me than I thought it would be. I talked and recorded as I prepared for bed, got undressed, and braided my hair. For thirty minutes, not three minutes! I said whatever came to mind, which is different from worrying whether a future reader can understand it or about the grammar, spelling, formatting, or scenarios. Some afterlife communication books report spirit messages are sometimes heard in the background when listened to carefully on cassette tapes and other recording devices.

4-7-2013. "A strong animal stands here next to you with love. You've been really opening up your soul recently, a lot over the past two weeks. By soul, I mean open your soul to other people. Helping other people. People need

CHAPTER 21: SPIRIT HELPS WRITE THIS BOOK

to know about your struggles. You need to tell your story because you're a very resilient person. People need to hear your story to know they can make it through hardships too."

11-3-2013. "You need to start writing down your prayers. Your prayers are powerful and inspirational to others."

2-9-2014. "I have someone here. Your mother, or someone like a mother to you. She says she's proud of you. She's glad you've decided to write. I don't know if you've begun to write yet, but at least you've decided to write. You'll be writing about grief and loss. A lot of people will be coming to you who have had losses."

4-27-2014. "I see three spirits here with you today. They're your new muses. They're helping you with your writing. There is art there too, but it is mostly writing. The spirit standing behind you brings you strength. You'll have more strength with the spring and summer."

6-23-2014. "Need to write and tell your story. It will be beneficial."

3-16-2015. "I see you doing great work with people after you graduate. You will be using your spirituality in your work. Later, not now, you'll be right there. Maybe in five years. There is a woman who was a writer who is helping you."

This came true in 2019 when I interned at a spiritually integrated psychotherapy clinic.

2015. "Keep writing, writing. Maybe journaling. Later it will develop into something else as you have more time. Maybe use your writing as a blog. Your writing will help others."

9-11-2018. "Then I want to look at the writing. I feel like the writing projects that you have in mind are off to the side of your desk. And again, that's okay. You can only do one thing at a time. But make sure you leave them on your desk, and they don't end up on the floor." The medium laughs and laughs. "Or under a pillow."

"Yeah." I laughed in agreement.

"Or forgotten. Like, 'I'll do this later.' Then it gets pushed off. So, with your writing projects, they want them on your desk. It's okay if they are not centered on your desk. But they don't want them anywhere other than on your desk. Because this is something, I feel like it's a calling. This is something that is calling to you. Something that would be really important for you. If you are not writing now, writing while you are waiting for this placement. It's kind of a nice thing to do. Even if it's writing about or journaling about the frustration of what this has been like in graduate school. You know?"

"Yes."

"The people that you are going to be helping are going to be facing the very same challenges. So, there could be some good inspiration there for a blog. Or something else that could be just as helpful."

While I was looking through my old journals, I found an email from 2004 from someone I met at a Chicago IANDS meeting. She had a near death experience after an electrical accident. In the email, she wrote:

When we were talking that day, I had such a strong feeling that you could affect many women. It is through these book tours and lectures that your book will become well known and your information will be helpful to others. I have never known anyone that can go from being homeless and still maintain a smile that lights up the universe. Your life is in a transitional state that is going to give you the courage to go back and capture all of the information that you have been collecting over the many years. I too have done the automatic writing. It has been put in manuscript form, and I'm looking for an agent with connections to a good publishing company. Please stay in touch. I want to hear more about your story. May the light of spirit shine on you the way your smile shines on us all. You will write a book and go on book tours, telling your story and teaching. I know a ghostwriter who can help! It is your light. People need to see your light, which they can't get from books. Love, Betty."

The books, yes. But I didn't like the idea of touring the country promoting a book! Neither Betty nor I knew then that I was about to be homeless again in 2005. My great-aunt-in-law, who persuaded me to move from the city to a small suburb to live with her, unexpectedly passed away. Her daughters from other states came in and wanted me out of their mother's house, not caring that affordable, wheelchair-accessible apartments were rare and had years-long waiting lists. They actually locked me out of the house. A day later, their brother called the police, who came and sent one of my cousins stomping out the door and down the sidewalk to her car and quickly driving away. Because my name was on the lease, I got to stay in the house until an apartment opened up six months later in the city. Three months after that, I moved again, to the apartment where I've been living for fifteen years now.

At some point during those fifteen years, I lost contact with Betty. There were ongoing health challenges with the paralyzing neuromuscular disease doctors had diagnosed me with only a year before I met her. The constant nerve pain was agonizing, especially at night. When I overdid activities during the day, my achy muscles and joints wouldn't let me sleep. Never knowing what was going to happen next with other parts of my body, I was depressed. With heaven's help, my health gradually improved. Instead of the doctors' prognosis of rapid decline, my health plateaued and kept improving.

Meanwhile, nighttime dreams and messages were nagging me to return to college because "A mind is a terrible thing to waste." In awe, and wondering how I was going to do it, I applied and was accepted to graduate school, first for a master's degree and then two years later for a doctorate too!

Understandably, I was mostly in survival mode, so I completely forgot about Betty until recently, in 2020. As she had predicted, my life was "in a transitional state that is going to give you the courage to go back and capture all of the information that you've been collecting over the many years," as I found twenty years of personal journals! My life was about to transition in 2004, but fifteen years later, I was writing my first book while in a new transitional state, along with the rest of the United States. I graduated with my doctorate in the midst of the COVID-19 pandemic. I hope that she will forgive me for forgetting her. Occasionally I had the opportunity to go to Chicago IANDS meetings. Thereafter I didn't see Betty.

Honestly, and I'm grateful, my life became incredibly busy, at times overwhelming, with even more twists and turns since then to add to the book that Betty predicted. I still wasn't thrilled know about traveling. Flying using a power wheelchair is often a nightmare. Airlines are known for damaging wheelchairs, this happened with mine, without paying any compensation or providing an identical or better wheelchair replacement. That is, of course, a whole other story. Along the way, I have become a better, more confident public speaker and writer. Until I had to write my dissertation/clinical research project, I honestly wasn't a great writer. What I wrote about was good and interesting, but I had no idea about grammar or organizing my writing. For example, in evaluating my final paper for an undergraduate advanced writing class in 1995, the teacher wrote:

"The many grammar, spelling, and punctuation mistakes, together with the syntactic errors hindered the outcome of your manuscript. You did, however, successfully extend and flesh out many of the original episodes in your chapters, which was a welcome addition, one that served to break up, what becomes elsewhere, a dry step-by-step narration of events. Your most recent chapters, while they have potential, are sketchy at best, both lacking sufficient development of idea and closure. Final grade = C (at 70%)."

Through writing graduate school research papers and exams, I gradually taught myself how to write well.

Finally I Began Writing Books

In 2018 I started writing a book about sandtray therapy but had to stop as I pursued and obtained a clinic training internship. Nearer graduation, in 2020, I heard the word "write" several times as I was falling asleep at night. Too tired, I really didn't want to be bothered! But then a month later, there was an urge and unseen push to write about the benefits of mediumship, especially with the coronavirus, with people's fears of dying and grieving for those who died. It was as if heaven was saying that my book was needed now, ASAP!

In midlife years, people that you know begin dying of aging and illness. The COVID-19 pandemic was a reminder that I too might not have many years left. I wanted to leave a legacy. Writing books was one way to share. But what if I didn't live that long? Graduate school—a master's degree and then a doctorate—took ten years out of my life. And there were ten years of being physically ill before that. What would happen in the next ten years to delay writing my books? If I die, will twenty years of my personal journals, along with five shelves of books, just get dumped in the dumpster in the backyard, similar to what happens to my elderly neighbors' books?

I started sharing my writing every day with someone, anyone. Words of encouragement and inspiration. I emailed or texted the spirit-inspired messages that came to me early in the morning soon after I woke. Short stories and ideas.

Facebook hasn't made sense to me as a form of communication because it is so impersonal when people post photos of themselves with only a few words. A cousin and I used to write long letters to each other and send them by snail mail. We vowed to save each other's letters and write a book about each other's life. But after emails and texts were invented, our words got shorter and shorter, and our personal letters ceased.

COVID-19 got me serious about writing this book, so I began. Rereading the spirit messages eight years later helped me keep going, especially through the tough, emotionally anxious memories that came up while writing a memoir. Every morning for six months, as soon as I awakened, I wrote for a couple of hours—whatever came to my mind relevant to the memories of my mother, our common experiences, and wisdom gained from life lessons. Then I typed these in the appropriate chapters. The writing process became easier and easier as I allowed spirit to show me what to do next, what was needed, and where to find information. I let go of worrying about the typical structure of writing books, and the encouragement from spirit kept coming.

Spirit Fest 2020

"Maya Angelou comes through for you. Did we talk about this? Or is she just telling me that you talk to her? You talk to her?"

"No. Maybe I should."

"But she is saying, 'Come talk to me.' She wants you to tell stories. You've got a whole life of stories. This is different from mediumship, your life story. Your life story would be interesting to children and adults. So, you might want to tell stories from your life, because you've seen a lot. It's very moving. You now just want to record what you've lived for others. It will bring you great joy. So, the spirit is saying, it's not just the book. The book is just part. Keep going on that book, but also do other things. Like those story hours on Zoom for the public library. You could tell stories about intuition and mediumship on Zoom. You could tell them about their heritage." (From the medium Janyce).

This is a new medium who really doesn't know me and hasn't heard my stories. In fact, very few people have heard my stories. The stories are coming out of me as I write this memoir about my mother and mediumship. Yet spirit is telling me that I need to share my stories in more ways than writing books. The medium may be psychically picking up on the fact that this past week, while co-facilitating postelection support groups, I observed that telling some of my life experiences was helping young people have hope for their future.

August 2020. More help from spirit. "Thank you for The Jungle Book! It literally fell off the bookshelf into my arms!" I caught it as I was gently pushing aside a stack of books to get to another book, *Heading towards Omega,* which seemed easy enough to get to since it was straight back and in the corner.

The adult version of *The Jungle Book*, by Rudyard Kipling, doesn't have pictures inside. The cover is pale green and has a sketched outline of a motionless elephant enclosed in a square. Aha! My fingers opened it to the middle, straight to the beginning of the Rikki-Tikki-Tavi story. I didn't even have to use the table of contents!

It happened again. I was looking for my journal or other earlier writings about the trauma of having my hair regularly combed or hot-combed when I was a young child. For a whole day, I couldn't seem to find anything. I couldn't find the journal dated for April and May 2019, when I did my presentation on hair for the Association of Black Psychologists. The next day, instead of finding the composition journal, I pulled a file folder from a lower shelf that contained what I wrote in 1998 about my second marriage. It brought up a lot of intense feelings. I did not feel like reading any more of it. I avoided writing for the rest of the day. The hair topic was traumatic enough, so I certainly didn't want to be reminded of what my abusive second husband did! But I breathed deeply and courageously typed up the information about life with him anyway. Healing wasn't done yet! Sigh!

Writing Help from My Dreams

In a dream, as I was waking up, I saw white notecards hanging on a clothesline. The cards in the middle of the clothesline each had a metal binder ring holding it up, giving me the flexibility to rearrange the order. Perhaps this was advice to add more information about the middle part of my life. I'd been writing and dictating voice-to-text on my iPhone and iPad, but I was afraid to risk using a touchscreen to move large sections of paragraphs to the appropriate chapters.

I'd been waiting for my new laptop so, hopefully, I'd be able to only see one page at a time and use a mouse instead of a touchscreen. Then I remembered that most laptops use a trackpad. Perhaps that's why the guidance from heaven was to use index cards first to get a better idea of how the chapters needed to be arranged before attempting this task on a computer.

The index cards were surprisingly helpful. It didn't take as long as I thought it would to write out the topics, chapter titles, and subtitles in pencil. The four-by-six index cards, however, were too big to fit on my small table. Later I added three-by-five index cards for the subtitles. Anyway, the cards helped me quickly arrange the titles in the order that events happened and add a few other headings. It gave me confidence that I was on the right track and reduced my fears.

During the COVID-19 crisis, while Black Lives Matter protests and other people's side agendas distracted from the real problems of the United States, frustrated looters caused nearby Apple and Best Buy stores to close. Instead of being able to go into either store, get advice, and take my computer home the same day, I had to order it online and wait three to four weeks for delivery to my home. After three years, my Windows 10 PC, which I bought from Best Buy, wasn't charging anymore. Although I paid $100 annually for Geek Squad coverage, I could not get an appointment by phone or online because of COVID-19 social distancing, extra cleaning, and staff shortages due to increased demand for electronic products and repairs as students switched to remote learning and employees worked from home. I needed other strategies while I waited for my laptop to arrive. My prayers were answered with the index card dream.

When I got scared while writing the middle part of my book, I wondered if I was doing it right. Did I have too few pages or too little information? Was I trying to do too much with three themes? Would the mediumship main title get enough space and emphasis? Would people think I was weird, and would my family disown me? Were my scenes exciting enough? Emotional enough? Would I lose sight of my overall focus? Finding the book, *Breaking Ground on Your Memoir,* got me going again. The authors helped me understand that these fears were common while writing a memoir. They also recommended several ways to structure my draft.

My best helpers were, of course, my spirit helpers. They were literally writing with me in my sleep. What was odd was that I would be excited to get this text that I was seeing very clearly onto paper as soon as I woke up. But with notebook in hand, my mind seemed to blank, and my pen was still. Then my mind filled with another different theme to write for that day instead of the dream messages. One day, spirit did give me direct instruction to put spirit messages from my journals into this book. I didn't argue with this new direction because it gave me a rest from writing about old memories from childhood, marriages, and graduate school which was, although wonderfully healing, also emotionally painful at times. From then on, I was content to follow the spirits' lead as I observed how each writing "assignment" fit neatly into the flow of the book's unfolding. I was beginning to write from my heart and soul. Most authors report that after a while, their books begin to write themselves. This was beginning to happen to me too!

***

My friend Ruth joined my other loved ones from the Other Side to help me write this book. She was also a mother that wanted to get through to her children and the rest of her family and continue to give them her love. It's still difficult to describe in writing what a spirit visit is like, so I guess she's giving me on-the-job training! As I wrote, her thoughts that became my thoughts, flowed so fast that I could barely keep up. I probably should've taken the shorthand class when I was in high school! I was anxious about whether people would understand these metaphysical happenings, but it was important for the family and the rest of the world to know as many people were grieving from the effects of the COVID-19 crisis and shutdown.

PART FOUR

WISDOM GAINED

Chapter 22: Coping with the COVID-19 Pandemic

Grieving

Six months into the stay-at-home and social distancing orders, was when my dear friend Ruth died. I initially met her at Chicago IANDS meetings and then we began going to the Church of the Spirit. We celebrated birthdays together and enjoyed hiking in the botanical gardens and forest preserves. Naturally, fears surfaced of the possibility of some of my other friends close to my age dying. The following week, two more friends were in the hospital. Both of them had serious illnesses, but not COVID-19. One friend had three procedures within one week, including a surgery. This brought up memories of a dear friend and neighbor James that went into the hospital, had several procedures, and never came home. He died a few months later. The theme of going away and never seeing people again made grieving for my friend very painful because it reminded me of the losses I'd had since childhood, like leaving Philadelphia and not knowing then that I was never going to see Grandma again.

Our only consolation is that people's spirits don't die, as Ruth joyfully showed me. She made a spirit connection with me soon after she died. So did my dear older neighbor friend, and Mother Dear, and my great-uncle a few years before her. Ruth was the fastest. She came to me the next day. That Saturday night, she came through the mediums at the Church of the Spirit with messages for a few of her other friends:

CHAPTER 22: COPING WITH THE COVID-19 PANDEMIC

"Our friend and our church healer, Ruth, is here. She's actually in this Zoom call, and I think that she wanted to come to all of us. She sends her love. I'm actually in communication with her. Haneefa, Ruth is saying that she values and loves the time that she spent with you. She wants to say thank you for your friendship with her. You are one of a handful of people who took time, outside of the church, to be part of her life. She says that you were very touched by her. It was very much a mutual sisterhood. You shared a lot with herbs and plants. She says to keep in touch. You are a natural medium, and she'll help you. She says, 'God bless you. Bless you.' Such a beautiful feeling I'm getting from her right now."

Ruth's spirit visited me three times at my home that week, more often than we usually visited each other in a year. I had to chuckle when I realized this. Her gorgeous smile, along with her large eyes, her face in front of my face, is in my mind's eye. I couldn't help but smile back. As I was journaling in my notebook while sitting on my bed, it felt as if she were sitting inside me as I wrote. Astonishingly, her mannerisms became my mannerisms, how she would just shake things off. As she stood and shook her spirit body, a wave of love and delight came over me.

I needed this encouragement to just "shake it off." I was depressed after Ruth passed away because I fretted over how many more activities we could have done together if I had not been immersed in graduate school for eight years. A few other regrets haunted me. The goals of earning a degree and gaining a profession are noble. However, you can almost lose your soul, family, friends, and community along the way because of all the ever-increasing, unnecessary, time-consuming tasks and commuting that are now expected. We've come to accept all this as normal. I felt guilty for not being a better friend and not having more time with her. Ruth felt my suffering and came to prove me wrong! She lifted my spirit and made me giggle. She also helped me experience the concept that time and space are illusions. So much for the excuse that I lived on the far North Side and she lived on the far South Side, miles apart!

Out of all the people I know who crossed over, Ruth's presence has been the strongest, perhaps because she was a medium and had had a near-death like experience. She came to me this morning while I was thinking about the Church of the Spirit's remembrance service for her. I was concerned and felt a little guilty for not saying to the family that it was normal for those closest to Ruth to not feel or experience her spirit presence as much as acquaintances would. I didn't want to make them feel worse by talking about Ruth's visits with me.

Ruth heard my dilemma and came again. Her face was directly in front of my face, smiling. I saw her beautiful, twinkling eyes. She laughed. Her laugh was contagious. Soon I was laughing. I thanked her. This was new for me, to experience a spirit lightly become a part of me. I wouldn't have known this was possible beyond the usual skills of seeing, hearing, and feeling spirits.

Early that morning, 4:30 a.m. to be exact, she helped me understand that she was coming to me to give encouragement to the family and let them know that she was still around. She could be with her daughters, her sisters, their children, and friends with enough love to go around—simultaneously, even! And maybe faster and better than when she was around. Of course, if you're hurting from grieving, you don't want to know that fact right away because you would have to acknowledge that she's gone. That hurts too much. Even mediums who have lost loved ones say they can't bring their own dear relatives' or friends' messages through.

Ruth came again a night later. I became conscious of her when I was sitting in bed, with my left hand holding my head up the way Ruth used to sit. It was as if Ruth's body impression was lightly on me yet a little in front of my body, not quite me. As I looked down at my body, it was as if she were again smiling and laughing. So I gleefully laughed too. There are some advantages to living alone!

Like Ruth, I often reach out and telephone people. They are truly grateful, staying on the phone with me for hours and, at the end, saying thanks for calling. I know what it feels like to be lonely, so I try to make sure others don't have to feel lonely. I have friends in nursing homes that can't get visitors now because of the COVID-19 shutdown. But this year I've needed to care for me too. Now I mostly call those who call me. Next to forgiveness, being able to receive as well as give love is probably at the top of the list of the most challenging life lessons. Friends passing or being seriously ill in hospitals or nursing homes gives us appreciation for all the people in our lives. We don't know who or what will still be existing when the COVID-19 pandemic crisis is over.

Learning Gratitude

Living in Zimbabwe for seven months during 1997 and 1998 also prepared me for coping with the COVID-19 crisis. The bare shelves in stores during the COVID-19 shutdown are a common occurrence in other countries. My international friends, new to the United States, would ask me to go to the store with them. They would point to the twenty or more brands of the same item, turn to me, and say, "Tell me which one I should buy."

Money does us no good if the food doesn't make it to the grocery stores. The shelves of small shops are bare on islands such as Jamaica if the ship is late coming in. This happened in England when the price of petrol was too high and delivery trucks couldn't bring milk to the shops. The dollar bill, since it is made of paper and cloth, might provide some nourishment, but you can't chew a credit or a debit card. You can't even see your money, don't even know if it's really in the bank! During the COVID-19 crisis, we didn't know how many people would have had money, as the shutdown continued. There was a shortage of money as well as of supplies. Some businesses went bankrupt within six months.

In the rural villages in Zimbabwe, I learned to be grateful. I was there as a student in the School for International Training study abroad program, as part of my senior year independent studies requirement for the bachelor's degree World Issues Program. An elder man there yelled at me once, "How can you say that you don't like guavas? How can you say that you don't like this or that? Here we are happy to eat whatever is in season!"

Eating what was in season meant delicious, steamed, buttered pumpkin with the leaves, spicy bitter greens, okra, plums, bananas, and monkey oranges. For protein, there were huge, coarse, tough corn on the cob, mopane worms—giant caterpillars, eaten fresh or dried—and strong-smelling dried fish. Otherwise, you ate the same meal for breakfast, lunch, and dinner: one plate of a stiff, boiled, finely ground cornmeal similar to grits with a couple of spoonfuls of cooked collard greens. Occasionally you had rice and potatoes. There were no second helpings. You were happy for what was on your plate. Zimbabwe had been in a drought for several years already. Their chickens, cows, and goats were very skinny as there was little grass to eat or money to buy grain or hay. They rarely had meat, except on holidays and celebrations a few times a year. Large families shared two very skinny chickens, and there was no such thing as "I want the leg, or breast, or thigh!" Yet physically, they were very strong. They didn't waste anything. Ate every part of the animal. There were no garbage trucks coming weekly to collect the garbage. Their homestead would end up littered, so they found creative ways to reuse what they had.

Due to the drought, women and girls walked for miles to fetch water from a river that dried up so much that they had to dig under the sand to get to the water. They also walked miles to gather small bundles of fallen branches from the few trees remaining. There was no electricity or running water or toilets in the villages. In the main cities, the water bills were so high that those who could not afford them, like my friend, had to ration their water daily. That meant that my friend gave me a small basin of water in the morning and another one at night to wash up in. No flushing the toilet after each use unless we had a bowel movement. There were no showers or baths, even though she had a bathtub and a shower in her beautiful ranch-style home. She took the dirty water from bathing and washing dishes and used it to do laundry, and although it was all soapy, she then took it outside to water the small vegetable garden. Her white neighbors next-door watered their lawns, gardens, and flowering trees with a hose, oblivious to others' suffering—they could have shared at least a little of their water!

But I am embarrassed and ashamed to say that the Zimbabweans also had to teach me how to share. Although every day they shared what little they had with me, many times I didn't think or know to share until they shyly asked me for something that I had. Young and naïve, I didn't understand about currency exchange, happily paying $35 to get my hair braided or giving a gift of ZWD$200, which sounds like a lot but was only US$3.50 and US$20, respectively, and didn't allow the Zimbabweans to buy much.

We take a lot for granted here in the United States. We complain and waste a lot. Yet each meal that we have is a feast, often with several servings of meat and choices of breads, pastas, rice, potatoes, fruits, and vegetables available all year. Each office party celebration, frequently several times a week, is a huge holiday feast in comparison. We absentmindedly let the water run in our sinks and our showers. Gallons of water used for wudu ablution before the five daily prayers is also a luxury, although the hadiths indicate that Muslims can use dust when water is not available. We are unaware that when we overuse the water in our areas, there is not enough to evaporate to make rain in other parts of the world. We throw away food because we don't like it, or it wasn't what we wanted, or—as my mother used to say—our eyes are bigger than our stomachs. What she meant, of course, was "Why did you put so much on your plate if you weren't going to eat it?"

Zimbabweans and several years of using a wheelchair have taught me to be grateful for whatever food I have in my cabinet and refrigerator and whatever anybody gives me. Twenty years ago, my Zimbabwean friend sat me down and gently explained that when you're invited to someone's home, you eat the food served to you because the host has sacrificed time, effort, and a few precious dollars for you. So I went on and ate the chicken, although I was vegetarian at the time. Her chicken was plump and tasty! I was especially aware during the COVID-19 crisis that many people did not have what I had. Unless homeless, we are all privileged with luxuries and conveniences—meaning most of what we have is not required for survival—no matter what skin complexion in the United States. Therefore, what I have is plenty enough. Satisfied, in gratitude, I humbly remind myself to eat and live in moderation. To share, whatever I have. Knowing that whatever I have is enough gives me peace and faith in times of uncertainty.

It Could Be Worse

The COVID-19 crisis also reminded me of when I became homeless upon returning from Zimbabwe. Imagine returning to the United States after doing everything together with lots of other people. We slept together in one room on the floor of the kitchen hut in the village, we ate together, we worked together, we talked together, and we walked miles together. The incredible unconditional love and caring we had for each other. Grateful for the opportunity to just be myself and not have to hide any part of myself, my skin color or my spirituality. We rode together in taxi minivans that did not move from the main pickup point until they were completely full of passengers. Squished together almost on top of each other, men and women, it didn't matter. The taxi did not move until even the trunk was full! This, of course, was uncomfortable for me at first, I had to get used to it. In the United States, we often try to have a whole seat to ourselves on the bus and are often the only passenger in a taxi. Yet now back here, I missed all of this togetherness and shoulder-to-shoulder contact.

I was living in a friend's apartment while I wrote my résumés and cover letters and went on job interviews. Eventually I didn't have any money left, and I had overstayed my welcome. Other friends paid for my rent at a rooming house for a few months, but I ended up homeless. So yes, it is true that we are all only one or two paychecks away from becoming homeless. Your education, physical attractiveness, or where you live, it doesn't matter. Homelessness can happen to anyone, along with social deprivation, the rejection and isolation from people, even more so during the COVID-19 crisis.

A case worker paid for me to get my belongings out of storage, and among them, I found my *Sacred Path Cards: The Discovery of Self Through Native Teachings,* book. Reading the interpretation of the card I pulled brought me out of the misery of loneliness and depression. The card was 38: Field of Plenty: Ideas / Needs Manifested. In my despair, I had forgotten the simple principle that it helps to be grateful to God as though you have what you need or want already. This belief is also part of Indigenous and ancient African cultures: what you imagine comes true, so be careful what you daydream about. Especially in a peaceful, meditative state, what you visualize does come true. Reading this restored my faith and reminded me of my many blessings thus far, although I was homeless.

In July 1999, three months after I became homeless, I was blessed with transitional housing, although it was only one room and I shared a bathroom with another woman. Sometimes she forgot to unlock the door on my side of the bathroom. It was one room with roaches and people who woke us up at night banging on doors, begging for cigarettes. But it was my space, and warm. No more having to walk the streets in the cold, waiting for the shelters to open, hoping there was room for one more. Hoping there was enough food I could eat at the soup kitchens. I truly had a lot to be grateful for. My needs had been met without me purposely visualizing anything, but I had been in too much despair and hopelessness to notice. I began expressing my gratitude and what

I wanted for my future that I could now believe was possible. Within a month after reading the *Sacred Path Cards* book, the homeless services agency moved me to a large, one-bedroom apartment with my own kitchen, where I could cook my own food.

These Native American teachings of the Field of Plenty were about, to the best of my understanding, showing the pilgrims how to have gratitude for sharing the year's harvest and give thanks every day, not just on Thanksgiving Day. Most important, it was about letting go of a fear of scarcity and poverty, knowing there is plenty for all when we share and only use what we need. We are blessed globally with ideas that come to mind for creative problem solving. We just have to have the courage to put these new ideas into action for us all, going forward, with what we learned from the COVID-19 crisis and civil unrest experiences.

The energetic powers of the Field of Plenty were increased during the Harmonic Convergence of 1987, the first global peace meditation on a day that coincided with the alignment of six planets and the Earth's moon all facing the Sun. The event was planned based on predictions from an ancient Mayan calendar that humans would enter a phase of greater harmony and manifestation ability.

Modern humans recently discovered this ability to manifest, proving these ancient traditional beliefs through science. Unfortunately, the New Age concepts described in The Secret about the ability to manifest focus on material gain rather than on gratitude and promoting positive human evolution. We are seeing now, through the COVID-19 crisis and civil unrest, that we must share with each other. That includes respecting and substantially compensating the Native Americans, Africans and other indigenous people whose wisdom, labor, land, water, and minerals are still being stolen. We must show gratitude for Mother Earth, who somehow continues to keep us alive, and gratitude to heaven, which provides us with guidance and ideas.

Chapter 23: The Healing Process

Healing has to be approached holistically, meaning physically (safe homes, healthy food, sleep, exercise), emotionally (all feelings and being accepted and appreciated in relationships, communities), and spiritually (having faith, a reason for living, peace, harmony, and morality). We can't leave any of these out. The problem with simply taking pills is they only give temporary relief, but the situations that caused the disease are still there.

People kept saying to me, "You should write a book."

So I asked them, "What would you like to see or read in my book?"

Most of my friends told me they wanted to know how I was able to keep going in spite of the traumas, racism, discrimination, and many other obstacles, including having a physical disability, and still graduate from an intense clinical psychology doctoral program. People witnessed my healing in leaps and bounds over twenty years' time. But it took me until the end of this book to really look back on my life and contemplate how I had coped to be able to answer that question.

To be honest, I believe it's because I do not take antidepressants or any other psychiatric medications or self-medicate with alcohol or street drugs. There are people who have severe mental illness that may need to take medication for psychosis or mania to function. But for the stressors of daily life, even trauma, there are natural ways of healing ourselves and society.

I agreed to take the antidepressant Zoloft (sertraline) after I became homeless in 1999. Initially I did feel much better mentally and emotionally, but after six months, I began to notice that it was as if I didn't have a conscience. I didn't have urges or thoughts of doing anything wrong. Just no inner or gut feelings. This really bothered me to not have what I now know is my intuition. I weaned myself off Zoloft. I didn't sink that low again, perhaps because becoming homeless opened the way for me to finally receive services and support that I didn't have previously.

I didn't even take medicine for pain. No aspirin (acetylsalicylic acid), no acetaminophen, no ibuprofen, no narcotics. My body was too sensitive for any of these. Aspirin, acetaminophen, and ibuprofen all gave me asthma attacks. I couldn't even take epinephrine for asthma attacks or as a local anesthetic to numb an area for stitches because a half hour later, I'd faint as my heart rate sped up too fast. I couldn't tolerate allergy medicine. One small dose of Sudafed or Benadryl at bedtime had me literally feeling high for forty-eight hours, as if I didn't know where my feet were, as if I were taking big steps high off the ground! I thought, "Is this what they mean by being high?" After procedures or surgery, I tried Ultram and even morphine, but I could only take the first dose. The second dose, and sometimes even the first, would have me very, very nauseated, with the room spinning even as I lay on my bed. Then I was irritable and cranky the next day.

Nerve pain is awful. Most people who have neuromuscular diseases or spinal injuries will tell you that there really isn't any medicine that relieves it. Burning, crawling, stinging, stabbing, electric shocks, tingling, throbbing, aching sensations—often all at the same time. Don't let us get too cold or too hot. Paralyzed legs often feel like they are on ice, being freezer-burned at night even when it's 80 to 90 degrees outside! I had to learn to live with the pain.

It is acknowledging and accepting the emotional and mental pain that promotes healing. Feeling the pain, not trying to push away or push down, nor trying to swallow the tears, snot, anger, frustration, joy, and pleasure. Cry, sob, scream, yell, shake, dance it in and out. Breathe it out. Then you are gently releasing the intense energy felt as pain. God gave each of us feelings for a reason, mostly for survival. We need to know when we are feeling afraid and disappointed because our frustration shows us when there is a problem to be solved. We also cannot have true intimacy and true love if we numb our feelings.

Connection is also feeling the other person's needs, hurts, and desires. All of our feelings, physical, emotional, sensory, and energetic, make up our connection as One. It is our natural radar for determining the weather and what to do next. Women were given stronger emotions because mothers have to intuit infants' needs, because babies can't talk. A mother has to keep the children safe, so she feels out the environment to determine who she can trust. It was the same with men, but somehow, during our history, men turned off their emotions and their intuition.

People mistakenly think they have to use hallucinogenic drugs in order to connect to the unseen. Indigenous people were able to see heaven, feel bliss, travel astrally, and get guidance naturally. We have a strong need to connect to each other and the universe. Perhaps this is the Tree of Knowledge in the Garden that we've been taught is forbidden, but mostly it was forbidden by Satan (Iblis) because it would fulfill our love for life and God.

So-called alternative medicine has been here for centuries. Ancient Chinese medicine, Ayurvedic medicine, yoga, homeopathy, and traditional Indigenous healing all take mind, body, spirit, and the social environment into consideration when treating a person who has illness or dis-ease. The goal is to restore balance. Often when a person is sick, it is because the family and the community are unbalanced. Psychology and sociology were already built into these ancient healing systems. How much unnecessary stress can people endure? Hello, COVID-19! Globally, people's prayers were answered because we needed a major event to get us to slow us down from an impossible pace of destroying ourselves and the Earth to hopefully to restore us to balance.

I've had acupuncture, and it helped, but even Chinese herbs were too strong for me. Homeopathic medicine is what I primarily use. It is only taken occasionally, when a dis-ease comes up, and then only for a couple of days or weeks, or if it's an old, chronic condition, maybe for a couple of months. Not every day for the rest of your life! The remedy prescribed by a homeopathic doctor is designed specifically for your body and life situation. Only one medicine is needed to treat you from head to toe, emotionally, spiritually, and socially too. Not a separate pill for your knees, then another pill for your headache, and another pill for depression, and another pill for anxiety, and another pill for your stomach, plus more pills for the side effects and interactions from pharmaceutical drugs!

CHAPTER 23: THE HEALING PROCESS

Homeopathy—along with prayers, psychotherapy, friends, family, and living life to the fullest, being balanced without going to extremes—has taken me from barely being able to walk or talk or even feed myself to doing it all—going from diapers to dry panties, from being on a ventilator at night to breathing freely.

From my religious and health experiences, I've learned the hard way that no extreme is better than any other extreme. Similar to going on a fad diet, this all-or-nothing behavior and thinking won't last long! In fact, it usually creates even worse problems in other areas of life. Balance is the key to better relationships, health, and true abundance.

Deep breathing through the pain—emotional and physical—will release its grip. Be okay with having quiet time alone. No TV, radio, cell phone, or computer—not even a book. Deep breathing, prayer, meditation. But then just be. Be okay with just being you. Doing something with your hands helps too, such as being totally involved in a creative project. Cooking, gardening, building—woodworking, Legos—jigsaw puzzles, counting a jar of pennies, and of course any type of art will work.

I have used my mother's gift of introducing us to art throughout my life, both as a healing distraction from the physical pain and also as a way to express emotional pain. Most of my watercolor paintings are colorful, beautiful, and optimistic. I've tried to capture and share with others the brilliant colors and incredible love and peace of visiting heaven during my near-death experience. Older paintings were of me looking calm and happy on the outside but symbolically showing that I was shattered, often with a broken heart inside from all the losses in my life. There are paintings of the burning physical pain too.

Art is also how I made it through the grueling pain of academic anxiety and isolation during my doctoral program. The isolation of being married to a computer screen with nonstop assignments, 24/7, even as I tried to sleep. Continuous planning, analyzing, and deadlines. And then there was the isolation of often being the only Black American in the classroom, not seeing my people's true culture, history, or strengths in textbooks and professional journals—instead we were represented only as stereotypes and "problems." Yet these problems were those that any oppressed people have regardless of complexion or location in the world.

Creativity was my way of connecting to myself and the universe. It gave me a sense of satisfaction that I could not only still create but I could finish the work. I was compensating for the otherwise awful feeling of never being good enough, especially as college students are given too many assignments and projects to ever complete with pride. Even during appointments with clients, we were rushed. What's that song lyric? "Can't get no satisfaction." So, I did art throughout graduate school. My knitting became a colorful canvas small enough to travel with me on buses and trains.

Being fully engaged in and outside of psychotherapy sessions also helps. I usually journaled or did art soon after therapy sessions to process understanding of what the therapist was trying to teach me. I also journaled in between sessions whenever I felt intense emotions to help myself calm down and think more clearly, and sometimes directly before sessions to choose what to talk about with the therapist. This way of journaling I discovered on my own, because often therapists did not understand how to help me. Life goes on; therefore, this is how I had to survive, somehow, the other six days of the week!

In spite of the anxiety and the fear, I kept going. Just as I kept going in spite of the physical pain, I kept going forward each day in spite of fear of more losses, rejection, and self-doubt. Gradually, fear was mostly replaced with self-confidence and continuous, wonderful calm and inner peace. I stay away from TV shows and movies so as not to retraumatize myself. Our collective fascination with violence is pure crazy making! Instead, I believe in surrounding myself with mostly the positivity that I want in my life and the world.

Gradually I let go of perfectionism, shame, guilt, and other bad habits that my mothers role-modeled and from my own overcompensation of being too independent and silent after surviving domestic violence. Healing and letting go allowed me to enjoy life and start to have fun again. For full healing, you have to have a reason for living and strong faith to keep going. As, hopefully, you have seen and experienced from reading this book of my journey toward real faith, love, and healing, it takes a huge leap of faith to trust the unseen—even to trust persistent mommas and other spirit loved ones, guardian angels, spirit guides, and God. To be able to rely on guidance and follow that guidance to do life differently, moving us forward toward true human evolution, knowing that heaven blesses us daily.

CHAPTER 23: THE HEALING PROCESS

I want to emphasize that I'm not special. We are all born with these abilities. We can all heal ourselves and others. Doctors weren't taught in medical school that patients could heal themselves, and doctors that did know—hid this information for decades. Now the truth is told in books such as, *Mind over Matter: Scientific Proof That You Can Heal Yourself* and *The Power of Eight*. Other doctors have seen miracles when, not knowing what else to do, they prayed for their patients. (See, *Physicians' Untold Stories*). We also have the ability to change the weather, know the future, and experience real love and connection. We've just forgotten. Nowadays, constant distractions take us away from our true nature as co-creators in the universe. Having more quiet time during the day and deeper sleep with dreams at night help us reconnect to wellness.

Chapter 24: Spiritual Growth

For a long time after the trauma of my second marriage, I shuddered every time I heard the name God or Allah. However, having witnessed the many miracles of Allah (Pure Love) for others and myself, my faith is restored. As I experience the wonder, awe, and fascination of the intricate workings of the unseen universe in removing something as seemingly simple as an eyelash from the eye. How the tears rinse the eyelash down and toward the corner of the eye. They have just the right consistency, neither too thin nor too thick, to naturally remove the whole, long eyelash. Other times, a little eyelash is neatly rolled up, carried to the corner of the eye, and left to harden, annoying us into removing it. When I was three or four years old, I remember crying and jumping up and down because I had an eyelash or lint in my eye. Momma would say, "Come here, Haneefa." Then she would blow on my eye. If she didn't get it out the first time and I was still crying, she would blow again and again until the little hair was out. Now that most of my eyelashes are white, I again have to rely on what is bigger and more powerful than myself. By now, I know that the tears will eventually move whatever is in my eye, and my eye will stop being irritated. I trust that relief comes in God's time, yet swiftly—especially when we are patient.

My awe is there for God, for Great Mystery, Infinite Intelligence (No one really knows how the universe functions, so why fight over a name?), YHWH, Yahweh, Olodumare and even Allah, as long as I see and experience the source as pure love, peace, and true abundance. I don't do the traditional five daily prayers anymore. I rarely read or finish the whole Quran during Ramadan. I sure tried, again and again. But after being immersed in Islamic culture last year, I could no longer prostrate myself on a prayer rug behind men, or even alone after listening to Muslim women's stories of continued domestic violence and knowing how men everywhere, regardless of religion, still support each other in continued disrespect, devaluing, abuse, and harassment of women. Yet men benefit enormously from women's unpaid labor, sacrifices, compassion, and unconditional love.

Besides, if you really think about it, would you really feel safe prostrating yourself with your butt and vagina up in the air after being raped and sodomized by men who said they loved you? How could you do that for a god who is portrayed as a man with a mixed, confusing contradiction of a loving, merciful, yet vengeful god that allows men to have their way for centuries, destroying the peaceful homes, families, and communities that women try to maintain?

Wait a minute! Weren't you raised a Muslim? What's a nice young woman like you doing going to a church like that? You have a Muslim name. Do you know what your name means? One cabdriver years ago told me, "You were born a Muslim. Anyone turning back on Islam is going to hell!"

The Quran does state over and over again the penalties for being or becoming a disbeliever with very terrible descriptions of being tortured over and over again in hell. In some Muslim countries you could be maimed or killed for breaking Islamic laws or being accused of leaving the faith.

Nevertheless, I have not lost my faith. My faith is even stronger than when I was a devout practicing Muslim or when I was with my Muslim family. I still do five daily prayers and follow the other pillars of Islam just in a different way. The point is to live the main goals of religious beliefs, not just quickly go through the motions. I give regularly of my time, talents, and abundance as well as money. With a history of health problems and anorexia, I no longer fast. I've done annual Ramadan fasts, spiritual retreats with three-day water fasts, and four- to ten-day cleansing fasts, eating only fruits and vegetables during the change of seasons at the equinoxes and solstices. This resulted in emergency room visits, but I'd dutifully fast anyway. For people who don't eat much, fasting is easy, not a sacrifice or hardship. Besides that, to be able to fast is a luxury. A poor person is already fasting! The iftars—the feasts at the end of the day—defeat the whole purpose of Ramadan, which is to know what it feels like to have to starve and to sacrifice one's personal urges and desires. Ramadan also builds self-discipline and stamina, but, as you have seen, I already had plenty of, if not too much, self-discipline, and faith that in excess was detrimental to my health, as well as to the rest of my life.

Having had a near-death experience, I know that it is only what we do toward learning love and being and sharing love that will be questioned on Judgment Day. Love is our greatest challenge and lesson to learn. When we die in the flesh, we can't take anything with us—money, status, the house, the car, or the people who seemed to make or break us. Gone are all of our excuses for not loving or caring or using the unique talents given to each of us.

All of my prayers throughout the day are for the whole world's and the universe's healing, and they go like this:

Upon waking: "Thank you, All That Is, for another day in this illusion of an Earthwalk, with opportunities to fulfill our destinies and our sacred contracts to help each other to experience love, be love, learn more love, accept love, and share that love."

At mealtimes: "Thank you, All That Is, for your nourishment and healing. I accept this nourishment. I ask that my partaking of this food is only for the good of All That Is. I am grateful for the necessary sunshine, rain, and soil to grow the gardens that feed the animals from whom I ask permission to share of their meat. I'm grateful to all those who plant, harvest, transport, and provide my food. I ask that All That Is, everywhere, has plenty of safe and healthy food, safe and healthy resources, and, most important, a safe and healthy environment that is filled with true love, along with peace and harmony and unity within all and with all, as we are all connected as One."

For global healing: "I pray that all who have chosen to be birthed with male bodies accept healing, their hearts opened and cleansed and now filled with true love, peace, and harmony from within, accepting loving relationships and emotions that bring us true intimacy and connection. A fullness, an aliveness, that awakens our full potential as One."

My Fajar prayer begins upon awakening, while I am still in bed, as I greet the day with gratitude to all creation and my ancestors. Then I write in my journals the dreams and thoughts that come to me early in the morning—usually before sunrise, but not always. It is the first activity I do, whatever time I wake up.

The second prayer is a combination meditation and physical exercise, such as gently stretching my body from head to toes or practicing qigong, which releases old, stagnant energy, negative thoughts, moods, and old beliefs and then gives fresh energy. We are less likely to sin when we have inner peace, calm, guidance, and faith that we can make a difference in our lives. Not blaming others for how we feel inside, or for what we have or don't have. Knowing that it is heaven that provides for us.

My third prayer is in the afternoon, when again I take time out of my busy schedule to acknowledge and express gratitude to creation and my ancestors. I do brief physical exercise followed by a deep-breathing meditation. But most important, I purposely seek higher loving, divine guidance. Speaking aloud, I ask for guidance and have pen and paper ready in front of me. This, of course, also helps develop my mediumship.

I'm usually exhausted by the end of the day, so my evening and night prayers are less specific. Mostly I express gratitude for the day and do wudu ablution or a shower, followed by a silent cleansing prayer and visualization meditation to wash away any negativity accumulated from the day. Although these personal rituals may seem like a lot, the routines are brief, naturally flow, and are done as I feel like it, and they are regularly, creatively changed. I definitely notice the difference if days go by and I haven't done these self-care activities. My mood and my energy suffer.

On the Day of Judgment, during my life review, I want it to show that I loved more than hurt people during this lifetime, that I learned what love is and how to receive, accept, and share that love. That I used the talents that God gave me at birth to help others. Over my lifetime, I've noticed that it really doesn't matter what religion or belief I try out. Heaven still provides for me in abundance. Perhaps this abundance comes from living love, faith, sharing, and gratitude and following heaven's guidance. It may also be because I live simply, and I'm satisfied with what I have and what I've accomplished—not in terms of my many academic degrees but in emotional and spiritual growth, healing myself, my family, and the universe.

I've borrowed the good from several religions, beliefs, and theories. This is because each group has a few pieces but is missing a lot of the rest of the puzzle. Therefore, none can see the whole puzzle. It's the same with people. We need each other. No one has all the answers or the best way to live. Together, we can spiritually evolve.

I am a Muslim because I truly submit to the will of heaven and pray several times a day. I am a Christian because I believe in the message of Christ's love and our human ability to heal, feed, and accept everyone. I am a Jehovah's Witness because I have experienced and believe in eternal life, and as a Spiritualist, I know that life continues after the change commonly called death. And that we are responsible for our own happiness and unhappiness as we obey or disobey Natural Laws of the universe and that the door to reformation is never closed. This is very similar to Indigenous beliefs. Therefore I am my Indigenous ancestors' spirituality, both Native American and African, because I choose to live in community with councils of wise individuals, including wise youth and the natural environment to lead us, making sure that everyone is taken care of and not hurt psychologically or emotionally. Because when one person in the community doesn't have and hurts, then we all hurt!

I believe in only having what you need, and no more, so that everyone can share of the Field of Plenty and Ma'at. And, of course, connection to the environment and the universe and other dimensions beyond the intellectual. Use of Indigenous divination methods to ask God for spiritual guidance to know what might happen so that together we are prepared ahead of time. Leaders then are guided by universal Natural Laws instead of their egos. We let go of blaming others for our troubles and each take responsibility for our individual lives, as well as for the community.

God's Grace

Life doesn't have to be all trials and tribulations. God showed me through gentle life experiences what true love is and how to get my needs met. God doesn't stand over us criticizing and punishing us all day. So why would a husband or parent do that? If a child is always in time-out or criticized, how do they ever know when they are doing something right?

After many Ma'at prayers, rituals, and meditations and much chanting in 1996, heaven began showing me how to live the right way by sending people to me who were role models of true love and caring and taught me how to get my needs met in the world. Ma'at is the spiritual principle of God's true love—unconditional love, acceptance, optimism, joy, and faith, knowing that heaven provides our needs and our desires. Therefore, we can share generously with others, not seeking anything in return from anybody while giving of ourselves—our individual, unique talents, time, wisdom, and experiences. This is more challenging than giving someone money occasionally. It is the belief in natural spiritual laws of what goes around, comes around, better consequences for good deeds versus bad deeds.

Gradually I understood that it wasn't necessary to go through the school of hard knocks and harsh consequences to learn my life lessons. Having faith and being gently shown new ways of perceiving and doing were enough to turn my life around and have fewer crises. Perhaps we are at the phase of human evolution when everyone no longer needs to go through the school of hard knocks to find out what we need to learn about what we are on this Earth to do.

We already know very well what violence, wars, greed, and extreme sex and pleasure are like, yet we try to push the limits even further. Enough is enough, already! Because we also know the opposite. There is a return to precolonial, Indigenous ways, cleverly disguised as New Age religions and women's ways of knowing. All over the world, people are healing and transforming spiritually as we all discover inner peace through better ways of communicating with each other.

Life Is Easier When We Allow Heaven to Help

I allow spirit to guide me, teach me, show me how to do technology, even take over my hands when I'm not sure how to do something. Lead me to the right place. All throughout the day, each of us is given guidance by the ideas and thoughts that come into our minds. Ideas and answers that there is no way anyone has previously taught you. You just know without knowing how you know. Automatically knowing measurements without understanding mathematics. Some people call this knowing—intuition. We say, "I should have followed my first mind," after we suffer the consequences of ignoring the quick, quiet advice. "I knew I should have listened and gone in another direction or grabbed that jacket or extra money or other item on my way out the door this morning. But I was in a hurry and didn't think I needed it anyway. Now I'm so sorry." We could save ourselves a lot of time spent redoing tasks if we listened to that quiet, inner voice of wisdom. And the more we pay attention, listen, follow, and thank aloud our unseen helpers, the more help is given.

When I was a little girl, younger than seven, I saw my mother say a prayer, then, with the spine of the Quran or bible facing down, lightly place her thumbs on it and allow the book to open at random. Whatever page it opened to, there she found her answer. A similar thing happens to me now, but not on purpose. I began to notice that my Kindle "randomly" opened to pages when I turned it on. If you consider that I have over five hundred books on my Kindle, what are the odds? When I read what's on the page in front of me, instead of being annoyed and rushing to the book I intended to read, it is the answer to whatever challenges I'm having that day! This phenomenon has been very comforting to me, mostly because the information validates my intuition, what I already know and have experienced.

Since 1998 a book on a shelf at the library or a bookstore would draw my attention, and I would check it out or buy it. Some people say that random books tend to fall off the shelf to the floor in front of them. That has only happened to me twice. Books come into my life usually after I've already gone through a crisis, done the problem-solving, and begun to see the light at the end of the tunnel. Exhausted, feeling like almost giving up, I had already gone through the dark night of the soul, which is a very lonely place to be. Sometimes I would get mad at God and say, "Why do you make me go through it alone? Then, when it's all over, you give me a book that is a story about someone who has gone through similar struggles. I never had a guru or mentor. I wish I'd had a real guru along the way!" Well, now, with the Kindle, I get guidance and support while I'm going through the current struggle. I no longer feel alone, as heaven sees and knows what I'm going through.

If I lose something, I stop, close my eyes, and ask spirit to help me find it. Then I'm led to where it is. One of my younger sisters misplaced her driver's license. She searched through her purse three times. She emptied out her suitcase items, one by one. I suggested that she stop, take deep breaths, and pray. She kept pacing back and forth, searching again through the items on the hotel bed.

She went to her previous hotel room to look some more, all the while thinking the worst. Finally she stopped and closed her eyes. She saw herself standing in the restroom of the restaurant where she'd eaten breakfast and lunch on the previous day. Then she heard "Cracker Barrel." She called the Cracker Barrel restaurant, and sure enough, someone had found her driver's license and given it to customer service! We went there and picked it up.

I also use a form of divination that is basically saying a prayer, asking God or heaven for help in making major decisions. Usually, if you are mindfully aware, connected, and fully participating in life, the answers you receive will validate what you already intuitively know. You may have heard of oracle cards or throwing cowrie shells and bones. These are Indigenous ways of consulting about personal spiritual growth and improving character and behavior. The elder council used divination to make the best decisions for the whole community. Often the answers gave predictions about the future, giving the community or country time to prepare. But divination is not for fortune-telling or a quick "yes or no" answer. The intent is to learn and do the personal work to grow, change and adapt to improve life and relationships. This doesn't mean there won't still be stressors and sorrows. You will just be better able to cope with life's natural ups and downs, including its joys.

Chapter 25: Accepting the Green Cloth

"Your mother is here, and she has a gift for you. The gift is wrapped in a green cloth. A shiny, satin, green fabric. She is handing it to you. Maybe get some green cloth and make yourself a scarf."

Reluctantly, I silently thought, Thank you, Momma. You heard my prayer this morning as I mentioned gratitude for expanding the role of women beyond what I observed of women during my childhood. An apology. I'm hesitant to accept the gift of the green cloth, but I sense you're showing me it is safe now to be a woman.

Domestic Violence

Domestic violence and sexual abuse occur in all types of family arrangements, in all religions, and at all income levels. Abuse occurs among same-sex couples too. Why? Because *globally* there are generations of trauma in families that hasn't been healed, such as refugees and immigrants who fled from wars and oppressive governments. Yet the grandparents and parents don't talk about how they were oppressed and discriminated against, often by people with the same complexion and birthplace. There have been long wars in Europe, and in Asia with the Japanese and Chinese atrocities against other Asian countries, and in the Middle East too—Muslims fighting other Muslims.

Conquerors privileged some tribes over others and made them fight each other. Corporations do the same with their employees today. The majority of

CHAPTER 25: ACCEPTING THE GREEN CLOTH

the world's population are people forced to go without money, status, power, and human dignity, put into positions of barely surviving—often repeatedly humiliated. Then there are men with money and status, but they are constantly aware of how fragile their status is in the pecking order of the hierarchy, aware that they could lose their position at any time and be cast out to live in poverty, despised.

It is difficult to know love or peace when living in these survival situations, surrounded by constant challenges and cruelty. The sickness of domestic violence and sexual abuse is passed down from generation to generation, leaving everyone with the feeling of not being connected to themselves or anyone. Fathers may be denied access to their families for many reasons, working too much or lack of adequate employment, be discouraged and walk away, have addictions or be unfairly jailed, killed, or injured and disabled. This leaves their sons to repeat the cycle of neglect and abuse. Women are overwhelmed with extra responsibilities, possible abuse, and lack of holistic support. Who, therefore, is to provide love and compassion to the community and families?

Domestic violence doesn't have to happen in the new millennium. Help and knowledge are available that our mothers didn't have. Now women, men, and children have the benefit of support groups, counseling, classes, self-help articles, books, blogs, movies, and YouTube videos. The main reason that domestic violence and sexual assault continues is we allow them to be kept secret, behind closed doors.

There is much that I wish my mother, grandmothers, and aunts had told me about life, men, and relationships. Beyond "keep your dress down and your panties up," girls were not told about sex. Some girls' mothers never even told them about getting their menstrual periods. Finding blood on their panties was a shock. My mother did tell me about sanitary pads, but no one told us about how charming boys and men could be, telling a girl how pretty she is and how much he loves her in order to get sex. Or how they could force sex on us and that it would most likely be a family member or friend doing this—not a stranger! Although in my situation, abuse occurred from strangers too. (TRIGGER WARNING).

On the way to junior high school one day, two teenage boys approached me and, while standing in front of me, quickly backed me into the alley. I usually walked through the large alley with garages on both sides to get home during lunch hour. The lunch hour was almost over, so I needed to return to school. I was confused as the tall teenage boys blocked my view and got in the way of me getting to school. They backed me up against a garage and told me, "Give me some pussy." I didn't know what pussy was. The leader put his hand between my legs and again said, "Give me some pussy."

A woman shouted, "What are you doing?" She scared them away. Then she took me to her house and called the police. The police came and asked me a lot of questions that I couldn't answer, embarrassing questions because no one, not my mother or father or anyone, had told me about sex. I was too frightened, confused, and in shock to even remember when my grandmothers took Kani and me into the pantry and told us not to let anyone touch us down there. The police took me home to my mother and told her what happened. Momma looked hurt and angry, but she didn't say much. We did not talk about the incident afterward.

When I was twelve years old, Momma told Kani and me about getting our periods. She explained and demonstrated how to put on a Kotex sanitary pad. This was a very complicated process with a thin elastic belt that went around my waist and had a metal clip in both the front and back. The pads had a long, thin paperlike tail on each end that I had to put through the small hole in the clip and twist it somehow so the pad stayed in place. In home economics, the teacher showed us a short cartoon about how girls have a menstrual period, what to do when you see blood, and how to mark a calendar so that you know when your period is coming. The teacher gave each girl a little Kotex booklet with Disney cartoon–style characters and calendar pages. I excitedly looked forward to getting my period. But still no one told us about sex.

Some men who see girl's vulnerability and lack of family protection take advantage of girls, and others force girls into prostitution for human traffickers. Yet it is only girls that everyone blames. Her reputation is ruined. If he gets her pregnant, she's the one that is sent away to a special school or a relative's house in the country until she gives birth. She is the one to have to make the decision to get an abortion or give the baby up for adoption, unless her family forces her into one or the other. Girls and women are always publicly shamed and blamed instead of the men. Since 2008, and pushed forward in 2018, we've had the beginnings of the MeToo movement and Time's Up!

It is time for women to stop accepting the many outrageous diagnoses of mental illness that doctors give us for being brave enough to say, "We hurt. We are tired of being hurt. We want the men to stop. We can't keep going on like this!" We are not the ones who are mentally ill. We are just crazy to keep going in spite of hurting, and for help others to not feel so hurt, and keep the world from completely falling apart!

Men have to do their part in their own healing and prevent domestic violence. First, men and boys must tell their stories of being molested, raped, and abused by other boys and men—and possibly women. Their competitive humiliation by other men at school and at work and being sexually assaulted by policemen while in custody. We need compassionate healing centers, not incarceration.

Writing this memoir made me aware of my own ongoing life themes of loneliness, isolation, and abandonment that started with domestic violence in childhood and continued in my second marriage. In pursuit of healing intergenerational trauma, I have sought ways to heal both myself and the world instead of passing violence on to the next generation. Indigenous cultures had ongoing healing rituals to help the whole community stay mentally well by jointly solving problems before conflicts became crises. Read *The Spirit of Intimacy: Ancient African Teachings in the Ways of Relationships.* Shamans also knew how to bring our ancestors' histories and past lives to our conscious awareness, therefore healing both our ancestors and us. Then we would be less likely to repeat our parents' and their parents' and their parents' mistakes. Modern therapists try to use some of these techniques with individual clients, but these are societal problems that need to be healed as a community.

Hopefully, we can flip the switch for awareness and change. We need national campaigns to talk about domestic violence and the ways families can learn to appreciate everyone, no matter their age, complexion, gender, identity, or culture. We need to be able to listen, to really understand the other person, and honestly tell our own stories too. How everyone can be treated with respect at home and at work, provided with a comfortable living wage and housing. We have taken women and poor people for granted by expecting free labor. But during the coronavirus pandemic, we don't know who would be left to care for us and our communities. Many women and poor people are now called "essential workers," although they were truly doing essential work long before the COVID-19 crisis.

Women's Spirituality

I learned faith and to love God by watching my mother and grandmothers. There is a difference between spirituality and religion. There's also a difference between women's spirituality and men's spirituality. The lived spirituality of my mothers was expressed in the love that glowed from their contented smiles and eyes. We saw Momma pray aloud. Her smile gradually replaced her worried look as she became peaceful and calm afterward. When my mothers told us that everything was going to be better, it was.

Perhaps women's faith and spirituality are stronger because men put women in such awful, impossible situations. They try to make us beholden to them as if they are God, and then they abandon us by withholding their money, protection, love, and presence. Left on our own in desperate situations, we pray, and our prayers are answered. The money, the food, and whatever else is needed simply appears. Even when I have money and am not in danger, whatever I need comes. This was a way of the universe saying, "Thank you for a job well done." Our unseen guardian angels save our lives miraculously by pushing us out of the way of danger just in time.

I allow spirit to guide me. Spirit wrote this book that you have in your hands right now. As I reread it while editing for typos and clarity, I was learning too. It was as if what was written was new to me! While I was typing this book, all my needs were met. Just a little thought of what I might need, even want, manifested within a day! And this time it came with a sense of humor. Recently, while clearing my apartment of clutter, I took down a box from the top of a bookshelf. When my friend who was helping me opened the small red-and-white party favor boxes, she discovered that each one was still filled with individually wrapped chocolates! All this time, I'd thought the little boxes were empty, and I was saving them for future parties. In spite of being across from the heater vent, the chocolates were still in great shape! The Ghirardelli name and logo were still etched in the chocolate. Somehow, it never melted in the four and a half years since my sixtieth birthday party. Two days before this, someone sent me a small box of chocolates hidden in packing paper in a big, $21 Priority Mail box, so I would receive it in time for Christmas! I think these were gifts from heaven, an acknowledgment of a job well done. Because I'm not really a chocolate person—usually I only eat it once every couple of months.

Recently, someone told me about the book *E-Squared*. For the first time in the thirty years that I have experienced miracles, this book explains miracles scientifically. I'd heard of popular book *The Secret*, but I never read it. The concept of making a vision board, putting on it pictures of what you want, and writing out a deadline and how much money you expect by that time—I didn't do any of that. The miracles just happen for me. Miracles can happen for everyone. I am not special. And no, it wasn't the jinn!

In the early 1990s, I read the Right Use of Will series. The author described our will as our feminine aspect. And as a part of human evolution in the future, which may be now in 2020, that there will no longer a need for performing religious rituals. This seems to have come true.

Sometimes, I wonder if men truly believe in God. Or were they taught that they have to always be the knight in shining armor, use force, and have all the answers? That would explain men's awful feelings of defeat and failure that become frustration and rage that they vent on their family. Perhaps they seek relief through alcohol, drugs, and sex instead of having faith and relying on God to provide guidance, basic needs, and the inner sustenance of a fulfilling life.

As I am filled with strong feelings of an expansive energy of love from those who passed on to the Other Side, sometimes I see a faint light around me with my eyes partially closed. I've had aha moments as I wondered, "Wow, is this what will heal the world? Those who passed on, even in war-torn places such as Syria, Afghanistan, and the Republic of the Congo to name a few countries. The ex-fighters and decreased family members are bombarding the current fighters and everyone else with bursts of love instead of revenge and obsession over losses. A love so strong that it brings us to our knees in awesome wonder! Overwhelming us. Humbling us!"

It is with this understanding of true femininity, including intuition, just knowing, beauty, harmony, compassion, nurturing, devotion, the magic power of miracles, spirituality, real intimacy in relationship and connection to all as one, that I accept my Mother's gift, the green cloth of full womanhood.

Human Evolution

Mother Dear, when she was in her 80's, told me, "The older you get, the more you realize how much you don't know." I was in my forties when she told me that, and I understood what she said was true. Life is ever-changing. What was true even two weeks ago is not true now. Many people in their late twenties and thirties come to therapy feeling they are in a crisis because whatever they were used to doing that previously allowed their lives to run smoothly no longer works. If you really think about it, it makes sense.

When I was six years old, I was tasked with memorizing my phone number and address and learning how to put two little fingers into the round hole of a rotary phone to dial the operator and relatives' or neighbors' numbers in case of an emergency. That was tough to do. My little fingers had to push hard enough while I remembered to turn the dial all the way around. Otherwise, I had to start over again. It was frustrating! There were also party lines to either assist or complicate the process further.

Now, no one would insist on going back to using rotary phones—we instead look forward to the next cell phone app to make our lives even easier. So why are parents, teachers, and preachers still trying to teach children and young adults what they learned thirty years earlier, which, like the rotary phone and phone booths, doesn't exist anymore? Why do we insist on enforcing ancient desert behaviors, traditions, religions, and rules that no longer make sense instead of only keeping what is helpful from the past and letting go of what harms us? We tend to stifle or neglect each other's growth and forward movement. Our families and institutions are stuck in the rotary phone age, going over, and over, and over, and over how the rotary phone was made and how to use it instead of coming out with better solutions so humans can evolve. We need to love and care for everyone and the environment of our current time. Technology has sped ahead of us, leaving us far behind. Taking hold of the future, we now have the internet to communicate and learn from each other, psychology to help us understand, heal, and improve our behaviors and relationships, and true spirituality to help bring us out of our dark ages.

Jigsaw Puzzle Metaphor

Everything we do or don't do in life teaches us a lesson, even putting together a circular, thousand-piece jigsaw puzzle on a sketch board that was too small. The board was twenty-three inches by twenty-six inches. The puzzle was twenty-six inches square. I knew that the sketch board was too small because I'd put the puzzle together previously. But somehow this time, the puzzle was way too big. The pieces on the edges repeatedly fell off the board onto the floor. Eventually I got annoyed and tired of picking up the pieces and putting them back together again and again.

Then I remembered I had a bigger board, but I was afraid it would be too much trouble and cause too many problems, so I didn't get it out. Of course, my pieces kept falling on the floor, so I had to repeatedly pick them up and put them back together again because the other board was just too small. I decided to push past my fears and get the bigger board out of the drawer, from under a lot of other stuff, including a large glass picture frame. It was much easier than I thought it would be! The big board was still too small. It was twenty-three inches by thirty-two inches. But I allowed my spirit guides to show me that I could tape a piece of heavy paper on the side where the puzzle was hanging off three inches. I propped it up underneath with a plastic sushi tray that I got from a restaurant. Now the whole puzzle fit.

This made me reflect on my life. The process of putting together the thousand-piece jigsaw puzzle reminded me of my younger years and missing out on life and doing without simply because I was afraid or thought it would be too hard to even try. I assumed everyone knew much more than I did because I thought I had to always catch up since my stepfather and foster father kept us isolated by not allowing us to do activities with friends.

Now I understand why this time, the puzzle was harder to fit on the sketch board. Since the puzzle is a circle, the outside is much larger than the middle. The first time I did the puzzle, I put it together from the inside toward the outside. Aha! It can be more of a struggle trying to cope with life from an outside perspective working toward the inner self!

Working the puzzle from the inside out was also difficult. When I finished, I felt like I'd come full circle. It was a very challenging puzzle, therefore an accomplishment. Yet I was also sad because in the rest of my life, there were many other long, drawn-out accomplishments and happy endings all happening at the same time. Just when we are starting to connect, participate, and share, then it's time to end. This book too will eventually come to an end. This is hard to believe because beginning this book was difficult. It was emotionally challenging to risk telling my story. However, I have benefited from reading many other people's memoirs over the years, so now I'm returning the favor, risking talking about culturally unspeakable topics that other people have not written about yet.

Finishing this book is also an accomplishment. At the beginning, I used the jigsaw puzzle as a distraction from the anxiety of the emotional memories trying to rise to my conscious awareness. The feelings were overwhelming. Too much, too soon. The puzzle was an addiction for me. There was no way for me to stay away from it. I told myself that I was going to stay away from it, yet I found myself in front of it even though my back and neck hurt from hours of sitting or standing over it. Often I would try several pieces, but only one or two pieces fit. Toward the end, the pieces went into place easily and fast.

That's the way this book came together. Slow at first, as I gathered all the pieces. Years of journals and audio recordings. Outlines for the chapters seemed to have too many pieces and too many holes. I didn't know how my mother's story would fit together. I prayed each night and early morning for my mother to help me write her story. She did. She sent me waves and waves of images and memories as I woke. Not only the pleasurable memories, but also the worst times in my life. While initially uncomfortable, the journey of writing this memoir is probably at the top of all the healing that I've done.

Conclusion: Mission Accomplished

Recently while talking to my sister Naimah, I was reminded of the automatic writing assignment given to me in 1998.

"You are to write a book."

"About what?" I asked.

"You."

"Me? What about me?" I had already started a memoir in 1995 as part of an advanced writing class. It was very tedious work trying to write my conflicting feelings about my past near death experience and having to make quality of life and end of life choices when several friends were either ill or had recently died from cancer.

"What part of my life should I write about?"

"Women."

"Women?" I asked. "What do I know about women? I don't remember my mother or my foster mother, my grandmother, or any other women telling me about womanhood. I have no children. I was married twice and divorced twice. I haven't gone out there and tasted life as other women have. What do I really know about womanhood?"

"Just write about your experiences."

"Okay, I guess I can do that. After forty-two years, I ought to know something."

I had recently returned from Zimbabwe and hadn't gotten a job yet. I was staying with a friend. On her bookshelf was the book Talking to Heaven. In the middle was a section on automatic writing. Some people may have experienced automatic writing while they were already writing a letter or story, then the pen or the typewriter or computer started to write by itself without them thinking about what was being written. A similar thing happens to artists, musicians, and scientists while they are creating and inventing.

I decided to try it. Beginning with a prayer and meditation, I held a pen in my right hand and allowed it to move on its own across the paper. The words I was writing with my eyes closed were much larger than usual, going up and down or on an angle, and it was difficult to see a whole sentence or its meaning. I eventually got a larger piece of paper. In the squiggly, barely legible writing was this message. To my surprise, my mother also came through with another message about my relationship with Kani.

Later came the insistent messages from mediums at the Church of the Spirit—from the very first year that I attended—of how important is was for me to write! Write poems, keep a journal, use audio recording to transcribe later, anything—just write about my life and share it.

After all these years—twenty-two, to be exact—I am now understanding Momma's automatic writing message. I also understand the second assignment she gave me from the medium at the Spirit Fest in 2015, that we women now have a choice and a responsibility to not allow ourselves to be abused. We have a responsibility to our children and for the evolution of the world to release our fears. The feeling of losing our souls is worse than the physical death of our bodies.

The return of the divine feminine is restoring balance to the Earth, the universe, and within each of us. It doesn't matter whether we are male or female, but it's especially important for the men because in rejecting the feminine within themselves, they push out their ability to receive love, to feel connected to others, to be connected to self, people, and the environment. Being connected to our feelings allows us to feel fully alive and passionate enough to fulfill our collective and individual potential, to have true intimacy in all our relationships.

Without the divine feminine, we know that we are missing something but are not sure what. Instead, we try to fill that inner emptiness with things and constantly change from one relationship, friendship, job, or location to another to try to bury that inner discontent and emptiness. What's worse is demanding that a woman could be your sister, girlfriend, or a prostitute, fill your empty space temporarily for you with "wham bam, maybe a thank you, ma'am" sex. Or using others to fill your responsibilities for you in order to gain more wealth and status—which you are terrified of losing in a patriarchal, competitive hierarchy. But true contentment and intimacy require cooperation and true collaboration, not constant competition. To truly collaborate requires the feminine qualities of nurturing, caring, and intuitively feeling what the other people around you are experiencing. Collaboration is also respecting and valuing everyone's wisdom and talents in order to come to the best solution for all.

Women need to reclaim and honor their feminine qualities. Everyone else needs to stop saying our feminine attributes are weaknesses. These are, of course, our strengths—very valuable strengths. Most important, women must not allow men to make us feel ashamed and take the blame for their bad behavior, especially since if it were not for women, most of the world would collapse and fall apart. There is a book titled, *Half the Sky*. I beg to differ. I think women are three fourths of the sky. We hold up the sky and everything else up to keep it from falling!

Some of my clients remind me of Momma. Some have postpartum depression. However, previous and ongoing verbal and emotional abuse from their husbands makes them sit or sleep most of the day, without the energy to do anything. For my mother, the domestic violence crushed her dream of being married, of having an ideal marriage. Her reputation as a great mother and "pious" Muslim changed to accusations that she was a terrible mother who didn't care about her children. A mentally ill mother.

I can believe my clients when they tell me they had all these plans for their children, but their husband would not let them do any of what they thought was best. So they ended up sitting or sleeping too much, hardly doing anything at all. I believe them because that is what happened to my mother! You have witnessed, through reading my life story, how my mother was before and after she married my stepfather.

But Momma found a way to be a mother anyway, and she made up for lost time. It's possible that Momma and my other loved ones in spirit have helped me all along. All these years prior she didn't even come to me in my dreams at night. It seems to me she stayed away. I wondered why I had vivid dreams of friends and even my stepfather and foster father but not her. I just wasn't aware until I found the Church of the Spirit and the wonderful mediums there. Momma's most precious gift is reminding me that I'm always loved as I reread her spirit messages and that she sees and feels how I'm doing and still guides me daily, along with guardian angels, spirit guides, and the rest of heaven.

I initially wrote this book because many children are angry and depressed growing up, believing that their mother chose a man over them, not knowing that it's possible to destroy a good woman and mother. But your mother loves you anyway. Even when it has to be from afar.

Epilogue

Life's Detours

One way to understand life's challenges is to remember what it's like when there is road construction. Sometimes road repairs last only a day, a summer or it could take a few years.

While the road is under construction you may stay on it bumping, shaking, and chattering your teeth. Good news is that it's a short stretch and doesn't last long. You continue onto smooth pavement.

Other times the road is closed with barriers and detour signs that send you off the main road. Lo and behold you discover that there's a new way. A shortcut, a faster route then you usually take. 'Why didn't I know of this street before?' You happily ask yourself.

There are detours that turn you around back in the direction you came from. A U-turn. Perhaps it's best to go back home. You forgot something anyway. Start out fresh the next morning. Maybe another day soon.

Or the detour takes you in the opposite direction— west instead of east—for a long distance with barriers not allowing you to go up or down sidestreets to go east. Now you're frustrated with the time it takes to find a way out. You eventually do. Perhaps a little late but you get there. And after all the being hot under the collar and worried – you usually get there on time. At the right time. Either the event is just starting, or you have to wait for others to get there anyway.

You do arrive at your destination. Whether you're the driver or the passenger in a car or on public transportation we usually don't complain long because we know eventually, we get there. In our minds is only that by the end of the day we will be there. Or perhaps on a road trip we've already planned using maps or GPS how many miles and how many minutes or hours it will take to get there. So an hour delay – what's the big deal? Your focus only on your goals.

Life is this way too. It may sometimes take longer to accomplish your goals. And the journey may seem longer to get there. Yet why do we give up so easily? Losing sight of our goals and the road up ahead? We do eventually get there. There are rest stops and flat tires along the way but we get there.

When I look back on my life, I now see and understand my many detours along the way. Thirty years ago, I declared I wanted to become a counselor or a therapist after my then sexual abuse therapist introduced me to the term PTSD. She explained, in 1989, that the diagnosis of PTSD posttraumatic stress disorder extended beyond only soldiers returning from war. Holocaust survivors and women survivors of domestic violence or rapes also had similar symptoms with flashbacks, painful memories, and nightmares. Women therapists were designing alternative, compassionate treatment for the traumas that women experience. They understood the normal reactions of shame and guilt seen as major depression and that extreme anxiety and fearfulness was not psychosis, schizophrenia, nor paranoia. Otherwise psychiatric treatment back then was brutal with strong medication side effects and electric shock treatments with long-term hospitalizations.

Psychiatrists and therapists were not trained in universities to understand and treat complex traumas. Alternative therapies and indigenous ways of healing were gradually replaced with the newer psychotropic anti-anxiety and antidepressants medications. Here, take a chill pill and go back home. Back home to fear for your life and dangerous working conditions for little pay. I was a registered nurse at that time helping patients to heal from medical conditions in hospitals or chronic illnesses in their homes. It occurred to me for both physical and mental illnesses people would be hospitalized less if their home and employment environments were safer, loving and supportive.

Back then I also heard through emotional and spiritual healing books and workshops that it was possible to reach a calm existence of "to just be." I initially didn't know what "to just be" meant but I wanted it. There is a saying, "be careful what you pray for— because you might get it."

No one told me that when you want something there is preparation and learning that comes first in order to have it. We say we want loving, healthy relationships. But do we know what love is? Do we know what a truly healthy relationship is? Most of us just copy off of what we saw our parents and grandparents do and from television or at the movies. We want well-paid, satisfying careers. Well when I was younger, I was told and believed that I should just be happy to have a job. In my naïve innocence I didn't know that women and people with darker complexions were paid less and expected to do hard labor or dirty jobs that nobody else would want to do. These jobs were also frequently understaffed which meant doing at least one other person's job in addition to one's assigned job. I did my best in all of these jobs because I had pride in whatever I did. Plus, we had to constantly prove ourselves to maintain employment.

It did not occur to me that further college education was an option until after my near-death experience and I had to recover mentally from an abusive second marriage. This first detour began as healing journey of exploring different alternative therapies, spiritual beliefs and religions. I focused more on healing than pursuing becoming a therapist. In fact, I did not know what education was required. While I continued working to pay my rent and have nice things, I experienced small miracles in my life as I spontaneously literally followed my nighttime dreams. An African American incredibly talented magician, with a learning disability who as a child struggled to read, came to an elementary school I was working at. His message to the students was it is never too late to follow one's dreams and goals. I spoke to him after his presentation and he me inspired to pursue my childhood passionate dream of illustrating children's books and now nonviolent video games. The School of the Art Institute of Chicago reviewed my drawing and painting portfolio and immediately accepted me. When I read that they also had a Master's in Arts Therapy program, I thought it would be great to combine my nursing background with psychology. However, I also learned the hard way what "starving artist" meant. Unlike other college majors, where you pay your tuition and buy textbooks at the beginning of the semester—art teachers expect students to purchase new art supplies at least twice a week. Good quality art papers and paints do help produce wonderful effects but are not cheap. I had to make a choice between buying groceries or buying art supplies!

As part of the art school's orientation I learned about their student study abroad programs. Previously traveling did not seem like an option because I thought only rich people traveled to other countries. A year later, after almost dropping out of the school because it was way too expensive, I inquired about the study abroad program when the spiritual group that I belonged to was going to go to Ghana in Africa in 1995. Couldn't I finish my bachelor's degree abroad? My nighttime dreams and whenever I closed my eyes showed me huge fields of spectacular sparkling red flowers that immediately filled me with peace similar to what I saw I during my near-death experience. I prayed and asked to go to wherever these flowers and also the high mountains and beautiful deep valleys were.

The art school explained that Ghana wasn't an option because it was an exchange student program meaning students from Ghana would have to come in my place and that was not likely to happen unless they were rich and could support themselves without working in the United States. Zimbabwe was an option. I never heard of Zimbabwe. Tearfully, I researched this country at the library and had more enthusiasm later when I learned that they actually did have fields of tulips and other flowers that the Dutch exported. It also had Victoria Falls. In addition, Zimbabweans used indigenous traditional healers. The tuition with scholarships and loans paid for my year on campus with room and board, and also included the flights to and from Zimbabwe during my senior year. This was the most important part of my healing journey as I received unconditional love and acceptance from the people in the villages and the city. Another prayer answered!

However as you learned from my memoir, I returned to the United States and became ill soon after. Another major construction detour as I had to heal physically and emotionally. An extended rest stop along the way. After navigating being homeless and eventually moving into transitional housing, I was given art therapy. This brought me back around to one of my passions and main road goals— but on a pleasant side street detour. With more permanent housing, I gradually adapted watercolor painting techniques by using large paint brushes and larger paper while semi-reclined in bed. Later I bought myself a computer and taught myself how to use it from bed. The Dragon Naturally Speaking software program that changes voice to text helped me to continue to be occupied and productive. The Dragon Naturally Speaking software program that changes the sound of voice to text helped me to continue to be occupied and productive.

It was when one of my doctors said to me, "You should be a counselor. Too many people with disabilities are depressed and bitter. You could help them" that I was reminded of my major highway goal of becoming a counselor or therapist. Still I didn't think it was possible for me my back still hurt a lot even while sitting. I had already applied for Social Security disability. However, for a couple of months prior I'd had recurrent nightmares of being in college, feeling lost because I arrived there late and in a few days was the first exam! Perhaps I could quickly study but would I really know the class lesson in enough time? I kept hearing in my head, "a mind is a terrible thing to waste."

So back onto the major highway and smoother pavement as I applied and was accepted into the Master's in Rehabilitation Counseling program. I wanted to help others have similar services that I was receiving as the State paid for transportation, school supplies, and home personal care assistants. I also received a full rehabilitation counseling scholarship for the two years program on campus and graduated on time.

However, another slight detour challenge happened as the United States economy collapsed in 2008. Rehabilitation counselors provide vocational counseling and training. But there weren't jobs to prepare clients for employment and a lot of mental health clinics also closed leaving me without job opportunities. This gave me another push to find a way back to the main highway because I wanted to do counseling—not find people jobs anyway. To me, people with and without disabilities have challenges. In fact, more able-bodied people have emotional challenges that prevent them from fulfilling their full potential. A common reason for people being stuck in fear is a past history of trauma and or ongoing exposure to trauma. I wanted to be able to provide therapy to anyone who needed it—not just people with disabilities. So I researched different doctoral programs and chose a university with health psychology and spirituality concentrations.

This major highway construction had very bumpy and torturous twists and turns. I don't think that the highway ever smoothed out except perhaps in the middle during the third year at the university. But I stayed on it.

In September 2021, I did officially become Dr. Mateen. Haneefa Mateen Psy.D., a doctor specializing in clinical psychology. A healed psychologist who does therapy. With the help from my spirit love ones, my mother, other relatives, friends and strangers with those in Earthly bodies encouraged me and were there to fix my flat tires allowing me to get back on the road.

COVID-19 caused another parallel road detour after all the shocks of 2020. A reflective yet productive rest stop for some people and yet full speed ahead for other people with few open exits to get off the busy highway. Either way we have had to reevaluate our priorities. Having survived so many shocking detour experiences in my life by now not much shakes me. Knowing that we will not return to "normal" we are inventing a new better world. I've learned true love and connection and now experience how to peacefully "just be."

Acknowledgments

I first want to thank Momma and my father and their parents and grandparents because without them I wouldn't exist. I wouldn't exist in physical body nor as the hard working, joyful, loving person I've become.

For all those seen and unseen family and friends who believed in me even during times when I didn't believe in myself. They encouraged me in the long haul through the wonderful and the terrible. They patiently waited saying, "I'll be glad when you graduate." Then had to miss me for another year as I diligently wrote this book.

Of course I'm grateful to the Church of The Spirit for all the mediums there that connected me to Momma and my other relatives, friends and love ones. Especially the spirit messages encouraging me to write books. And for the love and caring the congregation gave me with the social activities that we did together. Pastor Marrice Coverson for the thirty plus years of service to the Church of The Spirit and the community. Without them this book wouldn't have been possible.

For Carla Golden, who I met as another "Philly gal" through the Association of Women in Psychology Older Women's Caucus. She became my unofficial editor as her insatiable curiosity had her asking question after question to get to know me better. Yet from her questions and critiques of my written drafts chapter by chapter is how this book became the best it could be.

My copy editor Denise Logsdon who trudged through 99,000 words of my manuscript draft while finding the inconsistencies and repetitions to make corrections and suggestions. But it was her comments about what was missing and possibly misunderstood that had me do a major revision to bring Momma's story through.

To all my beta readers who read the first draft e-book version of this book and gave me recommendations based on what it was like for them to read this book. For their patience and commitment through the rough parts of the book, the trauma stories as well as my initial confusing timeline of when events happened.

To the members of the Association of Black Psychologists (ABPSI) who with their activities kept me grounded in African American and diaspora culture. Reminded us of what our true purpose for being on this Earth is, with living the principles of Maat daily. That we are always to remember our ancestors who came before us, those who walk with us now, and for us to prepare for those not yet born. Acknowledging the mental sickness of the promoters of global racism spread through European colonialism. ABPSI has given me support for over 11 years. Helped us through being the only one, in too many situations.

Gratitude to my academic advisors, professors Dr. Zoline and Dr. Wilson who assisted me in fulfilling graduation requirements for the doctoral program, and most importantly helped me write my dissertation about African Americans' experiences with posttraumatic growth. From these professors I gained courage and confidence along with insight and writing skills.

Appreciation for Mahala Bacon and members of the United Spiritual Council of Nations who regularly attend her Zoom spiritual, mediumship, and healing classes and Sunday services. They also encouraged me along the way in completing this book.

Books Mentioned in this Book

I purposely did not write this book in a scholarly way, with huge academic words, book quotes and citations. This is because we all have this knowledge and information within us. Books are just one way to share and communicate with each other. I believe there really is no such thing as an expert, it is simply one person sharing their opinion and experiences. The so-called expert may have done the research and statistics to find how many other people might agree. And they had the money and the time to get published. But life is always changing. Meaning what was true two weeks ago, may not be true today. And the authors may live in a completely different situation than yours, and therefore the advice may make no sense for your current life situation. Books are a way to have a long-distance conversation. Often with a stranger. But inside us is enough commonalities that we don't feel alone. Here is a list of books whose authors think similar to my experiences, and some who don't.

Ahmadou Bambu: A Peacemaker for Our Time. By Michelle R. Kimball. (2019).

Beyond the Light: What Isn't Being Said About Near-Death Experience. By P. M. H. Atwater. (1994, 2009).

Breaking Ground on Your Memoir: Craft, Inspiration, and Motivation for Memoir Writers. By Linda Joy Myers, PhD, and Brooke Warner. (2015).

Company of Prophets: African American Psychics, Healers and Visionaries. By Joyce Elaine Null. (1992).

Dreams and Visions in Islamic Societies. By Ozgen Felek and Alexander Knysh, editors. (2012).

E-Squared: Nine Do-It-Yourself Energy Experiments That Prove Your Thoughts Create Your Reality. By Pam Grout. (2013).

Good Clean Dark: African-American NEAR DEATH Experiences. By Lloyd Rudy & Nalo Halloway. (2015).

Half the Sky: Turning Oppression into Opportunity for Women Worldwide. By Nicholas Kristof and Sheryl WuDunn. (2009)

Heading Towards Omega: In Search of the Meaning of the Near-Death Experience. By Kenneth L. Ring. (1985).

How to Interpret Your Dreams and Discover Your Life Purpose. By Michael Sheridan. (2007). Aisling Dream Interpretation.

Inside the Soul of Islam: A Unique View into The Love, Beauty and Wisdom of Islam for Spiritual Seekers of all Faiths. Mamoon Yusaf. (2017).

Legends of the Fire Spirits: Jinn and Genies from Arabia to Zanzabar. By Robert Lebling. (2010).

Men Who Hate Women & The Women Who Love Them: Why Loving Hurts and You Don't Know Why. By Susan Forward. (1986).

Merriam Webster Dictionary. "Quintessential" Merriam Webster.com Dictionary, Merriam Webster,

http://www.merriam-webster.com/dictionary/quintessential Accessed 25 Nov. 2020.

Mind Over Matter: Scientific Proof That You Can Heal Yourself. By Lissa Rankin, M.D. (2013).

No Visible Wounds: Identifying Nonphysical Abuse of Women by Their Men. By Mary Susan Miller, PH.D.

Peaceful Families: American Muslim Efforts Against Domestic Violence. Juliane Hammer. (2019).

Phoenix Rising: No-Eyes' Vision of the Changes to Come. By Mary Summer Rain. (1987, 1993).

Physicians' Untold Stories: Miraculous Experiences Doctors Are Hesitant to Share with Their Patients, or Anyone! By Scott J. Kolbaba, M.D., with 26 other Physicians. (2016).

Sacred Path Cards: The Discovery of Self Through Native Teachings. By Jamie Sams. (1990).

Shifting: The Double Lives of Black Women in America. By Charisse Jones and Kumea Shorter-Gooden, Ph.D. (2003).

Spirited: Connect to the Guides All Around You. By Rebecca Rosen. (2010).

Spiritual Emergency: When Personal Transformation Becomes a Crisis. Edited by Stanislav Grof, M. D. and Christina Grof. (1989).

Talking to Heaven: A Medium's Message of Life After Death. By James Van Praagh. (1999). Berkley.

The Holy Quran. By Yusuf Ali. (2012).

The Jungle Book. By Rudyard Kipling. (1894, 2008).

The Last Frontier: Exploring the Afterlife and Transforming Our Fear of Death. By Julia Asante, PhD. (2012).

The Near-Death Experience: A Vehicle of Shamanic Initiation. By Nashid "Koleoso" Fakhrid-Deen. (2011).

The Power of Eight: Harnessing the Miraculous Energies of a Small Group to Heal Others, Your life and the World. (2017). By Lynne McTaggart.

The Spirit of Intimacy: Ancient African Teachings in the Ways of Relationships. By Sobonfu Somé. (1999).

The Soul's Journey After Death. An Abridgement of Ibn Al-Qayyim's Kitabar-Ruh. Layla Mabrouk (1987, 2011).

The Way of Sufi Chivalry. Futuwwah. By Ibn al Husayn al-Sulami. Translated by Tosun Bayrak al-Jerrahi (1991).

The World of the Unseen. By F. Amir Baiyg'e. (2019).

About the Author

Haneefa Mateen has a wealth of life experiences and knowledge from exploring healing methods for mind, body and soul. A natural teacher, healer, and artist she shares of her wisdom.

She has an associate's degree in registered nursing, bachelor's in International Studies, master's in Rehabilitation Counseling, and a doctorate in Clinical Psychology. She currently does spiritually integrated therapy and healing, and is active in African American community cultural events.

Her books are accessible, easy on the eyes, available in large print format.

www.ingramcontent.com/pod-product-compliance
Lightning Source LLC
Chambersburg PA
CBHW052134070526
44585CB00017B/1822